Poetic Investigations

Poetic Investigations

Singing the
Holes in History

PAUL NAYLOR

Northwestern

University Press

Evanston

Illinois

Northwestern University Press
Evanston, Illinois 60208-4210

ISBN 0-8101-1667-7 (cloth)

ISBN 0-8101-1668-5 (paper)

Library of Congress Cataloging-in-Publication Data

Naylor, Paul, 1957–
    Poetic investigations : singing the holes in history / Paul Naylor.
        p.   cm.
    Includes bibliographical references (p.   ).
    ISBN 0-8101-1667-7 (cloth). — ISBN 0-8101-1668-5 (paper)
        1. American poetry—20th century—History and criticism.
    2. Literature and history—United States—History—20th century.
    3. Literature and history—Commonwealth countries—History—
    20th century.   4. Philip, Marlene Nourbese, 1947–   —Criticism
    and interpretation.   5. Brathwaite, Kamau, 1930–   —Criticism
    and interpretation.   6. Mackey, Nathaniel, 1947–   —Criticism
    and interpretation.   7. Experimental poetry, American—History
    and criticism.   8. Commonwealth poetry (English)—History and
    criticism.   9. Hejinian, Lyn—Criticism and interpretation.
    10. Howe, Susan—Criticism and interpretation.   I. Title.
    PS310.H57N39   1999
    811'.5409358—dc21   99-29032
                                                        CIP

FOR MY FATHER,
KEN NAYLOR,
AND IN MEMORY OF MY MOTHER,
GLORIA NAYLOR

Contents

Acknowledgments

One of the unique pleasures of writing about contemporary poetry is that your subjects are often more than texts. All five poets I discuss in *Poetic Investigations*—Susan Howe, Nathaniel Mackey, Lyn Hejinian, Kamau Brathwaite, and M. Nourbese Philip—are very much alive and writing, and I thank them all for their willingness to answer questions about their writing and to respond to mine. Roy Harvey Pearce and Michael Davidson taught me about the power and importance of "making poems"; I hope this book makes them proud. I owe special thanks to Marjorie Perloff. Her enthusiasm for my work at a crucial stage made it much easier to finish. Many of my colleagues at the University of Memphis have read my work and listened to me yap—thanks especially to Theron Britt, Tom Carlson, Gordon Osing, Susan Scheckel, and Jennifer Wagner-Lawlor. John Duvall, in particular, was frequently successful in talking me off the ledge of rhetorical excess. My debt and gratitude to my parents, to whom this book is dedicated, and to my wife, Debi Kilb, are best expressed in private.

Some of the work in *Poetic Investigations* appeared, in somewhat different form, in the following publications. Many thanks to the editors.

Part of my introduction and part of chapter 1 appeared as "Writing History Poetically: Walter Benjamin and Susan Howe," in *Genre* 28, no. 3 (Fall 1995).

Part of chapter 1 appeared as "Where Are We Now in Poetry?" in *Sagetrieb* 10, nos. 1 and 2 (spring and fall 1991).

Part of chapter 2 appeared as "The 'Mired Sublime' of Nathaniel Mackey's *Song of the Andoumboulou*," in *Postmodern Culture* 5, no. 3 (May 1995).

Introduction

Writing History Poetically

Although most Americans first met him as a pitch man for Coke, he began his "career" in 1982 as a VJ on a British music video show. Then HBO financed a movie about him, and a television series soon followed in both Britain and America. By 1985, he was a hot commodity: product endorsements, guest appearances on late-night talk shows, T-shirts, coffee mugs. Not bad for a simulation. Max Headroom had everything going for him—everything, that is, except "being." Or did he?

In the movie and television versions of Max Headroom's story, both of which are set "twenty minutes into the future," Edison Carter, an investigative television reporter, is about to expose an advertising technique (known as "blipverts") designed to stop television viewers from changing channels during commercials. Carter is not only concerned with the obvious moral implications of coercing viewers to view; he has also discovered that blipverts may cause those who are obese and sedentary to spontaneously combust. Since Carter is a prominent on-air personality, he cannot be "eliminated" without causing suspicion, so the advertising and network executives decide to replace him with a computer-generated simulation. In an attempt to escape those trying to capture him, Carter is seriously injured in a motorcycle accident (he crashes into a traffic barrier that reads "Maximum Headroom"). His brain waves are then fed into the computer-generated model. The resulting "personality," Max Headroom, takes on a life of its own, beyond the control of its programmer, an adolescent computer genius named Brice. Since Max's program contains Carter's personal history, Max knows about the dangers of blipverts, which he exposes on an underground television program.[1] It seems as if Carter's ethical code was transferred to the simulation as well. Complete with a personal history and an ethical code, is Max simulating a person or is he one? What kind of a "being" is he?

The story has one more permutation. In his comic strip *Doonesbury*, G. B. Trudeau plays a variation on the Max Headroom theme with his character Ron Headrest, presidential candidate in 1988. Headrest is clearly a caricature of Ronald Reagan, and the implication is equally clear: there is little difference between a simulated candidate, Headrest, and a "real" one, Reagan. Headrest is the result of an attempt to download Reagan's personality into a computer-generated model of the president, which will then stand in on television for the real president. "It's a painless way to increase your accessibility and your Q rating!" an aide tells him. Besides, "It's just television, sir. No one will know the difference." Due to a power surge, however, the White House loses control over Headrest. He's "at large" and able to appear on any television at any time. We can now, we learn, "enjoy vivid, high-resolution leadership for just pennies a day." The immediate groundswell of support for Headrest implies that America would rather have a simulation of the Reagan presidency than see the "real" one come to an end. On one hand, this suggests that, since Headrest is running for president while Reagan is still in office, Americans are nostalgic for the Reagan presidency even before it's over; on the other hand, it also suggests that Americans do not see too great a difference between Reagan and a simulation of Reagan.

In short, many Americans were aware that in some sense Reagan always was a simulation—an advertisement for a past that no longer exists and probably never did—and they were not troubled enough by this to forgo electing him twice. As Garry Wills concludes, "The power of [Reagan's] appeal is the great joint confession that we cannot live with our real past, that we not only prefer but need a substitute" (458). Haynes Johnson, in his important study of the 1980s, *Sleepwalking through History*, makes a similar point: "Reagan's ability to show Americans what they wanted to see had been perfect at a time when America wanted to escape past problems and growing national doubts. Maybe Ronald Reagan was just another sound bite in a series of prime-time programs that America was addicted to" (447). The question, of course, is how big a step is it from a prime-time president to a simulated one, from Ronald Reagan the great communicator to Ron Headrest the great simulator? But an even more important question arises as well: does the American public really want a simulated president to present a simulated history—a history that reflects America's image of itself rather than its "real past"?

The Reagan years do, after all, coincide with the rise of "revisionist" history in American universities. The American public's desire for someone like Reagan could then be seen as a reaction against these revisionist attempts to debunk the myth of America as the sole source of democracy and freedom in the world, as a culture with an unstained history of moral and economic progress. In this case, Reagan would be, as Wills contends, "the demagogue as rabble-soother, at a time when people do not need to be stirred up but assuaged, to have anxieties dispelled, complexities resolved"; thus, Reagan "not only represents the past, but resurrects it as a promise of the future" (447). Reagan is the great enabler, encouraging America to continue "sleepwalking" through the past in order to maintain its image of itself in the present and to project that image into the future. He is the corporate spokesman for a wave of cultural nostalgia that tried to convince the American public that it didn't need to live in the America of the 1980s, that the America of the 1950s was still available. The ideology at work here is highly invested in representing contemporary culture as part of a seamless narrative of progress, obliged to cover up any of the "holes"—the erasures, gaps, and tears—in the fabric-ation of history.

This nostalgic trip back to the 1950s was, therefore, much more than a whimsical wish to return to an earlier, more prosperous, and orderly era of American history—to a time when, according to the simulated version of history Reagan offered, America fought to preserve democracy (which meant any opposition to the march of market capitalism would be met with an armed response); nuclear families were intact (which meant that women would be consigned to domestic and reproductive duties); and minorities knew their place (which meant they would not eat, sleep, drink, or learn in the same places as whites). More significantly, it was a concerted attempt to erase the effects of the 1960s. The foreign, domestic, and economic policies of the Reagan era enforced a ruthlessly coherent program for revitalizing the military-industrial complex, for rolling back the advances made by women, minorities, and the impoverished, and for ensuring that even more wealth became concentrated in even fewer hands. In short, the effects of Reagan's administration have proven to be much more than a simulated return to a bygone time. The salesman may have been simulated, but the product was not. And that product turns out to be an America that seems to believe that all of its best interests will be served if the best interests of a few wealthy men are served first.

Ron Headrest, however, is ultimately rejected by his viewing public. In the final panels of Trudeau's series, Headrest loses his cool on TV when he learns he won't receive the Republican party's nomination: "Am I teed off? Hey, who wouldn't be? I gave them great picture! I gave them even better sound bite. They gave me d-d-diddly squat, squat! Well, they won't have Ron Headrest to flip off anymore!" In the world of *Doonesbury*, the public sees past the great picture and better sound of the simulation and chooses the real candidate, George Bush. Although this isn't quite the utopian ending we might hope for—Bush certainly was not as good a salesman as Reagan, but they both peddled the same product—it does portray the American public as able to discern the difference between the real and the simulated. Unfortunately, in this case, life has yet to imitate art; America has yet to reject Headrest's real-world model or the public policies he promotes.

It is tempting to see in this scenario another example of contemporary culture teetering on the Baudrillardan abyss of hyperreality. According to Jean Baudrillard, there is no "real" space from which a critique of existing conditions could proceed because the difference between a simulated and a real world has been completely effaced. And "simulation is no longer that of a territory, a referential being or a substance. It is the generation by models of a real without origin or reality" (1983, 2). Baudrillard's diagnosis of American culture during this period seems all too accurate: "In Reagan, a system of values that was formerly effective turns into something ideal and imaginary. The image of America becomes imaginary for Americans themselves, at a point when it is without doubt profoundly compromised" (1989, 114). While contemporary culture is indeed moving in the direction Baudrillard maps out, I resist his conclusion that we have reached the point where there is no longer the possibility of a "place" from which a critique of contemporary culture can be launched. I am as suspicious of the seamless account Baudrillard constructs as I am of the one constructed by Reagan and his handlers. Note that both accounts hinge on erasing "reality" from the equation of contemporary culture, and that both ultimately advise resignation. I agree with Baudrillard that contemporary culture is "profoundly compromised" by the mediation of mediation. But I do not think it has been completely compromised. Baudrillard follows in Michel Foucault's footsteps and offers often brilliant descriptions of the systems that control contemporary culture. But I believe they both over-estimate the competence of the actual humans that staff Big Brother. They may be good, but not good enough to cover up all the seams.

Furthermore, accounts like those of Foucault and Baudrillard seem to fall prey to an "all or nothing" mentality—complete freedom or complete subjugation. I prefer a "some is better than none" approach that sets up a continuum of practical events that occasionally disrupt the systems of control. My approach reflects the highly "compromised" potential for true revolt in contemporary culture; it admits that the forces of consumer capitalism have virtually eliminated the possibility of a significant revolution waged against it. We are left with little more than the possibility of guerrilla tactics—subversive forays into the means of mediation. Writing in the wake of Foucault and Baudrillard, Michel de Certeau contends that because "the grid of 'discipline' is everywhere becoming clearer and more extensive, it is all the more urgent to discover how an entire society resists being reduced to it" (xiv). The answer, for de Certeau, is that societies and individuals can resist their reduction to a manipulable point on the "grid of discipline" by deploying "tactics" rather than "strategies," the latter having been compromised beyond use by contemporary consumer capitalism. A tactic, however, "insinuates itself into the other's place, fragmentarily, without taking it over in its entirety, without being able to keep it at a distance. It has at its disposal no base where it can capitalize on its advantages, prepare its expansions, and secure independence with respect to circumstances" (xix). "Dwelling, moving about, speaking, reading, shopping, and cooking," according to de Certeau, "are activities that seem to correspond to the characteristics of tactical ruses and surprises: clever tricks of the 'weak' within the order established by the 'strong,' an art of putting one over on the adversary on his own turf, hunter's tricks, maneuverable, polymorph mobilities, jubilant, poetic, and warlike discoveries" (40). In *Poetic Investigations: Singing the Holes in History,* I argue that the five writers discussed in this book—Susan Howe, Nathaniel Mackey, Lyn Hejinian, Kamau Brathwaite, and M. Nourbese Philip—create and use innovative forms of poetic writing as tactics to seek out the seams and other tears in history.

My argument, then, proposes that these tactics not only exist but are available for use, and that, consequently, a "place" exists from which a fragmentary and partial yet potentially effective critique of contemporary culture can arise—a place of "maneuverable, polymorph mobilities." *Doonesbury*, after all, does serve as a site for a critique of contemporary culture. I suspect Trudeau's strip is the most subversive work of art many Americans confront on a regular basis, which is why it is consigned to life among the classifieds in the *Commercial Appeal*, our daily paper here in Memphis. Trudeau has probably angered more politicians more times and compelled more editors to acts of censorship than any other artist working in America during the last twenty years. But a comic strip, no matter how pointed, cannot provide enough of a critique to counteract an information diet high in the unsaturated fat of the status quo. If a democracy survives to the extent that it allows expressed dissent, then a sustained critique of existing conditions should be the lifeblood of an advancing culture. By affirming the existence of tactics, we can avoid the optimistic passivity of the Reagan/Headrest model of history as well as the pessimistic passivity of the Baudrillardan model.

Unfortunately, one of the troubling effects of the Reagan administration's monopolistic corporate policies was the consolidation of media ownership. According to Ben Bagdikian, there were more than fifty national and multinational corporations that owned most of the major media in 1983. By 1992, there were fewer than twenty (ix). And the major media mergers of the late 1990s have left the power over much of America's information in even fewer hands. This consolidation makes the production and distribution of information critical of contemporary culture, of American corporate culture in particular, very difficult. "As competition declines through growing monopoly, and as the smaller voices that create diversity are drowned out by the overwhelming power of the giants," Bagdikian argues, "the dominant media corporations have ever greater freedom to shift the balance of news and popular culture away from reflecting what exists in American political, economic, and social culture, and toward creating what they would prefer to exist" (xviii). It is those "smaller voices" that speak for diversity that concern me most because their expressions of diversity often create dissent, and dissent does not sell or is not given the chance to. How do those smaller voices get heard if the means of production and distribution are owned by those invested in stifling dissent?

And what about those who express dissent formally as well as thematically, those who advance a critique of the *way* information is represented in contemporary culture as well as *what* is represented? If Walter Kalaidjian's claim that contemporary poets "are fated to write either for an audience largely oriented to the homogeneous representations of a monolithic culture industry or for fringe readerships pushed to the edge of America's cultural scene" (17) is accurate, and I believe it is, then the five poets I discuss in this study clearly choose the latter option. Their work challenges those "homogeneous representations" of contemporary culture that characterize much of the poetry published by the major trade presses, such as Knopf, Atheneum, Norton, and Penguin, and distributed by the equally homogeneous chain bookstores found in virtually every mall in America. As a result, it is often difficult to find the books of the poets examined in the pages that follow. Books published by small presses such as Awede, Ragweed, Lost Roads, and Kulchur are often available only through special order.[2] Douglas Messerli's Sun & Moon Press—which has published work by Howe, Hejinian, and Mackey—has recently been added to the lists of major book distributors, but that success story is a rare exception in today's market.

This situation is not merely a matter of these writers saturating their poems with statements critical of contemporary America. Many mainstream poets—Mark Strand, Adrienne Rich, Lucille Clifton, and Yusef Komunyakaa, for instance—offer thematic critiques of the values of contemporary American culture; there is, however, little dissent in terms of the form their poems take. For the most part, their poems continue the romantic lyric tradition in which a single and singular voice struggles to express and defend an authentic "personality" that stands over against an inauthentic social world. As Kalaidjian contends, "most contemporary poets and their critics succumbed to a kind of inward migration. In their writing, America's rich, contentious history was reduced and contained in personal narratives of private existential angst" (9). The poets discussed in this book, on the other hand, refuse to take part in that "inward migration"; more often than not, they turn their attention away from the personal and toward the social—or, to be more precise, they turn their attention to the intertwining of the personal and social. In short, these poets refuse to "sleepwalk" through America's history. And this refusal entails much more than making a critique of contemporary culture the thematic basis of their poetry: they insist on a formal as well as thematic critique of existing conditions.

Before I turn directly to the kind of poetry examined in this book, we should look more closely at the kind of contemporary poem that takes the "inward migration" to the mainstream. Here are two pieces by two highly regarded contemporary writers; the first is by Mark Strand, the second by Sharon Olds.

A Morning

I have carried it with me each day: that morning I took
my uncle's boat from the brown water cove
and headed for Mosher Island.
Small waves splashed against the hull
and the hollow creek of oarlock and oar
rose into the woods of black pine crusted with lichen.
I moved like a dark star, drifting over the drowned
other half of the world until, by a distant prompting,
I looked over the gunwale and saw beneath the surface
a luminous room, a light-filled grave, saw for the first time
the one clear place given to us when we are alone.

(149)

Miscarriage

When I was a month pregnant, the great
clots of blood appeared in the pale
green swaying water of the toilet.
Dark red like black in the salty
translucent brine, like forms of life
appearing, jelly-fish with the clear-cut
shapes of fungi.

That was the only appearance made by that
child, the dark, scalloped shapes
falling slowly. A month later
our son was conceived, and I never went back
to mourn the one who came as far as the
sill with its information: that we could
botch something, you and I. All wrapped in
purple it floated away, like a messenger
put to death for bearing bad news.

(25)

The first person pronoun (the first word in Strand's poem and the second in Olds's) controls and organizes both of these poems, and that "I" narrates episodes of recollection. The "I" in "A Morning" looks back on a monumental experience in his life. A youthful morning spent in splendid isolation in nature with the uncle's boat provokes a muted existential epiphany: I looked and saw I was alone. The "I" in "Miscarriage" is somewhat less generic; the recollection seems more visceral and particularized. Yet the muted domestic epiphany is no less obvious: "that we could / botch something, you and I." Both poems are vehicles that intend to transport their authors' recollected experience relatively untrammeled to the reader by employing the language of easy consumption, "The Plain Style," as Robert Pinsky dubbed it. The language in both poems readily conforms to the rules of normative discourse; there is little to divert our attention away from the representation of the authors' experience, which is the usual goal of a great deal of mainstream poetry. And both poems all too successfully privilege the personal at the expense of the social or historical.

Susan Howe, Nathaniel Mackey, Lyn Hejinian, Kamau Brathwaite, and M. Nourbese Philip write poetry that has very little in common with the work of Mark Strand or Sharon Olds. Rather than an exclusive offering of poetic representations of personal experiences, these five writers produce what I call contemporary investigative poetry in order to explore the linguistic, historical, and political conditions of contemporary culture.[3] These writers trace out and track power in the form of the poetic. Like scientists or district attorneys or philosophers, they *investigate* the cultural conditions under which they write. Ezra Pound advises poets to "Consider the way of the scientists rather than the way of an advertising agent for a new soap. The scientist does not expect to be acclaimed as a great scientist until he has *discovered* something. . . . He does not bank on being a charming fellow personally" (1968a, 6). Poets should, in other words, investigate and discover something rather than craft another representation of themselves "personally." But unlike most scientists, these poets primarily examine cultural rather than natural phenomena. So their work may be more similar to that of a district attorney or a private detective, since these poets investigate the causes that sustain the social and economic conditions that produce contemporary culture. As Susan Howe puts it, "Sometimes my poetry is only a search by an investigator for the point where the crime began" (Beckett, 21), and, to a great degree, this holds true for the other four poets I discuss. Yet poetic investigations take place as and in language, which makes them more like philosophical investigations, particularly the kind conducted by Ludwig Wittgenstein in his *Philosophical Investigations*.

I use the phrases *poetic investigations* and *investigative poetry* to characterize this approach to poetry and to underscore some of the concerns these contemporary poets share with science and criminology. But I use the term primarily to suggest some of the similarities between the ways these five poets investigate poetry and the way Wittgenstein investigates our uses of words as they move in and out of various "language-games." For Wittgenstein, a language-game consists "of language and the actions into which it is woven" (5). By including sociohistorical "actions" in his definition of language-games, his inquiries into our uses of language are open to cultural as well as linguistic matters, which is why, for Wittgenstein, "to imagine a language means to imagine a form of life" (8). Those inquiries are also open to the production of new language-games — new forms of poetry, for instance — since their "multiplicity is not something fixed, given once for all; but new types of language, new language-games, as we may say, come into existence, and others become obsolete and get forgotten" (11). The five poets discussed in this book, I argue, investigate disparate language-games in order to produce new poetic forms that articulate new forms of life — new instances of what I call writing history poetically. These new ways of writing challenge readers to stop "sleepwalking through history" by interrogating the forms of representation that make that somnambulism possible; as a result, these new ways of writing also challenge Baudrillard's contention that the difference between the real and the simulated can no longer be discerned.

I use the term *poetic* as a way of including more than "verse" in these investigations. Verse is a subset of the poetic, as is the prose poem, essay poem, visual poem, and combinations thereof. This book concentrates on poetic investigations that take the set, rather than subset, as their field, and that assume the boundaries between genres are permeable. All five of the writers treated in this book produce a variety of texts, most of which I would call poetic but not all of which are verse. Susan Howe has written two stunning works of poetic scholarship, *My Emily Dickinson* and *The Birth-mark,* in addition to more than ten books of verse. Nathaniel Mackey has recently completed his third volume of epistolary fiction, *From a Broken Bottle Traces of Perfume Still Emanate,* as well as his third volume of verse. Lyn Hejinian's *My Life* has become a model for the genre-bending contemporary prose poem, but her novel in verse, *Oxota,* is just as transgressive. If we compare the visual appearance of any page in Kamau Brathwaite's first book of poetry, 1967's *Rights of Passage,* with any page from 1994's *Trench Town Rock,* it is obvious that the boundaries between poetry and prose and between writing and graphics have become increasingly permeable in his work. And M. Nourbese Philip moves back and forth among verse, fiction, and essay in any number of her works — between verse and fiction in *Looking for Livingstone,* and among all three in "*Dis Place* The Space Between." We miss much of these writers' critique of the *way* contemporary culture is represented in language if we only attend to their verse.

Furthermore, we miss the ways in which these transgressions of form enact critiques of contemporary culture—which is to say these poetic investigations do have aims. My focus in this book will be on one of these aims: writing history poetically. My use of the term *history* is meant to include the social, political, and economic dimensions of culture, just as my use of the term *poetic* is meant to include verse, prose poetry, fiction, and essay. Both terms point toward writing that challenges the exclusionary boundaries that often define the social and aesthetic domains of contemporary culture. I propose that the five investigative poets I discuss write history poetically by deploying tactics to disrupt our culture's systems of control, the "language" systems in particular. In this introduction, I expand on de Certeau's notion by drawing it into dialogue with the work of Wittgenstein, Walter Benjamin, and Ernesto Laclau and Chantal Mouffe to gain a more specific understanding of the tactics investigative poetry has at its disposal.

Wittgenstein's notion of multiple language-games enables us to see resemblance across genre boundaries. Resemblance—not essence. Particularly in the first half of *Philosophical Investigations,* he interrogates the discourse of essence that dominates Western intellectual history, discards it, and offers a discourse of resemblance in its place. For Wittgenstein, we can identify the similarities among different kinds of games—"board-games, card-games, ball-games, Olympic games, and so on"—not because we detect a singular essential trait: "For if you look at them you will not see something that is common to *all,* but similarities, relationships, and a whole series of them at that" (31). Rather than identifying an essence shared, we gather phenomena together by identifying *family resemblances* —those "various resemblances between members of a family: build, features, colour of eyes, gait, temperament, etc. etc. overlap and criss-cross in the same way" (32). In this book, I gather five contemporary writers together in terms of family resemblances, not all of which are present in each writer, but enough of which are to perceive similarity. Rather than posit a single trait, an essence, that all five poets share, I propose to investigate the "overlap and criss-cross." Although there is no essence uniting the language-games of my five investigative poets, "something runs through the whole thread," as Wittgenstein contends—"namely the continuous overlapping of those fibres" (32). I use the phrase *writing history poetically,* then, as a metonymy for that which overlaps when these writers are considered as members of a family; it is not intended to indicate an essence. The multiple meanings of this phrase, as well as the phrase *poetic investigations,* will unfold as my argument progresses, and I will return to the other thinkers mentioned earlier, Benjamin and Laclau and Mouffe. But perhaps the most productive way to begin a discussion of family resemblance is to proceed inductively by taking a brief look at each of the five poets and at some of the "overlap and criss-cross."

Susan Howe's writing investigates the power relations at work in the construction of meaning; more specifically, it investigates the construction of meaning in and by history. She is "drawn toward the disciplines of history and literary criticism but in the dawning distance a dark wall of rule supports the structure of every letter, record, transcript: every proof of authority and power" (1993, 4). Howe's writing presents a sustained critique of the authorized interpretation of history and of the cultural forces, the "dark wall of rule," that authorize that interpretation. For Howe, "poetry unsettles our scrawled defence; unapprehensible but dear nevertheless" (1993, 2). She unsettles history by disrupting the sequential narrative style of traditional historiography with a highly paratactic and elliptical form of writing that frustrates the desire to uncover the "original" version of the story.

> Left home to seek Lost
>
> Pitchfork origin
>
> tribunal of eternal revolution
> tribunal of rigorous revaluation
>
> Captive crowned tyrant deposed
> Ego as captive thought
>
> Conscience in ears too late
>
> Father the law
> Stamped hero-partner

> pledge of creditor to debtor
>
> Destiny of calamitous silence
>
> (1990a, 25)

A number of thematic hints arise here—hints about oppressive relations between tyrants and the tyrannized, between creditors and debtors, between patriarchal law and its gendered subjects—but the hierarchical grammar and syntax that would organize them is absent, unrepresented. Instead, the order of the rulers, not the ruled, is silenced. Throughout Howe's poetry, the silence of the ruled is made manifest by drawing attention to their absence from the authorized narrative of history: "I wish I could tenderly lift from the dark side of history, voices that are anonymous, slighted—inarticulate" (1990b, 14).

As an African-American writer, Nathaniel Mackey shares Howe's concern for the silenced voices in history. For Mackey, however, "there has been far too much emphasis on accessibility when it comes to writers from socially marginalized groups. This has resulted in shallow, simplistic readings that belabor the most obvious aspects of the writer's work and situation, readings that go something like this: 'So-and-so is a black writer. Black people are victims of racism. So-and-so's writing speaks out against racism'"; reading this way tells "us only what we already know [and] is a symptom of the social othering such readings presumably oppose" (1993c, 17–18). Mackey is not out to discourage poets from writing about race, but he is asking them not to sacrifice the complexity of the issue for accessibility. The problem with simplicity is that it all too often simplifies by eliminating what he calls "noise": "whatever the signifying system, in a particular situation, is not intended to transmit, be the system a poem, a piece of music, a novel, or an entire society" (1993c, 20). These systems tend to reduce noise by homogenizing difference—formal difference, in particular—in order to produce a unified effect. Mackey advances a poetics that includes "a gesture in the direction of noise" (1993c, 20). A few lines from "Song of the Andoumboulou: 12" show how he investigates race in a poetic form that does not oversimplify it, thematically or formally:

> Cramped egg we might work our
> way out of,   caress reaching in
> to the bones underneath.
>
>   Not even

                    looking. Even so, see
                                thru.

               Watery light we tried in vain
                  to pull away from.   Painted
                                     face,
               disembodied voice. Dramas we
                  wooed, invited in but got
               scared of.   Song so black it
                                     burnt
               my lip . . .   Tore my throat as I
                  walked up Real Street. Raw beginner,

                                               green
                  attempt to sing the blues . . .
                                        (1993a, 9–10)

This passage seems to depict a birth scene, an emerging from a "cramped
egg," and the movement from the first person plural to the first person
singular suggests that this birth may be both communal and individual.
It may also be read as the birth or development of racial consciousness
signaled by the shift from minstrel songs ("Painted / face, / disembodied voice") to the blues as a form of African-American expression. Yet the
"noise" in this passage, the silent static created by the paratactic gaps between phrases and sentences, makes a number of alternative readings both
possible and plausible.

    In both Howe and Mackey, there is a formal as well as thematic chal-
lenge to the structure of authority under which history has been written.
And the structure of authority under which history has been read has
also been questioned. Lyn Hejinian adds to this list a challenge to the
structure of authority between writer and reader. She advocates a form of
writing history poetically called the "open text." According to Hejinian,
the open text "invites participation, rejects the authority of the writer over
the reader and thus, by analogy, the authority implicit in other (social,
economic, cultural) hierarchies"; in short, the open text "resists reduction and commodification" (1985, 272). The authority to commodify the
writer, the reader, and the processes of composition derives from a complex of practices that teach us to cede power to the normalizing forces of
culture, practices that teach us not only what to read and write but how
to read and write. The open text resists this authority by disrupting the
relation between writer and reader that presupposes an understanding of

language in which meaning passes relatively unmediated from person to person. In an open text, then, the reader as well as the writer must make meaning, not just receive it. Hejinian's collaborative, participatory model of composition draws previously stable notions of authorship and ownership into question. The opening stanza of "The Guard" can serve as an instance of an open text:

> Can one take captives by writing—
> "Humans repeat themselves."
> The full moon falls on the first. I
> "whatever interrupts." Weather and air
> drawn to us. The open mouths of people
> are yellow & red—of pupils.
> Cannot be taught and therefore cannot be.
> As a political leading article would offer
> to its illustrator. But they don't invent
> they trace. You match your chair.
>
> (1994, 11)

The paratactic arrangement of these sentences makes an authoritative reading of the passage virtually impossible. How can the reader be even fairly sure that he or she has successfully reconstructed the author's intended meaning? Given that this passage depicts the "I" as " 'whatever interrupts,' " not as the first person narrator who authorizes an interpretation, the satisfactions of reading this kind of poetry derive from being involved in the production as well as the consumption of meaning.

Kamau Brathwaite, an African-Caribbean poet from Barbados, writes history poetically by deploying "nation language"—his term for the variant of English, used in parts of the Caribbean, that is infiltrated with the linguistic "noise" that signals the remnants of diasporic cultures. This variant is not to be equated with dialect, which, Brathwaite argues,

> has a long history coming from the plantation where people's dignity was distorted through their languages and their descriptions that the dialect gave them. Nation language, on the other hand, is the submerged area of that dialect that is much more closely allied to the African aspect of experience in the Caribbean. It may be in English, but often it is in an English which is like a howl, or a shout, or a machine-gun, or the wind, or a wave. It is also like the blues. (1993, 266)

If dialect represents the subservient dimension of language in the anglophone Caribbean, nation language represents its subversive dimension. For Brathwaite, nation language serves as much more than a linguistic site of nostalgia for an unrecoverable past, as we can see from the opening lines of "X/Self's Xth Letters from the Thirteen Provinces":

> Dear mamma
>
> i writin you dis letter/wha?
> guess what! pun a computer o/kay?
> like i jine de mercantilists!
>
> well not quite!
>
> i mean de same way dem tief/in gun
> power from sheena & taken we blues &
>
> gone . . .
>
> say
> what?/get on wi de same ole
>
> story?
>
> okay
> okay
>
> okay
> okay
>
> if yu cyaan beat prospero
> whistle?
>
> (1987, 80)

The "creolization" (another key term for Brathwaite) of English is obvious to both the eye and the ear. Yet the passage is governed not by nostalgia but by a critique of the pastness of the present: technology may have changed, and the underclass may even have occasional access to it ("i" now writes "pun a computer"), but the "same ole / story" is still in demand, for the "same ole" conditions still persist—Prospero, "Shakespeare's plantation owner" (1987, 127), is still in charge. Although Brathwaite recognizes the significant changes in the strategies of colonial domination, his poetic investigations expose the naïveté of using terms such as "postcolonial" to describe Caribbean culture.

M. Nourbese Philip is also an African-Caribbean, born in Tobago and now living in Canada. And, like Brathwaite, she confronts the traditions of colonialism that endure in contemporary culture. For Philip, "The place African Caribbean writers occupy is one that is unique, and one that forces the writer to operate in a language that was used to brutalize and diminish Africans so that they would come to a profound belief in their own lack of humanity" (1989, 19). The English language was imposed on the anglophone Caribbean in and by slavery at the expense of the "mother" tongues of Africa. Given that those tongues have been all but lost, Philip contends that the challenge for African-Caribbean writers "is to use the language in such a way that the historical realities are not erased or obliterated, so that English is revealed as the tainted tongue it truly is" (1989, 19). The final lines of "Testimony Stoops to Mother Tongue" investigate this complex challenge and raise what may be an unanswerable question:

> in my mother's mouth
> shall I
> > use
> the father's tongue
> cohabit in strange
> mother
> > incestuous words
> > to revenge the self
> > > broken
> upon
> > the word
>
> (1989, 82)

Philip figures the relationship between colonizer and colonized as analogous to the relationship between men and women in patriarchal cultures: "the father's tongue" imposed on "my mother's mouth." Her use of the first person possessive to indicate the speaker's relation to "mother" and only a definite article to relate the speaker to "father" is telling: the speaker possesses a mother but not a father. Yet "the father's tongue" has been imposed with all too much success, and it seems that the only chance of revenge is through an "incestuous" relationship with the imposed language.

Even this brief first look at the five investigative poets I discuss suggests patterns of resemblance. All five tend to write formally and thematically subversive forms of poetic history in order to confront the forms of cultural power that use language to use people. The place of the author in the strategies of authority—strategies of race, class, and gender—that guide history and govern contemporary culture is of great concern to these writers. To differing degrees, they all practice disruptive forms of writing that foreground the subversive tactics of "noise" and dissonance. Although they argue that it is possible to subvert the cultural conditioning that takes place in and by language, none of them would claim that he or she could escape that conditioning altogether. Not complete subversion; but, again, some is better than none. The formal disruptions that characterize much of the poetry discussed in this book create some of the conditions for this subversion; thus, this poetry amounts to much more than just formalist experimentation: it carries a "message" consonant with its form. Refusing to write poetry that is formally and thematically conventional needs to be recognized as the political gesture that it is, and I will discuss shortly the ways in which investigative poetry is political. For now, I want to situate my claims about these five contemporary writers in terms of their resemblance to specific modern and contemporary models of writing history poetically.

Howe, Mackey, Hejinian, Brathwaite, and Philip continue the modernist assault on the ossification and commodification of language in conventional form, the form in which ideology lies lowest. They take up many of the modernist textual practices that characterize the innovative work of writers such as Gertrude Stein, Guillaume Apollinaire, Ezra Pound, William Carlos Williams, H. D., Aimé Césaire, and Louis Zukofsky, to name only a few. These contemporary poets inherit the modernist preoccupation with language; they investigate innovative ways of writing about the past in the forms of collage and montage; and they explore the political implications of poetry and the poetic implications of politics. Yet they submit those modernist practices to considerable criticism and revision, and the result is a disparate body of poetic work that is more than a mere repetition of an earlier movement.

A brief contrast between a quintessential modernist, Ezra Pound, and one of the five contemporary writers I discuss, M. Nourbese Philip, will demonstrate some of those revisions. In "The State," a short essay published in a 1927 issue of *The Exile,* Ezra Pound sets forth his position on the way in which an artist engages with his or her culture:

> The artist, the maker is always too far ahead of any revolution, or reaction, or counter-revolution or counter-reaction for his vote to have any immediate result; and no party programme ever contains enough of his programme to give him the least satisfaction. The party that follows

him wins; and the speed with which they set about it, is the measure of their practical capacity and intelligence. Blessed are they who pick the right artists and makers. (1973, 215)

Here we have many of the doctrines of "heroic" or "elitist" modernism on full display. The artist is ahead of but never alongside his or her contemporaries—too far ahead, in fact, to see an "immediate result" or to derive much "satisfaction" from his or her labors. The responsibility of the poet is to bring intuitions to form; the responsibility of the citizens and leaders of culture is to recognize and follow the artist to the extent that their "practical capacity and intelligence" will allow. "Blessed are they" who know whom to follow. Pound's characterization of the relation between artists and their cultures is fairly typical of many modernist variations on this theme: the artist is isolated from his or her culture because of the demands of genius; but by virtue of that isolation, the genius can transcend culture and return to intervene invested with the authority of the gods or muses. As Bob Perelman notes, many modernist visions of the writer "displayed a hierophantic conception in which writing floated down from a higher world of order that was fully accessible only to the genius-writer and that could be only partially revealed even to the devout reader" (14). Pound's vision is no exception and does not represent all or even most modernist writers; it is a position most of the contemporary poets I discuss criticize and reject.

A passage from the introduction to Philip's *She Tries Her Tongue, Her Silence Softly Breaks,* which won the Casa de las Americas prize in 1988, sets out a very different understanding of the relation between writers and their culture:

> Only when we understand language and its role in colonial society can we understand the role of writing and the writer in such a society; only then, perhaps, can we understand why writing was not and still, to a large degree, is not recognized as a career, profession, or way of being in the Caribbean and even among Caribbean people resident in Canada. (1989, 11–12)

For Philip, the writer cannot transcend culture or choose not to write "about" it, as if culture were no more than a theme or a background one may or may not address. The writer, in short, is not ahead of culture but within it. So the "career" choice of writing and the politics of being an "other," of being an African-Caribbean woman, are inseparable for Philip. That choice situates her work within specific social practices—practices that failed, whether intentionally or not, to recognize either the possibility of that choice or the complicity between the languages of the Caribbean and the politics of colonialism in concealing that possibility. In this account, the writer is isolated as a result of racist and sexist social practices, not as a result of his or her genius. The remedy for this kind of isolation involves a particularized investigation of language, history, and ideology so that the writer understands the conditions of his or her vocation.

The emphasis on the local and the specific in Philip's diagnosis stands in stark contrast to the more universal and general emphasis in Pound's. Philip embeds the issue of the relation between poetry and politics in a specific moment in history, neocolonialism, and a specific place, the Caribbean. Pound's diagnosis marks neither time nor place—which may seem odd since his poetry is so deeply engaged with the particularities of history, yet this dichotomy is present in many other modernist writers. From Pound to Philip, then, we see a shift from an image of the poet as genius and augur of universal truths to an image of the poet as ethnographer and witness of particular practices. This shift in analytical focus from the universal and general to the specific and local marks one of the significant differences between a great deal of modernist poetry and the poetry of the contemporary writers I discuss.

Pound's are not, of course, the only modernist responses to questions concerning how one can write history poetically and how much one may or may not intervene in culture as a result of that writing. Walter Benjamin, although he was only seven years younger than Pound, responds to these questions in a way which is almost diametrically opposed to Pound, a way which has much more in common with the five contemporary writers I discuss. As such, Benjamin's response serves as an alternate link to the modernist past for these contemporary writers. Whether Benjamin's work directly influenced any of the five writers I treat does not concern me; the alternative he provides to Pound, however, does. In "Surrealism" (1929), in "Theses on the Philosophy of History" (1940), and throughout his furtive Arcades project, Benjamin presents an aphoristic manifesto on the practice of writing history poetically that not only distinguishes itself from Pound's practice but can also serve to foreground some of the tactical resemblances that occur in the work of Howe, Mackey, Hejinian, Brathwaite, and Philip.

Benjamin's project arose from questions that have become increasingly important for contemporary writers: Who and what compose history? How do they do it? And how do they gain the power to impose their say on others? His answers are impacted within his understanding of the image, which for Benjamin, like Pound, is the fulcrum of both his theory and practice of writing. "History breaks down into images, not into stories" (1989, 67), Benjamin contends, and, in doing so, he presents us with a philosophy of history grounded in poetics rather than narratology. For Benjamin, narration has its place but mostly as commentary on the history of the image being presented. The image underwrites Benjamin's philosophy of history and his philosophy of history writing, a point best evidenced in his "Theses on the Philosophy of History."

To appreciate Benjamin's image-based philosophy of history, we need, first, to understand just what he means by an image; second, to see how his notion of the image differs from some of his modernist contemporaries; and, finally, to explore the implications this notion has on the role of the author in writing history poetically.[4] For Benjamin, images are not windows that let us look into an atemporal or ahistorical realm of universal truths; they do not allow us "to distil the eternal from the transitory," as Baudelaire thought (12). In Benjamin's practice, images illuminate material configurations in all their transience; they illuminate the profane world of the everyday, the world in which one's desire for happiness meets its match in those who impose their word on others. As he puts it in the second of his "Theses," "Reflection shows us that our image of happiness is thoroughly colored by the time to which the course of our own existence has assigned us" (1968, 253–54). In other words, our images of utopia are necessarily grounded in and derived from the material and historical conditions in which we find ourselves. Thus, Benjamin concludes, these utopian images of happiness, because they originate in real rather than ideal conditions, contain the seeds, latent within the image, of a revolution that would bring about actual utopian conditions. Benjamin calls the image in which these two moments intersect the "dialectical image."

According to Benjamin, dialectical images illuminate the real and ideal as well as the ways in which the two are woven together and deployed by those who compose history. More specifically, dialectical images illuminate the ways in which the images a culture has of itself are used by those with power over them to impose their own image of the present. Benjamin's conception of the dialectical image is obviously indebted to Hegel, but the two are not identical. As Susan Buck-Morss points out, the difference between Benjamin's image-driven dialect and Hegel's concept-driven dialectic is that Benjamin's "does not form a discursive system in a Hegelian sense. The moment of sublation reveals itself visually, in an instantaneous flash wherein the old is illuminated precisely at the moment of its disappearance" (146). Benjamin's dialectical image represents the moment of tension between the thesis and the antithesis rather than the moment of resolution. In Benjamin's words, "an image is dialectics at a standstill" (1989, 50)—and it is at that moment that a dialectical image serves as a tactic to investigate the holes in the seamless narrative of history.

"Thesis 17" provides the epistemological backing for this understanding of the image. "Thinking involves not only the flow of thoughts, but their arrest as well. Where thinking suddenly stops in a configuration pregnant with tensions, it gives the configuration a shock, by which it crystallizes into a monad" (1968, 262–63). The dialectical image delivers that shock to the configuration of history that Benjamin seeks to disrupt: history configured as progress. At the moment in which one of the dialectical oppositions succumbs to the other, something gets covered over—what the other had and has to say before and after being "sublated." Progress can only proclaim itself if what the other says is suppressed. The dialectical image disrupts the story of progress, a story that, like most stories, encourages continuity in both its form and content. Dialectical images discontinue "the flow of thoughts" that compose the narrative of progress; they reveal that which has not progressed as well as that which has regressed. In other words, they "arrest" progress. As we will see, the five investigative poets I discuss present work that tactically disrupts the narratives of progress.

Benjamin's preoccupation with arresting progress in and with an image reveals the modernist moment in Benjamin's historiography. I have already mentioned Baudelaire's dictum that the modernist should seek "to distil the eternal from the transitory"; we also see this preoccupation in James Joyce's aesthetics of "stasis" and in T. S. Eliot's doctrine of the "still-point." But the best foil for Benjamin's conception of the image is Pound's. "An 'Image,'" according to Pound, "is that which presents an intellectual and emotional complex in an instant of time. . . . It is the presentation of such a 'complex' instantaneously which gives that sense of sudden liberation; that sense of freedom from time limits and space limits; that sense of sudden growth, which we experience in the presence of the greatest works of art" (1968a, 4). For both Pound and Benjamin, the image is "complex" since it is composed of conflicting, juxtaposed elements; for both, the image is presented "instantaneously"; and for both it liberates. The difference between the two lies in just what it is that the image liberates us from. For Pound, it liberates us from the limitations of space and time; in short, the image liberates us from the material constraints that space and time impose on history. In Pound, the image seeks to set us free *from* history; in Benjamin, the image seeks to set us free *in* history. For Pound, "all ages are contemporaneous" (1968b, 6); for Benjamin, all ages are different since truth changes over time, and truth in transition is fleeting. Benjamin calls for an "emphatic refusal of the concept of 'timeless truth' " (1989, 51); consequently, his dialectical images present the transitory rather than the eternal. They arrest history in progress as progress.

According to Benjamin, "When thinking reaches a standstill in a constellation saturated with tensions, the dialectical image appears. The image is the caesura in the movement of thought. . . . The dialectical image is, accordingly, the very object constructed in the materialist presentation of history" (1989, 67). As we have seen, Benjamin contends that the image marks out the tension inherent in a moment in history, and, as such, it represents the "caesura" in the dialectic rather than its resolution. More important, the dialectical image becomes the object the historian, the materialist historian, not only studies but constructs and presents as well. If the dialectical image is indeed the object of the materialist historian's attention, then what would the principle of construction of such an object be? Benjamin's answer to this question occurs in a note on his own attempt to construct such a text—his book on the Paris Arcades. "Method of this project: literary montage. I need say nothing. Only exhibit" (1989, 47). He found this principle of montage at work in the texts of many of his contemporaries, but those of the surrealists proved the most influential.[5] He uncovered, in a number of their works, the dialectical image in its predialectical moment.

To a much greater extent than other practitioners of modernism, the surrealists investigate the dream state and the possibilities of representing that state in language. And like their fellow modernists Joyce, Pound, and Eliot—although again, to a much greater extent—the surrealists juxtapose images from the realm of dreams with images from the realm of myth. In these juxtapositions the surrealists, like most modernists, seek to unite the realms of dream and myth in the image. The difference between the surrealists and most other modernists is that the surrealists want to bring these disparate elements together, as Buck-Morss points out, "in such a way that myth's claim to express transcendent, eternal truth is undermined" (257). Note that the difference between the surrealists and modernists such as Joyce, Eliot, and Pound is strikingly similar to the difference between Benjamin and these same modernists on the nature of the image. Benjamin follows the surrealists in his attempt to present the permanence of transience in dialectical images. In both instances, the ground beneath any claims for a notion of truth as atemporal and transcendent begins to shift.

One of the first transcendent, eternal truths that needs undermining, both Benjamin and the surrealists agree, is capitalism's claim for the precedence of the individual—of the self as a cogito that has as its essence an inalienable right to consume. The implications Benjamin's notion of the dialectical image will have on the role of the author in thinking and writing history poetically become most apparent in relation to this issue. I take Benjamin's description of the surrealists' position on this issue as a fairly accurate description of his position as well: "Language takes precedence. Not only before meaning. Also before the self. In the world's structure dream loosens individuality like a bad tooth" (1978, 179). Before meaning gets a chance to translate language into traditional discursive patterns, the self encounters it as imagery in the dream state. The self as a site of dream imagery precedes the self as a consumptive cogito. And the principle of montage gave the surrealists and Benjamin a technique with which to present this precedence in writing.

Yet Benjamin offers a critique of surrealism as well as an endorsement. For Benjamin, surrealism, by focusing on the dream state exclusively, fails to investigate not only that state's opposite, the state of being awake; it also fails to investigate the dialectical relation between those two states. The surrealist emphasis on only one of these two states, the dream state, will, as Terry Eagleton points out, "bring calamity, since folding history back into the unconscious . . . rob[s] both past and unconscious of their emancipatory force, which is to be always elsewhere" (43–44). The unconscious and the conscious quickly become charged with political connotations for Benjamin: he identifies the former with the dream of a utopia, while he identifies the latter with the activity of revolution. While the dream state supplies the waking state with an image of its desire, the latter attempts to actualize the former in history. Benjamin wants to illuminate the dialectic of awakening in order to complete the surrealists' task of loosening the grip the capitalist construction of the individual has on the self.

"Such awakening," however, "began where the Surrealists and other avant-garde artists too often stopped short, because in rejecting cultural tradition they closed their eyes to history as well" (Buck-Morss, 261). Benjamin finds in the discourses of theology and Marxism a way of bringing history back into play—a way which allows his dialectic of awakening to move beyond the dream state of the surrealists. Although the discourses of theology and Marxism seem at odds with each other, Benjamin discovers, in their encounter in a dialectical image, grounds of similarity. The two share a desire for the dissolution of the constructed category of the individual and a utopian sense of community. The surrealists clearly share the first desire with theology and Marxism, but their hostility to history leaves them without the image of a utopia from which to address the second desire. Thus, the crucial difference between Benjamin and surrealism: if language loosens the "tooth" of individuality when presented in surreal images, Benjamin's dialectical images go a step further and extract that "bad tooth." Loosening the tooth is necessary but usually only prolongs the pain; extracting it provides a cure.

Benjamin's philosophy of history, then, turns out to be a philosophy of history writing. The intimate link between Benjamin's way of thinking and writing history and the technique of montage, as practiced by the surrealists, lies in the shared desire to bring disparate elements into opposition with each other and illuminate the identity among the elements as well as the difference. In practice, Benjamin's philosophy of history writing works by juxtaposing quotations with other quotations as well as with his own commentary.[6] The latter allows Benjamin to overcome the contradiction he exposes in surrealism: commentary opens the text up to revolutionary contents, while the method of montage opens the text up to revolutionary forms.

Yet this is precisely where the dialectic of authorship, a dialectic that remains unreconciled in Benjamin's writings, begins: commentary brings the author as individual on stage, but this move contradicts the principle of montage, which attempts to remove that same author from the stage. And it is this contradiction in Benjamin's philosophy of thinking and writing history poetically that generates many of the questions that animate Benjamin's work. Is it possible to actually say nothing and only exhibit history through a montage of images? And, given this possibility, is it also possible to present a revolutionary content through this montage without the author stepping on stage? The answers for Benjamin—answers that recognize rather than reconcile the contradiction—are contained in his concept of the dialectical image, which reduces the role of the author as arranger and commentator to a bare minimum.

The central example of a dialectical image in Benjamin's "Theses" is the image of the angel of history, and it is also his central image of the author. As his friend Gershom Scholem remarked, "If one may speak of Walter Benjamin's genius, then it was concentrated in this angel" (86).

This image of the angel of history, inspired by a Paul Klee painting, appears in the ninth of the eighteen "Theses" and presides over the whole in the same way Benjamin believes an author presides over a text—not as a creator or dictator but as a witness and a messenger. According to Benjamin, the angel of history's face is

> turned toward the past. Where we perceive a chain of events, he sees one single catastrophe which keeps piling wreckage upon wreckage and hurls it in front of his feet. The angel would like to stay, awaken the dead, and make whole what has been smashed. But a storm is blowing from Paradise; it has got caught in his wings with such violence that the angel can no longer close them. This storm irresistibly propels him into the future to which his back is turned, while the pile of debris before him grows skyward. This storm is what we call progress. (1968, 257–58)

Benjamin's image of the angel of history illuminates the oppositions that produce much of the tension in his work: the opposition between the past and the future, as the angel looks back to the former while being propelled into the latter; the opposition between the theological impulse that posits a "paradise" from which the angel arrives and the Marxist impulse that condemns the "pile of debris" the angel finds when he arrives; and the opposition between the message of "awakening" the angel would like to pass on and the "catastrophe" that message seems too late to avert. In short, the image of the angel of history presents the dialectic of redemption and destruction that marks virtually every page Benjamin authored.

The reader of Benjamin's "Theses" confronts this dialectical image at the moment between redemption and destruction, and Benjamin's image illuminates the complicity of one with the other. Note, after all, that the storm the angel encounters, the storm that pushes the angel away from those who most need his message, "is blowing from Paradise," not from hell or the earth. Note also that "this storm is what we call progress." I believe Benjamin's image of the author of history is very similar to his image of the angel of history. The author of an image-based history is not an antiquarian recounting the past for posterity's sake; rather, he or she delivers a message of warning for the present. The author of a materialist history who attempts to think and write history poetically, like the angel, witnesses the catastrophe of history and tries to deliver a message.

But that message cannot take the form of traditional historiography since so much of the message concerns that which a continuous, seamless narration of history leaves out: the voice of the other, of those "sublated" by the narrative of progress that underwrites most modern methods of historiography. Benjamin's insistence on the image as the ground of an alternative poetic historiography, then, is much more than a matter of adopting a more "ornamental" or "literary" style when one writes history. For Benjamin, traditional narrative historiography, which aims at the "establishment of continuity," "breaks down and thus misses those jags and crags that offer a handhold to someone who wishes to move beyond them" (1989, 64–65). Those jags and crags that traditional methods of thinking and writing history miss are the dialectical images embedded in the past, and they provide history's mountaineer a chance to move beyond a presentation of history as the continuous story of progress and completion.

Benjamin's model of writing history poetically highlights a number of resemblances with the work of Howe, Mackey, Hejinian, Brathwaite, and Philip. His concern with the weave of the real and the ideal in the dialectical image, which is at odds with the erasure of the real in the Reagan/Headrest and Baudrillardan models of history; his concern with the ways in which such images can arrest the hegemonic narrative of history, with the desire to be set free in rather than from history by awakening the unconscious (utopian) and the conscious (revolutionary) forces of language; and his concern with the image of the author as witness all bear striking resemblance to many of the concerns of the five investigative poets I discuss. In short, the desire to awaken those that are "sleepwalking through history" and to disrupt the simulation of history as progressive joins these writers together in their poetic investigations of contemporary culture.

Yet they also share with many innovative writers of the modernist period, including Benjamin and Pound, an aesthetic of difficulty. Ignoring the difficulty of their work is a disservice to the poets and their poetry, as is the suggestion that all this poetry needs is a few good critics to uncover the simple truth beneath the difficult surface in order to make it accessible to the "common" reader. As I argued earlier, these contemporary writers do continue the modernist assault on the ossification of language, which results in an assault on conventional forms of poetry, which results, in turn, in a "difficult" text. This shared aesthetic of difficulty sets both modern and contemporary investigative poetry at odds with another modernist tradition that offers very different answers to the questions of how one writes history poetically and how much a writer may or may not intervene in his or her culture.

In *Repression and Recovery*, Cary Nelson reclaims a modernist movement of poetry based on the premise "that traditional forms continued to do vital cultural work throughout this period," a movement opposed to "formally experimental but politically disengaged modernism" (23, 22). Early in his study, Nelson offers "How Much for Spain?"—written in 1937 by Mike Quinn, "perhaps the quintessential Communist Party poet" (24)—as an instance of a poem that does "vital cultural work."

> The long collection speech is done
> And now the felt hat goes
> From hand to hand its solemn way
> Along the restless rows.
>
> In purse and pocket, fingers feel,
> And count the coins by touch.
> Minds ponder what they can afford
> And hesitate—how much?
>
> In that brief, jostled moment when
> The battered hat arrives,
> Try, brother, to remember that
> Some men put in their lives.
>   (Nelson, 24)

Nelson values Quinn's poetry, and work like it, primarily because it is "highly accessible" (24), a judgment grounded in the Marxist tenet that art addressing the working class is the most valuable. Only basic reading skills are necessary to decode not only Quinn's call for money but to feel the "justness" of that call, given the price paid by those mentioned in the final line. And since the form—the predictable meter, the symmetrical stanzas, the simple diction—is conventional, it is likely to be familiar to more potential readers, which may translate into more contributors to the cause. The way a poem like this intervenes in culture, then, is to recruit members for working-class organizations, to generate solidarity (and funds) within those organizations, and to memorialize the anonymous heroes of the social struggle.

However, if we judge either the innovative modernists or the five investigative writers I discuss by this measure, both groups will surely be found wanting. Innovative poetry, whether modern or contemporary, is usually not addressed to the working class. This is no surprise in the case of many modernists, some of whom were right-wing zealots, but the contemporary poets I discuss have far more in common with Marx than Mussolini. All five are clearly left wing when it comes to politics, yet their poetry does not primarily address the working class in forms that group would be familiar with. Brathwaite's "nation language" poetry probably comes the closest to this measure, but the difficult form his poetic critique of colonialism takes, with its dense historical allusions and its fragmented narrative, requires a reader that probably is not part of the working class. A certain level of education and a certain amount of leisure time are assumed in order to read and understand a book like *X/Self.* Although I do not mean to suggest that one has to have a college education to read contemporary investigative poetry, I suspect most of its readers do.

If most contemporary investigative poetry does not primarily address the working class, does that mean it cannot intervene in any way on behalf of those who have been oppressed by the economic and social conditions of contemporary culture? Answering this question calls for a more contemporary model of writing history poetically—one that, by including the issues of race and gender, includes more than class in its determinant categories. In this respect, the limitations of Benjamin's model for my purposes are apparent, for he too situates the category of class at the center of his analysis. Although Adorno criticized Benjamin's theory of the dialectical image, particularly Benjamin's notion of a "collective unconscious" grounded in Freudian and Jungian psychology, because Adorno thought it led away from a Marx's theory of class (113), I concur with Buck-Morss that "class differentiations were never lacking in Benjamin's theory of the collective unconscious" (281). "The class struggle," according to Benjamin, "is always present to a historian influenced by Marx" (1968, 254). My point is not that Benjamin, or Marx for that matter, are "wrong" to focus exclusively on the category of class but that the movements of contemporary history no longer allow us to exclude or subordinate the categories of race and gender. We need a more inclusive model of writing history poetically if we are to address the question of whether contemporary investigative poetry can intervene in contemporary culture. The work of Ernesto Laclau and Chantal Mouffe serves well as such a model.

Although Nelson presents a compelling case for the importance of poetry in American working-class culture during the historical period he surveys, 1910 to 1945, I doubt anyone could offer an equally convincing argument about the importance of poetry in contemporary working-class culture. The years following those Nelson covers mark the consolidation and expansion of the reign of the "culture industry," to use Max Horkheimer and

Theodor Adorno's term, which has certainly subordinated the consumption of poetry and the other "high" arts to the consumption of television, movies, and prerecorded music. The lyrics of popular songs are probably the closest many people, not just working-class people, in contemporary culture get to an encounter with poetry. In short, our culture hardly encourages anyone, let alone the working class, to consume either innovative or mainstream poetry. Thus, if the claim that the working class no longer (assuming it once did) reads very much poetry is correct, then in what ways can we expect investigative poets to intervene by writing history poetically?

First, we need to determine if contemporary investigative poetry's relation to the working class should be the measure by which one decides if it does any vital cultural work. If it is not, as I contend, then we need to map out a new understanding of the way artists intervene in culture. My argument begins from a post-Marxist position, one that recognizes, with Laclau and Mouffe, that

> What is now in crisis is a whole conception of socialism which rests upon the ontological centrality of the working class, upon the role of Revolution, with a capital "r", as the founding moment in the transition from one type of society to another, and upon the illusory prospect of a perfectly unitary and homogeneous collective will that will render pointless the moment of politics. The plural and multifarious character of contemporary social struggles has finally dissolved the last foundation for that political imaginary. (2)

Three important claims arise here. First, the working class, as an analytic category, no longer has the "ontological centrality" assigned to it by Marx and his followers. Because late capitalism has so effectively seduced and accommodated it, the working class is not likely to lead a revolution, which is why it is no longer ontologically "central." Nor is "revolution," which is the second of Laclau and Mouffe's claims, for it is no longer seen as the "founding moment" that governs the narrative of social struggle and change. Read optimistically, their claim implies that cultures can transform themselves without a full-scale revolution; read pessimistically, though, their claim also implies that, given the grip capitalism has on contemporary culture, a revolution that overthrows it has become virtually unimaginable. Their third claim, that the "plural and multifarious character of contemporary social struggles" is the solvent of ideology, not only exposes the widespread exclusions that occur when the category of class is given "ontological centrality"; it also implies the coming of age of new agents of change, new groups that just may have constructed, and continue to construct, a new "political imaginary" in contemporary culture.

Laclau and Mouffe's generalized diagnosis of contemporary culture fits well with the historical particularities of postwar America.[7] As Stanley Aronowitz points out, "The New Deal coalition born after 1936 was a major instance where a section of the ruling class joined with the workers, blacks, women and other groups to constitute an alternative *within* the frame work of late capitalism"; as a result, "a mass socialist party could not emerge since its political space was occupied by a party committed to both capitalism and social reform" (17). When the New Deal took effect, the American working class, for the most part, became reformist rather than revolutionary since the impetus for change now came from within that which the working class no longer wanted to overthrow—capitalism. Because of this reformist turn, the working class lost its "ontological centrality" as the privileged agent of revolutionary change. And a look at the status of the working class in contemporary culture only confirms earlier fears of its ultimate pacification through consumptive co-optation. Organized labor probably has less influence now than at any time since the Depression. Big business, now that it has finally gotten the government off its back, has gorged itself on the spread provided by deregulation, the primary digestive effect of which has been the "downsizing" of the American workforce. Thus, in the United States, "the working class has barely succeeded in constituting itself as an independent force for its immediate economic interests, and has not attained the level of political class-formation within capitalism, much less constituting itself as ideological oppositional" (Aronowitz, 107).

The question now is not whether any "class-formation" within late capitalism can constitute itself as oppositional but whether "plural and multifarious" groups can take on and transform that oppositional role. And indeed, a constellation of newly legitimized groups did emerge in the United States after the dissolution of the "political imaginary" that scripts the working class as both rescuer and rescued. These groups began to gather strength in the late 1950s and early 1960s, and by the last years of that decade, they had entered, by force as often as by consent, the cultural dialogue, addressing matters of race and gender as being of equal significance to matters of class formation.

I believe poetry must address these "plural and multifarious" groups and their concerns if it is to do any vital cultural work in contemporary culture. That address, however, cannot and should not be directed primarily at the working class for reasons both practical (it consumes very little poetry) and theoretical (it can no longer serve as the central category in an analysis of late capitalism in the United States). Whom, then, should contemporary investigative poetry address? This question brings me to the most troubling part of my argument—not because the answer is difficult, but because it is easily misconstrued. Simply put, poetry can address the intellectuals that constitute the core of those "plural and multifarious" groups, the teachers within and across those groups, and the curious students on the inside and outside of those groups and still perform vital cultural work. I certainly do not want to imply that only those in one of my categories should or do read poetry; nevertheless, I am presuming a "trickle-down" model of dissemination. Although this model is not at all inviolable, it does seem to be the most common way in which art that dissents formally and thematically from the dominant values of contemporary culture finds its audience. I would prefer my answer be taken as a realistic assessment of the potential audience rather than as an elitist proclamation of aesthetic value, but admittedly those judgments are not easily separated. One could conclude that the limited audience is an effect of the elitist tendencies of innovative art or that the limited audience causes artists to abandon the hope of reaching many people and to substitute the adventure of innovation. However we choose to explain it, the audience for contemporary investigative poetry consists, for the most part, of a small group of intellectuals, not all of whom are associated with universities, who believe that the development of critical interpretive faculties among those emergent groups is necessary for a viable critique of contemporary culture to occur and that familiarity with the arts fosters that development.

But what kind of tactical intervention into contemporary culture can poetry with such a limited audience hope to effect? To answer this question, we need to explore the implications for contemporary poetry and poetics of the post-Marxist argument I am advancing. Laclau and Mouffe's position "accepts the structural diversity of the relations in which social agents are immersed, and replaces the principle of representation with that of *articulation*. Unity between these agents is then not the expression of a common underlying essence but the result of political construction and struggle" (65). If social relations cannot be subsumed under one analytic category, then no necessary "essence" can be identified and represented as an "expression" of a unified subject. The diversity of social relations in contemporary culture requires a method of articulation rather than representation. Articulation, according to Laclau and Mouffe, designates the moment when divergent language-games make contingent connections that are transformative since "their identity is modified as a result of the articulatory practice" (105). Investigative poetry intervenes in contemporary culture during and as a result of this moment of modification, and this modification serves as a tactic to illuminate the holes in history. Howe, Mackey, Hejinian, Brathwaite, and Philip explore a multiplicity of language-games within which and across which articulations and modifications occur. These articulations, like de Certeau's tactics, are the result of contingent rather than necessary forces, and it is this desire to articulate contingency that I believe animates the highly paratactic writing practices of the five writers I discuss.

To understand how this tactic of articulation constitutes an intervention in contemporary culture, we must first deal with the most controversial portion of Laclau and Mouffe's argument—the fact that their "analysis rejects the distinction between discursive and non-discursive practices" (107).[8] This distinction involves "an assumption of the *mental* character of discourse. Against this, we will affirm the *material* character of every discursive structure" (108). Denying that discourse is a mental phenomenon does not necessarily lead to the collapse of the nondiscursive into the discursive or the real into the simulated, to use Baudrillard's terms. It does lead, however, to the claim that the discursive and the nondiscursive are both material phenomena. And it is at this point that Laclau and Mouffe articulate their own position with Wittgenstein's, for, they assert, "It is evident that the very material properties of objects are part of what Wittgenstein calls language-game, which is an example of what we have called discourse" (108). Recall that Wittgenstein defines a language-game as "language and the actions into which it is woven"; Laclau and Mouffe's equation of "discourse" with Wittgenstein's language-games suggests that actions are also woven into their notion of discourse. It also suggests that both positions begin by denying the "mental" or "ideal" character of language-games or discourse, which brings with it a denial of the traditional philosophical oppositions between mind and matter, thought and reality.

But what effect does this philosophical argument have on our understanding of how investigative poetry intervenes in contemporary culture? "The main consequence of a break with the discursive/extra-discursive dichotomy," Laclau and Mouffe contend, "is the abandonment of the thought/reality opposition, and hence a major enlargement of the field of those categories which can account for social relations" (110). Abandoning the thought/reality dichotomy has significant repercussions on the way we think about the base/superstructure dichotomy that grounds traditional Marxist accounts of how artists intervene in culture. According to these accounts, artists represent or reflect in the cultural superstructure the struggles that emanate from the contradictions in that culture's economic base; thus, the base (typically associated with the "reality" component of the thought/reality opposition) determines the superstructure (typically associated with the "thought" component of the thought/reality opposition). But if we deny the distinction between the discursive and the nondiscursive, between thought and reality, then we must also deny the distinction between the base and the superstructure as well, which suggests that talk of one term of either opposition determining the other or representing the other is meaningless. Thus, Laclau and Mouffe conclude, "the field of politics can no longer be considered a 'representation of interests,' given that the so-called 'representation' modifies the nature of what is represented" (58). If the representation can modify the represented, the superstructure can modify the base, which unsettles the determinant relation most traditions of Western thought establish between those oppositions.

As we have seen, Laclau and Mouffe abandon these traditional oppositions in order to effect a "major enlargement" of the categories that "account for social relations." That enlargement occurs when the causal connection between the represented and the representation is replaced by an articulated connection between material practices. This enlargement also unsettles corollary distinctions between form and content, style and theme, since neither term of the opposition exclusively determines or represents the other. Although Laclau and Mouffe do not fully develop the connection between poetics and politics, they do provide a point where I can articulate my argument concerning the ways in which investigative poetry intervenes in contemporary culture with their argument concerning the relation between the discursive and the nondiscursive. For Laclau and Mouffe, "Synonymy, metonymy, metaphor are not forms of thought that add a second sense to a primary, constitutive literality of social relations; instead, they are part of the primary terrain itself in which the social is constituted" (110). Rather than classify literary tropes as discursive superstructural manifestations of the latent content inherent in the nondiscursive economic base of contemporary culture, Laclau and Mouffe insist that those tropes are part of the constitutive process that produces contemporary culture. The tactics of poetry, in other words, are not "secondary" representations or illustrations of a "primary" extradiscursive reality; they participate and intervene in the constitution of that reality.

My list of poetic tactics, however, is much more expansive than Laclau and Mouffe's. Granted, they are not out to produce a theory of poetry, so their list—"synonymy, metonymy, metaphor"—is meant to be illustrative rather than exhaustive. Nevertheless, their list contains only rhetorical elements. We need to consider matters of grammar and rhythm, syntax and sound as well, for they intervene in culture in the same way rhetorical figures do: they do not simply represent or reflect that culture; they participate in its constitution by articulating it. Enlarging the list of poetic tactics, furthermore, expands Laclau and Mouffe's already "major enlargement" of the categories that "account for social relations." And I believe this enlargement of both the poetic and political fields is particularly necessary in order to account for contemporary investigative poetry. Take a quick look back at the short samples cited earlier from the five poets I discuss. Howe's substitution of the paratactic phrase for the hypotactic sentence brings the politics of erasure to bear on the form and the content of her work. Mackey's juxtaposition of mythic and historic moments of dis-integration in the rhythms of jazz and blues music certainly advances a sociopolitical critique that is at once formal and thematic. The disjunctive movement of the lines from Hejinian's "The Guard" enacts both an unsettling and a modification of identity, which occurs, according to Laclau and Mouffe, during the moment of articulation. And Brathwaite's and Philip's use of nation language and the demotic cannot be accounted for without taking the formal implications into consideration. All of these distinct poetic tactics, moreover, can be understood as ways poets articulate contingency—the contingency of meaning and identity, of the boundaries between social and aesthetic categories, of the past's relation to the present and the present's relation to the past and future.

I suggested earlier that this desire to articulate contingency animates the writing practices of the five investigative writers I discuss, but we are just now in a position to explore that suggestion more fully. According to Laclau and Mouffe, "The presence of the contingent in the necessary is what we earlier called *subversion,* and it manifests itself as symbolization, metaphorization, paradox, which deform and question the literal character of every necessity" (114). In short, contingency subverts necessity— the necessity of historical teleologies, of social normalization and absorption, of writing that represents rather than articulates reality. By extension, contemporary investigative poetry questions the necessity of grammar and syntax, of univocity and coherence by articulating the contingencies within and between those terms. Again, we need to expand Laclau and Mouffe's list of poetic tactics beyond symbolization, metaphorization, and paradox to include the nonrhetorical dimensions of language; and again, this expanded list enlarges our understanding of how the formal as well as the thematic dimensions of language can be used to intervene in culture. If one of the imperatives of contemporary investigative poetry is, as Charles Bernstein asserts, "to dismantle the grammar of control and the syntax of command" (202), then the political content of form shows itself when we see grammar and syntax, among other things, as points of articulation within and among the disparate language-games that help constitute the heterogeneous culture that emerges in contemporary history. Bernstein's imperative strikes a note similar to Laclau and Mouffe's call for subversive infusions of contingency in discourse in order to "deform and question the literal character of every necessity." Both draw attention to ways in which language intervenes in culture through a practice of dismantling or deforming the business-as-usual mode of communication. And both draw attention to what we might call the ideology of the literal or normative.

This last point can best be made in conjunction with Laclau and Mouffe's rejection of the distinction between discursive and nondiscursive practices. The dichotomy between the figural and the literal that grounds the ideology of the normative is predicated, as are the discursive/nondiscursive and the superstructure/base distinctions, on the thought/reality dichotomy, which insists on the mental essence of the first term and the material essence of the second term in each opposition. By denying the mental character of discourse and affirming its material character, Laclau and Mouffe avoid many of the ontological and epistemological problems of Western thought. They no longer have to explain how a mental or ideal substance interacts with a material or real substance, or how one of the two terms of the opposition determines the other, or how the discursive and figural represent or reflect the nondiscursive and literal "external world" of objects. However, for Laclau and Mouffe, and this point is crucial, "What is denied is not that such objects exist externally to thought, but the rather different assertion that they could constitute themselves as objects outside any discursive condition of emergence" (108). What is denied is that we could ever experience objects prior to or outside of a cultural context constituted in and by discourse.

What Laclau and Mouffe accomplish here is the completion of Marx's attempt to turn Hegelian philosophy "upon its head; or rather, turned off its head, on which it was standing, and placed upon its feet" (Engels, xxi). As is well known, Marx and his followers effect this turn by replacing Hegel's idealist ontology with a materialist one. Yet, as Tony Bennett contends, this turn is never fully realized since Marxism reinscribes the oppositions that plague idealism in the base/superstructure opposition, which underlies the discursive/nondiscursive opposition. According to Bennett, Marxist thought "has been held in check or deflected from what might have been more productive avenues of inquiry by dint of its susceptibility to the idealist categories of bourgeois aesthetic discourse"; furthermore, these "idealist deformations are constitutive of Marxist aesthetic discourse; they *define* the tradition rather than comprising its incidental and, therefore, easily corrigible by-products" (34). Thus, Bennett, in agreement with Laclau and Mouffe, concludes that the distinction between the discursive and nondiscursive is the remnant of idealist ontology and epistemology and that this remnant is definitive for Marxism rather than incidental. With this argument in mind, we can see how it is possible to complete the materialist turn by restaging, on the discursive rather than ontological or epistemological plane, Hegel's argument against Kant's distinction between phenomenal and noumenal realms.

Although Laclau and Mouffe do not specifically mention Hegel in this context, I believe they follow the logic of Hegel's argument denying Kant's distinction between phenomenal and noumenal realms,[9] but instead of asserting the ideality of the remaining phenomenal realm, as Hegel does, they assert its materiality. Thus, just as Hegel argues against the possibility of achieving a perspective outside of phenomenal experience from which to determine the existence and nature of a noumenal realm of objects, Laclau and Mouffe argue against the possibility of achieving a perspective outside of discourse to determine the existence and nature of a nondiscursive realm. If they are correct, then it would be impossible to experience "literal" or "real" objects as they "constitute themselves as objects outside any discursive condition of emergence."

The implications of this argument for Marxist and post-Marxist thought, as well as for my sense of the ways in which investigative poetry intervenes in contemporary culture, are far-reaching. First, it becomes impossible to assign a determinative relationship between the various dichotomies we have been discussing. We can no longer assert that reality or the base or the nondiscursive determine and constitute thought or the superstructure or discourse. Second, and this point pertains more directly to my concerns, the literal can no longer be seen as determining or constituting the figural—a distinction that grounds what I earlier called the ideology of the normative. Thus, if thought, the superstructure, and discourse all participate in the constitution of reality, then figurative language must be seen as constitutive as well and not as a set of devices that reflect, represent, or ornament the literal. Clearly, these distinctions between the ideal realms of thought, discourse, and the superstructure and the material realms of reality, the nondiscursive, and the base underwrite the aesthetics of socialist realism that dominate Marxist thought in the 1930s and 1940s in which art is seen as a reflection or representation of the real social conditions that are determined by the economic base of a given culture.

Yet these distinctions continue to underwrite certain contemporary accounts of the ways in which artists intervene in their cultures. Nelson's judgment that poetry like Mike Quinn's does "vital cultural work" while the poetry of a "formally experimental but politically disengaged modernism" does not, for instance, rests on two assumptions: first, that simpler language reflects and represents real social conditions more accurately than formally experimental poetry does, and second, that poetry that is "accessible" to more people does more vital cultural work. I grant that accessible poetry can be and probably is read by more people, but both of Nelson's assumptions hold only if we concede that simple or normative language more accurately reflects or represents social conditions, which in turn holds only if we concede that those social conditions are in themselves simple. But if those conditions are not inherently simple, then accessible poetry may in fact oversimplify and hence distort those conditions. This line of reasoning not only confirms Mackey's suspicion cited earlier that an aesthetics of accessibility often results in "shallow, simplistic readings" of poetry; these simplistic readings may in fact unintentionally reify existing conditions. In other words, privileging the simple and accessible may end up affirming rather than critiquing a culture that values immediate gratification. More people may indeed read "accessible" poetry, but that does not guarantee that it does vital cultural work.

Given the complexity of contemporary culture, with its "plural and multifarious" social struggles being fought on the terrains of race and gender (to name two of the more prominent sites) as well as class, I believe we need forms of poetry that engage with rather than simplify this complexity. Furthermore, the nostalgia for a return to the values of a supposedly simpler time in American culture that animates contemporary culture needs to be critiqued for what it is: a desire to roll back the advances made as a result of these diverse social struggles in the 1960s and 1970s. Reducing the complexity of these struggles to simple forms of representative or reflective poetry may provide a thematic critique of contemporary culture, but a corresponding formal critique is necessary in order to foreground the ways in which the ideology of the literal or normative tends to affirm existing conditions. Thus, poetry that "dismantle[s] the grammar of control and the syntax of command," to recall Charles Bernstein's words, may be doing vital cultural work by offering a formal as well as thematic critique of contemporary social and discursive conditions rather than an intentional or unintentional affirmation of them. I do not want to overstate the case for the poetry I am discussing in this study; the audience for this kind of writing is probably between five hundred and five thousand readers. Yet we need to be careful not to judge the effect of this work by the standards of mass consumption it intends to critique. Sales figures alone cannot determine whether or not contemporary investigative poetry does vital cultural work. If the audience for this kind of poetry is, for the most part, located in and around universities and colleges, we need to look toward those institutions to gauge its impact on contemporary culture.

Alan Golding's assessment of the possible cultural effects of "language poetry" is particularly useful on this point. He argues that judgments about the political efficacy of this kind of writing are often grounded in an "unstated assumption that the Language writers' ideological claims for their project are best measured instrumentally, in terms of direct results in the 'real' world." Rather than accept this instrumentalist criterion, Golding suggests that the impact of this kind of writing is more "usefully discussed in institutional rather than more globally political terms" (153, 157). The primary institution he refers to is the university, which, as I have argued, contains the principal audience for contemporary investigative poetry. This kind of poetry intervenes in the institution of the university, Golding contends, by drawing into question the ways in which canons are formed, a situation that is particularly evident in the attempts to open the canon up to culturally diverse work. As Bernstein rightly points out, "Too often, the works selected to represent cultural diversity are those that accept the model of representation assumed by the dominant culture in the first place"; as a result, cultural difference "is confined to subject matter and thematic material, a.k.a. local color, excluding the formal innovations that challenge those dominant paradigms of representation" (6). A look at the selections of contemporary poetry in the dominant anthologies for the collegiate market supports Bernstein's contention. Of the women and minority poets born after 1930 included in these anthologies, the same names appear almost without variance: Sylvia Plath, Audre Lourde, Amiri Baraka, Michael Harper, Simon Ortiz, Nikki Giovanni, Louis Glück, Rita Dove, Alberto Ríos, Lorna Dee Cervantes, and Cathy Song. With the exception of Amiri Baraka, most of these poets produce work that has far more in common with the kind of mainstream poetry written by Mark Strand and Sharon Olds discussed earlier than with any of the five poets examined in this study, none of whom are included in any of the prominent anthologies I consulted.[10]

Inclusion in the canon may be one way contemporary investigative poetry intervenes in culture, but the more important effect this work has is to question the notion of a canon in the first place. As Robert von Hallberg argues, the formation of a canon plays an important role in imperialistic cultures. "The nations that most need to demonstrate coherence," he contends, "are those that are most open to diverse influences and are yet striving to assert hegemony, which is the situation of the colonizer"; thus, an imperialistic nation uses canons "to validate in one not altogether abstruse way its right to global superiority" (28). The United States was and continues to be an imperialistic culture "open to diverse influences," and canons are one way of containing and homogenizing this diversity. I do not share von Hallberg's enthusiasm for this use of canons, but I think he is correct in claiming that this is how and why the canon of American poetry following World War II was shaped: "after the war America took over the military guardianship of Europe, and with it came a challenge: could Americans measure up culturally as well as they had militarily?" (3) In other words, postwar America needed canons to back up its cannons. If this is indeed what canons are for, I doubt any of the five poets I discuss would want to be included. They are clearly not, like the writers von Hallberg most admires, "Poets who wish to speak from the center" (4). Howe, Mackey, Hejinian, Brathwaite, and Philip, on the contrary, engage in poetic investigations that seek to question and dismantle that "center," and that engagement involves a formal as well as thematic critique of the imperialistic ideology that the postwar canon of American poetry seeks to validate.

Although von Hallberg's discussion concerns canon formation in the late 1940s and early 1950s, it has particular relevance for my discussion of the place of poetry in contemporary culture since the period he is concerned with is the very one for which Reagan and his followers were and continue to be nostalgic. Yet this certainly was and is not a passive nostalgia for an empire of the past. The attempt to recreate "Morning in America" and reassert the "global superiority" of the United States required an intensification of the arms race to defeat the Soviet Union, covert and overt military operations to keep communism out of "our backyard" (also known as Central America and the Caribbean), and, in the Bush years, a massive display of force in the Middle East to protect "our national interests" (also known as oil). On the domestic front, the right-wing assaults on affirmative action and reproductive rights, on multiculturalism and revisionist history, on the National Endowment for the Arts and the Humanities that began during the Reagan administration and continue into the present are rather transparent attempts to contain diversity and reassert the hegemony white, middle-class males continue to enjoy. Yet if we see the "culture wars" that rage within and outside academia as merely reflective of larger economic and cultural developments, then the constitutive role the academy has and does play in these wars gets obscured. The vitriolic reactions of the right-wing coalitions in the United States show that they understand that these culture wars continue a critique begun in the 1960s of American imperialism at home and abroad. As Michael Bérubé points out, "we know what's most feared by the country's reactionary and anti-democratic forces, for it underwrites their obsessive and indiscriminate hatred of the 1960s: political and cultural alliances among progressive university intellectuals, students, new 'social movements'" (34), and, I would add, those who question a canon that seeks to reinforce the "center."

Contemporary investigative poetry is an active participant in these struggles against American imperialism and the attempts to roll back the gains made in the last thirty years by underrepresented groups. And those struggles often occur in and around universities and colleges, which, again, constitute the principal audience for this kind of poetry. In the chapters that follow, I examine the poetic investigations in which Howe, Mackey, Hejinian, Brathwaite, and Philip articulate these struggles by writing history poetically. In this respect, these five poets compose works that run counter to Fredric Jameson's contention that contemporary or postmodern cultural productions are characterized by "the emergence of a new kind of flatness or depthlessness" in their representation of history in which "the past as 'referent' finds itself gradually bracketed, and then effaced altogether, leaving us with nothing but texts" (9, 18). Jameson ends up, albeit unwillingly, in the same position as the Reagan/Headrest and

Baudrillardan models. As we saw at the beginning of this introduction, Baudrillard contends that the difference between a "real" and a simulated world has collapsed in contemporary culture and that, consequently, there is no place from which a critique of existing conditions could occur. I suspect that Jameson's and Baudrillard's assessments of most or many contemporary works of art are all too accurate.

My concern in the pages that follow, however, will be to demonstrate that those assessments do not apply to the five investigative writers I discuss. Their approach to writing history poetically is not flat or without depth and does not bracket or efface the past to the point where history is nothing but a simulation. Furthermore, if contemporary culture does represent history as a depthless simulation, it is because, to recall Garry Wills's contention, "we cannot live with our real past, that we not only prefer but need a substitute." Howe, Mackey, Hejinian, Brathwaite, and Philip consistently and creatively confront us with that preference, and this confrontation serves notice that a critique of contemporary culture is still possible. By deploying the constellation of concepts derived principally from de Certeau, Wittgenstein, Benjamin, and Laclau and Mouffe, *Poetic Investigations: Singing the Holes in History* seeks to show that writing history poetically in contemporary culture can and does provide a viable alternative to "sleepwalking through history."

I wish I could tenderly lift from the dark side of history, voices that are anonymous, slighted—inarticulate.

—Susan Howe

I. Susan Howe

Where Are We Now
in Poetry?

"My poems always seem to be concerned with history," says Susan Howe.[1] "No matter what I thought my original intentions were that's where they go. The past is present when I write" (Beckett, 20). Her poetry ranges across vast tracts of English, Irish, and American history in the service of a resolute investigation of the "dark side" of colonialism and imperialism. Clearly, Howe sees her poetic investigations as ways of writing history poetically. Yet, as we saw with the brief excerpt from her poetry in the introduction, her work is highly paratactic, which makes it difficult for a reader to find his or her way in her poetry. I suspect that many readers, when first confronted with Howe's poetry, as well as with most contemporary investigative poetry, ask a simple yet important question: Where are we? Where is it that the author of the poem intends us to be? What "imaginative space" or landscape does he or she want us to occupy?

In the case of many poems, the answer is relatively simple. In book 6 of Wordsworth's *Prelude,* for instance, it is clear that where we are is in the Alps with the young Wordsworth, or that in Pound's third *Canto* we are in Venice, sometime in 1908. Even in the poetry of an experimental writer like William Carlos Williams, the answer is generally straightforward: where we are in a Williams poem is usually next to a refrigerator or beside some white chickens. These poems all occupy what I call "real world" landscapes: none of them asks us to stray too far from a "naturalistic" perspective in order to participate in the world of the poem. In short, the shared landscape of the real world is presupposed by both the writer and reader of such a poem.

But what about poems that make different kinds of claims on a reader's imagination? Where are we supposed to be when we read a poem by, say, Edgar Allan Poe or Emily Dickinson? With poets such as these, we enter the ethereal world of what is often called "pure" poetry. There are, of course, many different definitions of pure poetry, and many of these definitions are in direct conflict with one another. And it is also clear that pure poetry is more of an ideal toward which, or away from which, poets strive rather than something achieved. Nevertheless, pure poetry is most often linked with an "art for art's sake" aestheticism. Definitions arising from Poe's "The Poetic Principle" usually denote a poetry purified of the semantic and referential dimensions of language—a poetry stripped of "ideas," a poetry of a purely sensuous, sonorous type, which has more in common with music than with prose. Other definitions, often associated with Stéphane Mallarmé and the symbolists, emphasize the autonomous, self-referential world of the pure poem—a world cleansed of the claims of mimetic representation in which the poem mostly has itself in sight. Despite the various and contradictory definitions of pure poetry, two characteristics do stand out. First, pure poetry seeks to separate and differentiate itself from what I have called the real world landscape; second, pure poetry seeks to separate and differentiate itself from prose. Rather than presuppose the landscape of the real world, pure poetry seeks to supplant the real world with a world of its own: an autonomous world of words, a self-referential linguistic or propositional landscape, purged of the prosaic elements that characterize the real world.

I am not going to argue that Susan Howe or any of the other four poets I discuss in *Poetic Investigations* can be strictly classified as "pure poets," but this particular tradition of poetry can provide us with one way to enter into the landscape of contemporary investigative poetry. With that caveat in mind, what I would like to do now is trace out one pathway that leads up to work such as Howe's and that helps answer the question of where we are when we read this kind of poetry. Before we tackle Howe's poetry, I would like to take a brief look at two American poets from earlier generations, Wallace Stevens and Jack Spicer, as a way of locating us in the terrain of contemporary investigative poetry. My focus here will be on the linguistic or propositional landscapes that characterize these poets in order to find out just where we are when we encounter poems of this type and to outline a shift from a pure to an impure poetry. I also will argue that this shift presents itself most clearly if we pay close attention to the kind of "poetic logic" governing the propositional landscape of each of these poems. By poetic logic I simply mean the manner in which phrases relate to each other in the poem. My claim, then, is that, as we approach the present, the "impurities" of both the real world and prose increasingly infiltrate this strain of American poetry. In other words, as we move from Stevens to Spicer to Howe, there is a move away from the kind of aestheticism that characterizes pure poetry and toward a more political and prosaic form of poetry—a form that creates new possibilities for writing history poetically.

In June of 1939, in one of the first of many letters he would write to Henry Church, Wallace Stevens states that "I am, in the long run, interested in pure poetry. No doubt from the Marxian point of view this sort of thing is incredible, but pure poetry is rather older and tougher than Marx and will remain so" (1981, 340). Stevens's statement sets up nicely the inherent opposition between pure and political poetry: if the former seeks to compose an autonomous world of words, a world detached from the strife and contingency of the real world, the latter seeks to immerse itself in that very world. "The great poem," Stevens wrote, "is the disengaging of (a) reality" (1957, 169). For a politically engaged writer or reader of poetry, pure poetry is not only incredible but irresponsible as well since, in seeking solace in an autonomous world of words, pure poetry lures both the poet's and the reader's attention away from the injustice that dominates the real world. In short, pure poetry does more than merely overlook injustice; because it provides a palliative rather than a solution for injustice, pure poetry can find itself in collusion with injustice. It should be noted that Stevens's letter to Church was written shortly after his only real attempt at political poetry, "Owl's Clover," was deemed a failure by friend and foe alike, so I suspect Stevens still felt the sting of criticism when he wrote to Church. Nevertheless, Stevens maintained his disdain for political poetry throughout his career. His primary objection to political poetry was that it simply would not endure time's test. As he said in a letter to Church's wife in 1952, "Nothing in the world is deader than yesterday's political (or realistic) poetry" (1981, 760). Given Stevens's attitude toward pure poetry, I now want to look at one of his later poems, "The Poem

That Took the Place of a Mountain." Although he wrote this particular poem near the end of his life, Stevens not only reaffirms the aesthetic that grounded his life's work, he attempts to "recompose" it once again.

The Poem That Took the Place of a Mountain

There it was, word for word,
The poem that took the place of a mountain.

He breathed its oxygen,
Even when the book lay turned in the dust of his table.

It reminded him how he had needed
A place to go to in his own direction,

How he had recomposed the pines,
Shifted the rocks and picked his way among clouds,

For the outlook that would be right,
Where he would be complete in an unexplained completion:

The exact rock where his inexactnesses
Would discover, at last the view toward which they had edged,

Where he could lie and, gazing down at the sea,
Recognize his unique and solitary home.

(1974, 512)

Initially, I would like to point out a few of the formal qualities of this poem. First, note that Stevens's poem emanates from the voice of a single, unitary speaker; in this sense, it fits the time-honored tradition of the romantic lyric. To borrow a term from Mikhail Bakhtin, Stevens's poem is an example of monologic discourse, which is a characteristic of most of Stevens's poetry. Second, note that the poem contains three complete, declarative sentences—the first two encompass two lines each, while the third sentence constitutes the final ten lines of the poem. Note also that the poetic logic governing the relations between these three sentences is hypotactic—which means that the connections between sentences or propositions signal a hierarchical or subordinate patterning. In this case, the logic of the poem moves from a general proposition to more specifically qualified propositions to a concluding statement that resolves the tension, at least the logical tension, in the poem. A second consequence of this particular type of poetic logic is that it seals the poem off from any impure, prosaic elements. Given the tight, seamless progression of the poem, how would it be possible for anything other than pure poetry to enter the text? That helps explain the "form" of the poem, but what about its "content"? The basic narrative line of the poem seems to go something like this. A poem—perhaps a newly composed poem, perhaps a poem from his youth—reminds the writer of what I take to be his lifelong project: that of transforming the world of "reality" into the world of "imagination," into the world of the poem. Those familiar with Stevens's poetry and poetics will recognize in my formulation the fundamental opposition that not only governs but generates most of his poetry: the opposition between the "imagination" and "reality." Throughout his career, Stevens attempted to reconcile dialectically the claims of both imagination and reality; he consistently asserted that reality was a necessary prerequisite for the transformative acts of the imagination that produce poetry. Yet this reconciliation was never very satisfactory, for Stevens or his readers, and it became even more tenuous in his later poetry. According to one of his most acute readers, Roy Harvey Pearce, "What has happened [in the later poetry] is that the dialectical compromise, although it is still wished for, is no longer conceivable. The poet will do one thing or the other. He will celebrate mind or celebrate things themselves." And, more often than not, Stevens chose to celebrate mind in such an intense and sustained manner that "'reality'. . . will surely turn out to be a kind of mind, the kind of mind which Stevens most often called 'imagination'" (277, 269).

This movement in which the imagination supplants reality is evident in "The Poem That Took the Place of a Mountain." The poem, the act of the imagination, "took the place of" reality (a "mountain" in this case) because the poem "had recomposed" reality. Stevens, in other words, offers a "subjectivist" form of pure poetry: the poet transforms the real world landscape into a landscape located purely in the imagination of the poet. Yet it is a landscape divested of companionship—a "solitary home" for the singular self of the poem, or, to be more accurate, the singular self that composes the poem. The distinction is important because Stevens still views language as a medium through which the poet "recomposes" reality. Thus, where we are in this poem is in the imagination of a poet who uses language, poetic language, to "transport" the reader into the propositional landscape of that imagination. The emphasis in this poem, as in virtually all of Stevens's poetry, is on the transformative power of the poet—the power to compose a world of one's own making, a landscape of pure acts of the imagination that appear, "word for word," in the poem.

When we turn to the poetry of Jack Spicer, however, we encounter a different kind of landscape since Spicer's primary concern is not with the transformative power of the poet but with the transformative power of language. For Spicer, language is not a medium through which a poet connects up with the world and, in the case of Stevens, moves beyond it; language is, rather, that which makes the world possible. Spicer, I suspect, would agree with Bakhtin, who argues that "language is not a neutral medium that passes freely and easily into the private property of the speaker's intentions; it is populated—overpopulated—with the intentions of others" (294). Language is, in short, a precondition of the relation between a subject and an object, not a passive or transparent medium flowing between them.

Spicer's work, in my opinion, has not received the attention it deserves. He bears some of the responsibility for this neglect since he adamantly refused to market, promote, or even copyright his work. But I suspect the main reason his poetry has been overlooked is that it is difficult to classify. For the last ten years or so of his life—a life that unfortunately ended at age forty—Spicer composed "books" rather than "collections" of poems. For Spicer, a "book" of poems had primarily a narrative rather than lyric intent, and this narrative, as Spicer practiced it, consisted of what he called "serial poems" combined with extracts from "nonpoetic" documents— particularly extracts from letters. This technique draws into question most traditional notions of poetry and of pure poetry in particular. Furthermore, Spicer argued that the writing in such a book was "dictated" from a source "outside" rather than "inside" the poet. As Michael Davidson puts it, Spicer "regards the poem not as originating within the individual but as a foreign agent that invades the poet's language and expresses what 'it' wants to say. The poet must clear away the intrusive authorial will and allow entrance to an alien and ghostlike language" (151). Because of his unorthodox ideas about the composing process, it is all too easy to dismiss Spicer as either a crank or an oddball mystic. Yet I believe Davidson is correct when he claims that Spicer's notion of a dictation from the "outside" is "more dialogical and social" than metaphysical or mystical; the "outside," Davidson contends, "has its base in human intercourse within a community and . . . its reception takes the form of a conversation" (155). This conversation, however, often takes place between Spicer and a "dead" poet. Yet Spicer was not claiming to be clairvoyant: the conversation takes place between the poet and the text of a previous poet. In other words, Spicer offers a rather eccentric account of how a tradition gets passed on from one writer to another.

For instance, Spicer's first such "book," titled *After Lorca* (1957), purports to be a series of translations of selected poems of Federico García Lorca. The book opens with a very dismissive "Introduction" supposedly written by Lorca himself—which is troublesome, since Lorca died in 1936. On the surface, Spicer's book claims to be a series of "translations" of Lorca's poetry, but as "Lorca" himself points out in his "Introduction,"

> Mr. Spicer seems to derive pleasure in inserting or substituting one or two words which completely change the mood and often the meaning of the poem as I had written it . . . [and] there are an almost equal number of poems that I did not write at all . . . and I have further complicated the problem (with malice aforethought I must admit) by sending Mr. Spicer several poems written after my death which he has also translated and included here. (11)

The end result of Spicer's composing process in *After Lorca,* then, is that the authorship of any one poem is drawn into question: Whose words are those, Lorca's or Spicer's? Whose images? And since we can never know just "who" wrote these poems, our attention shifts away from the author and toward the words and poems themselves. Again, a comparison with Bakhtin's theories of language and authorship is fecund—a comparison Burton Hatlen has already worked out in detail. Spicer's *After Lorca,* Hatlen argues, "at once acknowledges the distance between 'Lorca' and 'Spicer' and systematically blurs that distance—just as the 'quasi-direct discourse' which Bakhtin sees as the distinctive idiom of modern prose narratives simultaneously acknowledges the differences between an authorial voice and the voices of his characters and breaks down these differences" (121–22). And because we are forced by Spicer's tactics to consider the possibility of coauthorship of the poems, we are in a propositional landscape that is populated with others, other voices and authors. Unlike the "unique and solitary home" that Stevens creates in his imaginative landscape, Spicer's linguistic landscape blurs the distinction between "unique" or individual compositions and moves toward a poetics of collaboration—of dialogue rather than monologue.

Spicer also included in this book letters he had written to Lorca, letters that not only create the sense of dialogue within the book but provide important clues to Spicer's own poetics. In his first letter to Lorca, Spicer gives his definition of tradition, one that seems to be cast in direct opposition to the view of tradition advanced by T. S. Eliot and the New Critics. According to Spicer, tradition does not consist of "an historical patchwork (whether made up of Elizabethan quotations, guide books of the poet's home town, or obscure hints of obscure bits of magic published by Pantheon)"; for Spicer, tradition "means generations of different poets in different countries patiently telling the same story, writing the same poem, gaining and losing something with each transformation—but, of course, never really losing anything" (15). Thus, if we keep this view of tradition in mind—along with the recognition that Spicer was, above all, a most playful poet—his comments on "dictation" from a source "outside" the poet will not seem as strange as at first glance.

More important for my purposes here, though, is the effect such ideas have on the notion of pure poetry. Not only do other voices infiltrate the supposedly autonomous world of the poem, but prosaic elements intrude as well. In other words, Spicer did not limit his definition of the poetic to verse. Spicer did not, however, interject these prosaic elements within the poems themselves; he kept the prose and the poetry in *After Lorca* separate. Yet a number of Spicer's letters to Lorca and many of his poems deal directly with the possibility ("impossibility" might be a more accurate word) of pure poetry. In his fifth letter to Lorca, for example, Spicer writes that "Loneliness is necessary for pure poetry. When someone intrudes into the poet's life . . . he loses his balance for a moment, slips into being who he is, uses his poetry as one would use money or sympathy" (48). Spicer's desire is to keep the autonomous world of the poem free from the intrusion of what he called, in the same letter, "the big lie of the personal." As a result, his version of pure poetry has a much more "objectivist" stance than Stevens's version—a distinction that will become more apparent if we look closely at one of the poems in *After Lorca*.

Spicer's poem "A Diamond" will help illustrate my point.

A Diamond

A Translation for Robert Jones

A diamond
Is there
At the heart of the moon or the branches or my nakedness
And there is nothing in the universe like diamond
Nothing in the whole mind.

The poem is a seagull resting on a pier at the end of the ocean.

A dog howls at the moon
A dog howls at the branches
A dog howls at the nakedness
A dog howling with pure mind.

I ask for the poem to be as pure as a seagull's belly.

The universe falls apart and discloses a diamond
Two words called seagull are peacefully floating out where the
    waves are
The dog is dead there with the moon, with the branches, with
    my nakedness
And there is nothing in the universe like diamond
Nothing in the whole mind.

                                                          (22–23)

As I argued earlier, Stevens's typical poem follows a poetic logic of hypo-taxis; Spicer's poetry, on the other hand, generally follows a more dis-junctive logic. Spicer preferred to separate and disjoin propositions rather than arrange them hierarchically. His poems usually offer sets of opposi-tions and alternatives that, again unlike Stevens, are rarely resolved. Note in lines 4 and 5 the offhand way in which Spicer offers two alternatives for that which cannot contain a "diamond": first the "universe," then the "mind." The movement is so rapid that we might conclude that the mind has usurped the universe, as in Stevens's poetry. Except that line 6 could easily stand as a manifesto for an "objectivist" rather than "subjectivist" poetics: the object—a "seagull"—takes over the poem rather than the poem taking over the object, as in Stevens's poem. But what kind of ob-ject is this poem? And what kind of a landscape surrounds such an object?

The key to these questions, as well as to the larger question of where we are in a Spicer poem, lies in line 13: "Two words called seagull are peacefully floating out where the waves are . . ." Here, Spicer places us in a world where objects are composed, literally, of words; as Spicer puts it in another poem, "Where one is is in a temple that sometimes makes us forget that we are in it. Where we are is in a sentence" (175). Thus, the landscape of a Spicer poem is a purely linguistic construct, but it is not a construct of a "unique and solitary" writer but of the interaction, in lan-guage, of two or more writers. Since a linguistic landscape, unlike a purely imaginative landscape, is by definition a shared landscape (no private languages, as Wittgenstein argues), Spicer can offer a poetics of inclusion rather than exclusion—a poetics composed of the many voices of a narrative rather than the single voice of a lyric. In this respect, Spicer's poetry veers away from a strictly defined version of pure poetry. Nevertheless, Spicer still wanted his poems to be "as pure as a seagull's belly."

Turning now to the work of Susan Howe, we see that she veers even further away from the kind of pure poetry exemplified by Wallace Stevens. Her books usually consist of lengthy serial poems that engage, on a very material level, various mythical and historical texts, yet it is most often an engagement with hidden or repressed texts. As the epigraph to this chapter indicates, Howe wishes she "could tenderly lift from the dark side of history, voices that are anonymous, slighted—inarticulate" (1990a, 14). Howe's 1990 *Singularities* contains one sequence of poems that illustrates both her peculiar way of encountering history and her relation to the tradition of pure poetry I have been tracing out. *Thorow* is a serial poem in three parts, introduced by a prose preface, the second half of which is entitled "Narrative in Non-Narrative" (1990a, 41–42). The preface helps articulate the complicity between the past and the present that animates so much of the poem. Howe composed *Thorow* during the winter and spring of 1987, which she spent at Lake George, New York—the site of William Johnson's 1755 victory in the French and Indian War—conducting a poetry workshop. She was repulsed by the crass commercialization of the area, finding "gift shops selling Indian trinkets, china jugs shaped like breasts with nipples for spouts, American flags in all shapes and sizes . . . a fake fort where a real one once stood, a Dairy-Mart, a Donut-land, and a four-star Ramada Inn built over an ancient Indian burial ground" (1990a, 41).

In many respects, *Thorow* seeks to uncover that burial ground lying beneath the commercial veneer of Lake George, to uncover the "Interior assembling of forces underneath earth's eye. Yes, she, the Strange, excluded from formalism" (1990a, 41). The feminine pronoun here has a dual role, referring at once to "mother" earth and to women, both of whom have been elided by the formalism of the "paternal colonial systems," which deploy a "positivist efficiency" to appropriate "primal indeterminacy" (1990a, 41). Howe's poem, then, brings to the fore three of the "anonymous, slighted—inarticulate" voices silenced during the conquest of North America: the voices of nature, of Native Americans, and of women. Throughout the poem, the "primal indeterminacy" of these voices is juxtaposed to the "positivist efficiency" imposing the "European grid on the Forest" (1990a, 45).

Yet we should not see this "primal indeterminacy" as merely a thematic element in Howe's poem; it permeates the form of the poem as well, a form opposed to the "formalism" from which "she" is excluded. The poem's title is just such an instance. First, it can be construed as a misspelling of Henry David Thoreau's name—a writer Howe was reading at the time. Second, it can stand as an archaic spelling of the word "thorough," meaning passing through as in thorough-fare; this possibility is reinforced by a quotation from Sir Humfrey Gilbert that Howe cites in her introduction: "To proove that the Indians aforenamed came not by the Northeast, and that there is no thorow passage navigable that way" (1990a, 42). Finally, the word can again be an archaic spelling of "throw," which appears in the sixth poem in the sequence: "Irruptives // thorow out all / the Five Nations" (1990a, 46). Although Howe's use of archaic word forms is certainly meant to lend authenticity and historicity to her poem—as Linda Reinfeld points out, a good deal of the "language of 'Thorow' is drawn from old journals and accounts documenting the history of the Lake George region" (98)—it also serves to destabilize the poem's language and enhance its "primal indeterminacy." Given these multiple possible meanings, it should be clear that Howe's approach to writing history poetically is anything but simple.

Howe's approach, however, is also anything but aimless or gratuitous. Here, in an interview with Tom Beckett, is her account of her concerns during the composition of *Thorow*:

> Recently I spent several months at Lake George where I wrote *Thorow*. . . . I think I was trying to paint a landscape in that poem but my vision of the lake was not so much in space as in time. I was very much aware of the commercialization and near ruin at the edge of the water, in the town itself, all around—but I felt outside of time or in an earlier time and *that* was what I had to get on paper. For some reason this beautiful body of water has attracted violence and greed ever since the Europeans first saw it. I thought I could feel it when it was pure, enchanted, *nameless*. There was never such a pure place. In all nature there is violence. Still it must have been wonderful at first sight. Uninterrupted nature usually is a dream enjoyed by the spoilers and looters—my ancestors. (Beckett, 20–21)

Howe's comments here are quite revealing. First, Howe's landscape is temporal, hence historical, hence linguistic, rather than naturalistic. In this sense, she participates in the tradition of pure poetry that seeks to create a world of words. As she told Reinfeld, *Thorow* consists of "a landscape out of bits of words" and is about "what time does in a landscape" (98). Yet the crucial difference between Howe and other pure poets such as Stevens and, to some extent, Spicer, is that she does not attempt to seal this world off from the real world of historical fact but to make visible the holes in traditional historiography. What happens to a landscape in time is, of course, history, and the history of the Lake George region in New York is a series of scenes of the appropriation of Indian territory by the European settlers. Second, note Howe's failed attempt to experience that landscape prior to the "violence and greed" that is its history; in other words, the hope of a "pure" encounter with a natural landscape, disengaged from the political realities of that landscape, is as impossible as the hope of creating an autonomous world of words, detached from the concerns of the real world, in poetry. In short, Howe has, in the course of her writing, come up against the limits of pure poetry and willingly transgressed them.

For Howe, tracking the equivocal and equivocating paths of language is one of the primary roles of the author, for "work penetrated by the edge of author, traverses multiplicities" (1990a, 42). If Benjamin, as we saw in the introduction, portrays the author as a witness, Howe portrays the author as a scout setting out to explore the "word Forest" for a path leading "back to primordial" (1990a, 49). Yet Howe's venture into the primordial is not motivated by an antiquarian's interest or a search for lost origins.[2] As the poem opens, the "Scout" is dispatched in search of the "Idea of my present" and the "Etymology" of "this / present in the past now" (1990a, 43). Howe's scout is not looking for the repetition of the past in the present. Her work as a whole repudiates such an ahistorical approach, and in this respect she is much closer to Benjamin's project of presenting the transitory in history than to Pound's project of presenting "all ages [as] contemporaneous." Thus, Howe's scout follows "The track of Desire" as a way of "Measuring mastering" (1990a, 45) as it occurs in different temporal and cultural contexts.

This act of "Measuring mastering" as a means of exposing the "European grid" imposed on the wilderness and its native inhabitants is indeed one of the primary themes in her poem, as is evident in the third poem from the second part of *Thorow*.

> Thaw has washed away snow
> covering the old ice

the Lake a dull crust

Force made desire wander
Jumping from one subject

to another
Besieged and besieged

in a chain of Cause
The eternal First Cause

I stretch out my arms
to the author

Oh the bare ground

My thick coat and my tent
and the black of clouds

Squadrons of clouds

No end of their numbers

Armageddon at Fort William Henry
Sunset at Independence Point

Author the real author
acting the part of a scout

(1990a, 51)

As this passage demonstrates, Howe's poetry is built on an aesthetic of
parataxis that makes "primal indeterminacy" an integral element in the
poem itself. It is a poetry of phrases and fragments best read as elements
of a collage in which the reader supplies the connections—connections
rendered even more indeterminate by the absence of punctuation. The elision of almost all hypotactic markers in this passage, furthermore, makes
it virtually impossible for the reader to "master" it by applying the grid
of traditional grammar. This act of hermeneutical resistance parallels the
kind of cultural resistance implied in Howe's critique of the European
traders who "discovered" Lake George—"Pathfinding believers in God
and grammar [who] spelled the lake into *place*" (1990a, 41). Naming is
an essential step in the capitalist process of appropriating and mastering
nature in order to convert it into private property. And regulating nature's
representation in language with the tools of grammar and spelling keeps

the lines of ownership and mastery well defined and open to adjudication by the "European grid" of property-rights law.

In the fourth line of the poem, the conflict between "Force" and "desire" recalls the "track of Desire" the author/scout sets out on in his or her task of "Measuring mastering." Clearly, "Force" and "desire" take on allegorical dimensions in this passage, yet the relation cannot be reduced to a single interpretation. These lines can be read as a political allegory in which "Force" is a figure for the European explorers, and "desire" is a figure for the Indians who were dispersed or "made" to "wander" by the wars of appropriation conducted by the European colonists. But if the word "subject" in line 5 is taken as a synonym for self—a reading supported by the opening poem in *Thorow,* in which the scout is sent out into the "domain of transcendental subjectivity" (1990a, 43)—then the passage can also be read as a philosophical allegory in which "Force" causes "desire" to "wander" from "one subject / to another." Finally, the language near the end of the poem suggests a theological allegory by citing the "Armageddon at Fort William Henry," which I assume alludes to the Indian massacre of British soldiers and their families after the British defeat and surrender to the French and Indian forces in 1757. Although these three readings cannot be reduced to a single line of interpretation, they do circle around the conflict of the "positivist efficiency" of European colonial forces as they attempt to impose their "grid" on the "primal indeterminacy" of the wilderness and its native inhabitants. The author, "acting the part of the scout," surveys the common terrain these three readings occupy and presents them in paratactic fragments that require the reader's own connective act of authorship. As Howe tells Lynn Keller, "I wouldn't want the reader to be just a passive consumer. I would want my readers to play, to enter the mystery of language, and to follow words where they lead, to let language lead them" (1995, 31).

Thus, the conflict between cultural and natural forces that runs throughout this passage of *Thorow*—figured in the metaphor of "Squadrons of clouds" and juxtaposed in the scenes of "Armageddon" and "Sunset" in lines 17 and 18—confronts the reader in a manner that resembles Benjamin's dialectical images. In both Howe's and Benjamin's texts, the reader mediates the opposed images to such a great extent that authorship becomes a collaborative event taking place between writer and reader rather than a hierarchical event in which the writer directs the reader to the "correct" interpretation of the text. In this respect, the aphoristic style of Benjamin's "Theses" and the paratactic style of Howe's *Thorow* both work by eliding the hypotactic elements of their texts—elements that direct the reader's attention along an "authorized" path of interpretation. Although this elision takes place between sections in Benjamin's text while it takes place between phrases in Howe's text, the result is much the same: without the reader's participation, the texts seem to be a jumble of phrases and paragraphs lacking in coherence and purpose.

These similar formal strategies signal similar thematic concerns in the texts of Benjamin and Howe.[3] As we have seen, Benjamin's dialectical image seeks to disrupt the continuous narrative of progress underlying the version of historicism that his poetic historiography critiques. Recall that Benjamin intends the dialectical image to "arrest" the "flow of thoughts" that compose the linear narrative of history as represented by traditional historicism, which "contents itself with establishing a causal connection between various moments in history" (1968, 263). I read a similar critique in lines 7 through 9 of the passage cited above from *Thorow*. The "subject" of line 5 is "besieged" by the logic that determines the "chain of Cause" in the mechanistic, progressive historiography that underwrites both the seventeenth-century rhetoric of the early European colonists and the nineteenth-century apologists for the doctrines of manifest destiny. Moreover, Howe's desire to represent "this / present in the past now" (1990a, 43) provides a critique of a less apparent form of progressive historicism, one that asserts that the present age has moved beyond the barbarism of past generations. Howe's preface surely stands as an indictment of the barbarism of contemporary commercial capitalism, but the most intriguing aspect of Howe's poem in this regard is the way in which she implicates the poem's "I" in her critique. "I am / Part of their encroachment," Howe writes, adding also that "My ancestors tore off / the first leaves / picked out the best stars" (1990a, 47, 52). The temptation to identify these first person pronouns directly with the author as traditionally conceived— as Susan Howe, writer—is great and not entirely inappropriate. Read this way, Howe is acknowledging her own complicity with the past.

Yet recall that for Howe the author "traverses multiplicities," and one of those multiplicities is the notion of the author. In *Thorow*, as we have seen, the "I" has a role as author, as does the "scout" following the "track of Desire," but a third reference remains a possibility. In "Incloser"—an innovative poetic essay composed of a collage of quotations from Puritan writers and her commentary on them—Howe remarks that the theocratic leaders of the first settlements in New England "tied themselves and their followers to a dialectical construction of the American land as a virgin garden preestablished for them by the Author and Finisher of creation" (1993, 49). God figured as author of the world is a familiar conceit in Puritan writing, one that Howe hints at in the passage from *Thorow* cited above. In lines 9 through 11, Howe invokes "The eternal First Cause" and proclaims that "I stretch out my arms / to the author." The allusion to Aristotle's synonym for his "Unmoved Mover," which medieval theologians appropriated as an equivalent for their conception of God, highlights the philosophical and theological allegories in the poem, and this "First Cause" may indeed be the author toward which the "I" stretches out. Thus, Howe's presentation of here notion of authorship confronts the reader once again with a volatile mix of philosophical, political, and theological language that marks most of her poetry.

Howe's project of "unsettling the wilderness in American literary history"—which is the subtitle of *The Birth-mark,* her collection of essays—has a great deal to do with her refusal to reconcile in one linguistic register the many voices, some acknowledged and some not, in *Thorow.* In both her poetry and prose, Howe constantly undermines the settled opinions of American history, opinions that have silenced all too often the voices she seeks to "lift from the dark side of history." As we have seen, one of Howe's primary tactics for "unsettling" history in *Thorow* is the elision of the hypotactic elements in her writing that allow readers to chart a clear and relatively unequivocal path through a text. Howe's "scout" forswears many of the traditional devices for keeping meaning on track in order to explore terrain in the "word Forest" that the "European grid" has either missed or covered over: "I pick my compass to pieces // Dark here in the driftings / in the spaces of drifting // Complicity battling redemption" (1990a, 55). The willful destruction of the compass stands as a figure for Howe's practice of writing history poetically. Yet Howe's subversion of normative discourse amounts to much more than a new compositional technique. On the contrary, *Thorow* investigates the "complicity" between normative discourse and the "progress" of history generating the conditions she confronted during her stay at Lake George: "Everything graft, everything grafted" (1990a, 41).

Thus, Howe's poetic investigations locate us in a linguistic landscape that is quite different from Stevens's and slightly less different from Spicer's —as the first poem in the second section of *Thorow* illustrates.

Walked on Mount Vision

New life after the Fall
So many true things

which are not truth itself
We are too finite

Barefooted and bareheaded
extended in space

sure of reaching support

Knowledge and foresight
Noah's landing at Ararat

Mind itself or life

quicker than thought

slipping back to primordial
We go through the word Forest

Trance of an encampment
not a foot of land cleared

The literature of savagism
under a spell of savagism

Nature isolates the Adirondacks

In the machinery of injustice
my whole being is Vision

(1990a, 49)

At first glance, the scene in this poem seems to resemble the scene in Stevens's "The Poem That Took the Place of a Mountain." Howe, like Stevens, does not attempt to offer a real world landscape: where we are in Howe's poem is on "Mount Vision," which apparently is located in, according to line 14, a "word Forest" rather than the real world of the Adirondack mountains. Yet there is a marked difference between Stevens's linguistic landscape and Howe's. For Stevens, the mountain becomes a promontory within the mind of the poet; the physical world of the mountain is usurped by the mind and transformed into an act of the imagination. For Howe, this movement appears to be reversed: as she says in her introduction, "The Adirondacks *occupied* me" (1990a, 41). In line 1 "Mount Vision" is something on which one can walk; but in the poem's final line, the poet equates that "Vision" with her "whole being." The word "vision," of course, has a number of connotations, ranging from simple perception to mystical apprehension, and I suspect Howe wants the word to resonate with these multiple possibilities. Yet there is a strong sense in which that "Vision" comes from "outside" rather than "inside" the poet. Thus, Howe's understanding of inspiration and composition is much closer to that of Spicer than to that of Stevens.

Howe's poetic landscape, then, like Spicer's, is a world of signs, yet hers is a world of signs seen in a larger context. If for Spicer, "where we are is in a sentence," then for Howe, where we are is in the "word Forest" of history. In other words, her unit of measure is neither the word nor the sentence but history. It is not, however, history presented intact; Howe's is clearly a fractured, fragmented history, both elided and effaced. Interestingly enough, one way to enter Howe's landscape of fractured history is through a comparison with Wallace Stevens. As she tells Keller, Howe finds Stevens's poetry to be "tremendously beautiful, and moving, and philosophical, and meditative, and all the things that words have the power to be, which is ultimately mysterious" (1995, 23). Her work is also a striking instance of meditative, philosophical poetry, but the differences between Howe and Stevens are just as striking. As she tells Janet Ruth Falcon, "Obviously I have a very different voice from Wallace Stevens, and he is a poet who means everything to me. I am unable to speak with as *sure* a voice. . . . Stevens has the assurance of centuries behind him. . . . I often think when I am overwhelmed by Stevens's achievement as a poet that my own work is doomed to be hesitant—breathy" (28). The key words here are "assurance," which she uses to describe the voice heard in Stevens's poetry, and "hesitant," which she uses to describe the voice heard in her own poetry. There is a "stuttering" or "stammering" quality to Howe's work that is not to be found in Stevens. As Peter Nicholls notes, Howe's "stammering keeps us on the verge of intelligibility, and in her own work Howe's emphasis on sound is coupled with a habitual shattering of language into bits and pieces" (597). As I argued earlier, the poetic logic in Stevens's poetry takes the form of complete, declarative sentences, ordered hypotactically, and there is very little, if any, shattering of language going on in his work. And it is the absence of such stammering, I believe, that gives Stevens's poetry its assurance—an assurance shared by the centuries governed by a similar logic.

Howe's poetry seeks out a different logic, a logic she believes has been repressed rather than assured by the centuries. Much of her desire for a different logic arises from her interest in history and with the voices in history "that are anonymous, slighted—inarticulate." Thus, in place of a logic of hypotaxis, which governs Stevens's poem, Howe offers a logic of parataxis. Note the absence of any punctuation in the poem cited above. How are we to know where a sentence begins or ends? At first, we might take the capitalized words as indicating a new sentence, but Howe, much like Emily Dickinson, capitalizes words in the middle of sentences— words like "Fall," "Forest," and "Vision." Which brings us back to my main question: where are we in a poem such as Howe's? What kind of a landscape is it? Given her paratactic approach to poetry, it is difficult to tell just where we are in her work since the connections between "things" in this landscape have been elided. Howe's landscape, though, resembles Spicer's landscape more than Stevens's: the landscapes in Howe and Spicer are composed of and by language.

However, the poetic landscapes of Spicer and Howe, despite this resemblance, are not identical. Although Spicer's sentences are often disjunctive, they are usually complete sentences. Such is not the case with Howe's sentences, which are better characterized as phrases rather than sentences. And since these phrases are arranged paratactically, it becomes difficult, if not impossible, to find our way among them. The map of this historical, linguistic landscape, in other words, has been effaced; key information has been elided, just as it has been in history—which I take to be the most important implication of the poetic logic Howe employs. As she points out in her interview with Beckett, "There are breaks in world-historical reason where forms of wildness brought up by memory become desire and multiply" (20). These breaks create gaps or holes in our understanding of history. In short, the events in history are not, despite appearances, woven into a seamless, hypotactic narrative; information has been, intentionally and unintentionally, left out. Without that information, without the normal hypotactic connections between elements within the narrative, we become, as Howe puts it in another poem, "Lost in language," although "we are language" (1990a, 99).

We proceed, therefore, with far less "assurance" when we are asked to negotiate a poetic landscape such as Howe's than we do when we negotiate a landscape such as Stevens's or Spicer's. This lack of assurance, this hesitancy, in Howe's work is a direct result, I believe, of the inclusion of history in the otherwise purely linguistic landscape of her poetry. After all, the landscape in the poem cited above is isolated "in the machinery of injustice," not from it, as in most versions of pure poetry. Howe's willingness to open up the text of her poetry to the silenced voices in American history not only distinguishes her work from most traditional instances of pure poetry; it also distinguishes her work from the type of pure poetry offered by both Stevens and Spicer. If we recall Howe's comments in the Beckett interview, she understands that a pristine, apolitical experience of a landscape, whether natural or linguistic, "is a dream enjoyed by the spoilers and looters"—people she readily acknowledges as her "ancestors." By acknowledging her own genealogical connection with the "machinery of injustice" Howe puts herself in the same situation she depicts in the final line of the second section of *Thorow*—a situation of "Complicity battling redemption" (1990a, 55), which, as she told Reined, is "what the history of America is" (100).

By opening up her work to these silenced voices, Howe also forges a poetic critique of contemporary culture that takes more than issues of class into consideration. Her poetry participates in the "major enlargement of the field of those categories which can account for social relations," to recall Laclau and Mouffe's words (110). Clearly, issues of race are of deep concern to Howe in *Thorow*, as her poetic investigation of the appropriation of Native American lands by the "paternal colonial systems" shows. But what about issues of gender in her work? Who is "she, the Strange, excluded from formalism," and what role does she play in writing history poetically? These questions are best answered by examining another of Howe's works that not only challenges received notions of gender but received notions of what counts as poetry as well—*My Emily Dickinson*.

Howe's groundbreaking study of Emily Dickinson puts forth a form of writing that willfully and skillfully transgresses the boundaries between poetry, criticism, and literary history. In an interview with Janet Ruth Falcon in 1986, she contends that her critical prose essays "are a kind of poetry. I have the same problem with meaning and sound when I write them that I do when I write a poem. I don't like separating things into categories" (32). *My Emily Dickinson* is, in fact, a treatise on the art of writing poetically as much as it is on one particular writer, and the book is itself a significant instance of that art. In short, the style or form of the book is very much a part of its "argument." As John Taggart notes, "What is authorized by her style and her own working knowledge is a picture of composition. The major importance of this book lies in the originality and depth of that picture and its potential for application by other poets" (173–74). A characteristic passage from *My Emily Dickinson* provides a glimpse of that picture:

> At the edge of unknown, the sacred inaccessible unseen—Lyric "I" is both guard and hunter. *We* and *We* prey on each other. Absence is the admired presence of each poem. Death roams the division—World's november. Two separate Questors have found nothing but noise of their own aggressive monologues echoing. Firm allegory has escaped into the heart of human cruelty, Love's unfathomable mystery. Into the desolate attraction of annihilation, dauntless they will turn and turn again telling. (1985, 70)

This passage occurs at the beginning of Howe's comparison of Robert Browning's "Childe Roland to the Dark Tower Came" and Dickinson's "My Life had stood—a Loaded Gun,—." Yet, as she does throughout her book, Howe allows her argument to arise out of metaphor and association, sound and rhythm. Note how the vowel sounds carry the first sentence toward its definition of the "I" in lyric poetry as both "guard and hunter"—a definition that then, by association, takes in oppositions between presence and absence, life and death, cruelty and love. The passage also contains an implicit critique of monologic poetry by the metaphoric equation of that kind of poetry with the "noise" of aggression echoing within the enclosed space of the lyric. So Howe clearly advances here a critique of a privileged form of verse; but the form in which she advances that critique also constitutes an analogous critique of a privileged form of criticism that is governed by hierarchy, rationalism, and explanation. Thus, the "picture of composition" we are given enacts an encounter, in both its form and content, between poetry and critical prose.

Furthermore, Howe's "style" in *My Emily Dickinson* carries within it a critique of the gender-specific boundaries that define writing about and of women. As Rachel Blau DuPlessis contends, "While content and theme have been sites of cultural change in recent years, where the representations of women are concerned, a naturalized set of language strategies, or nice, normal presentations of material seemed to partake of the same assumptions about gender that they would claim to undermine. So it has seemed crucial for feminist writing to reexamine and claim the innovative writing strategies for which our century is noted, turning collage, hetero-glossia, intergenres, and self-reflexivity (to name just some) to our uses" (viii). Although Howe has certainly made great use of the innovative writing tactics DuPlessis cites, her work has not received the attention it is due from feminists. When Falcon asks how she feels about the fact that feminists have "embraced" her, Howe retorts that feminists "haven't embraced" her because "They don't know about me. If you are not doing hardcore political writing, and you are not in the confessional school embraced by so many women's studies programs or departments in universities you are *not*" (39). This situation is also typical of the way other female innovative or avant-garde poets have been treated, or not treated in this case, by mainstream feminist criticism.

One reason for this neglect is that innovative women poets often refuse to encase their critiques of gender issues in traditional, easily recognizable forms of writing. Unlike the "confessional" poets that gain the attention of feminist critics in the academy, investigative women writers rarely produce monologic, lyric poetry in which the "I" recounts personal experiences of injustice based on gender inequities. As Howe bluntly puts it, "I do not like confessional poetry. These days, in America, confession is on every TV program, let alone in most poems" (1995, 33). For her, "a poet is like an ethnographer. You open your mind and textual space to many voices, to an interplay and contradiction and complexity of voices" (Beckett, 24). As we have seen, Howe achieves this "interplay" of voices in her work by deploying many of the innovative writing tactics DuPlessis cites. Howe's use of "collage, heteroglossia, intergenres, and self-reflexivity," among other tactics, leads to forms of writing that are admittedly difficult and do not lend themselves to the kinds of feminist readings that focus primarily on the content of poetry.

Howe, like many women who compose contemporary investigative poetry, frequently questions the assumptions of some of the more prominent versions of feminism, and this questioning puts her at odds with the critical establishment. "I think that women who take a theoretical position are allowed to take a theoretical position only as long as it's a feminist theoretical position, and to me that's an isolation. I would be extremely wary of being put in the category of writing about 'women's problems,' because then you get, I think, shifted out" (1995, 21). In the opening pages of *My Emily Dickinson,* for instance, Howe sets her reading of Dickinson apart from the feminist approaches of Hélène Cixous or Sandra M. Gilbert and Susan Gubar. Howe is uncomfortable with Cixous's prescriptive declarations of what women's writing "must" do, and she is even more uncomfortable with Gilbert and Gubar's treatment of Dickinson. Howe's book on Dickinson, according to DuPlessis, "is mounting a critique of the tendency of *The Madwoman in the Attic* to a 'victimization' hypothesis, which underplayed the agency of women. Yet despite this attack, Howe is notably a feminist" (134). Rather than cast Dickinson as a victim of patriarchal Victorian culture, Howe's Emily Dickinson is a woman of immense strength who chooses to radically limit her participation in that culture. For Howe, Dickinson "built a new poetic form from her fractured sense of being eternally on intellectual borders, where confident masculine voices buzzed an alluring and inaccessible discourse, backward through history into aboriginal anagogy" (1985, 21). This portrait of Dickinson being on "intellectual borders," far from the "masculine voices" of her culture, is also consonant with Howe's portrait of her own position as a poet. By taking a close look at the first few pages of *My Emily Dickinson*, we can see how her critique of received forms of critical prose meshes with her critique of the ways in which women writers have been treated by literary critics, a critique that I believe includes not only Dickinson but Howe and other women writers of innovative poetry.

"My book is a contradiction of its epigraph" (1985, 7). So begins Howe's introduction to *My Emily Dickinson*. The epigraph she refers to is from *In the American Grain* by William Carlos Williams. In that book he claims that "there never have been women" poets and that "Emily Dickinson, starving of passion in her father's garden, is the very nearest we have ever been—starving. Never a woman: never a poet. That's an axiom" (1985, 6). Rather than simply asserting that Williams is wrong in his judgment, Howe takes a more intriguing path: "I think he says one thing and means another. A poet is never just a woman or a man. Every poet is salted with fire. A poet is a mirror, a transcriber. *Here* 'we have salt in ourselves and peace one with another'" (1985, 7). In reading Williams against his own "grain," Howe simultaneously points at and beyond gender. Throughout *My Emily Dickinson*, she sustains a poetic assault against essentialist notions of gender that would reduce humans to only "men" and "women." Instead, she posits a more inclusive category, "poets," and list qualities that obtain in both men and women poets—being "salted with fire," being a "mirror" or "transcriber." As she writes in the final paragraph of her book, "poetry is the great stimulation of life. Poetry leads past possession of self to transfiguration beyond gender" (1985, 138). It would be a great mistake to see Howe's move "beyond gender" as a lack of concern with gender;

there is in all of Howe's work a persistent investigation of how gender both confines humans to and releases them from assigned roles.

As we see in the opening paragraph of the first part of *My Emily Dickinson*, Howe is very concerned with the ways in which issues of gender affect literary history.

> In the college library I use there are two writers whose work refuses to conform to the Anglo-American literary traditions these institutions perpetuate. Emily Dickinson and Gertrude Stein are clearly among the most innovative precursors of modernist poetry and prose, yet to this day canonical criticism from Harold Bloom to Hugh Kenner persists in dropping their names and ignoring their work. Why these two pathfinders were women, why American — are questions too often lost in the penchant for biographical detail that "lovingly" muffles their voices. (1985, 11)

Howe's words here are charged with agency, with active verbs that readily assign praise or blame. She does not portray Dickinson and Stein primarily as victims of neglect; it is their work that "refuses to conform," and that refusal contributes to their marginal place in literary history. Yet they are not the only agents responsible for this consignment; canonical critics "persist" in ignoring their work or in subordinating an assessment of that work to an account of their lives. For Howe, both of these strategies leave the important question unasked: why was this writing produced by American women? This is a complex position Howe takes up. Her point about male critics like Bloom and Kenner is as simple as it is accurate, but this passage also offers a subtle critique of those who do attend to the work of Dickinson and Stein. Assigning agency to Dickinson and Stein in the first sentence strikes me as an implicit criticism of Gilbert and Gubar's " 'victimization' hypothesis." And the scare quotes around "lovingly" in the last sentence warn against a sympathetic encounter that may do more harm than good. Thus, Howe's feminism is best approached with caution and care, for, as DuPlessis notes, "Howe continually proposes at least a feminism of cultural critique while declaring strong opposition whenever she suspects unitary (undialectical, uncritical) feminist enthusiasm. The only danger is that Howe's precise kind of feminism may be misread by a- or anti-feminist commentators" (135).

This "precise kind of feminism" produces an account of why such strong American women writers like Dickinson and Stein are consigned to the margins of literary history that succumbs to neither a " 'victimization' hypothesis" nor uncritical "enthusiasm." For Howe, Dickinson and Stein are marginalized because they "conducted a skillful and ironic investigation of patriarchal authority over literary history. Who polices questions of grammar, parts of speech, connection, and connotation? Whose order is shut inside the structure of a sentence?" (1985, 11) These two women writers pursue feminist projects designed to uncover the sexist foundation of literary history in their times, which is very much what Howe pursues in her work. Furthermore, Howe argues that Dickinson and Stein conduct these investigations on the field of discourse by exploring how power inheres in grammar, syntax, and semantics. Recall Laclau and Mouffe's contention that individuals and groups intervene in their cultures by "articulating" or connecting divergent language-games in order to account for the divergent social relations that occur in cultures, and that these articulations take place on the field of discourse. This line of thought allows them to understand that the poetic elements of discourse do much more than adorn reason. Thus, "Synonymy, metonymy, metaphor are not forms of thought that add a secondary sense to a primary, constitutive literality of social relations; instead, they are part of a primary terrain itself in which the social is constituted" (110). In short, Howe's version of feminism involves an investigation of poetic form as a means by which women writers intervene in culture. Thus, one of the reasons why writers such as Dickinson and Stein were and continue to be marginalized in our accounts of literary history is because they intervene in ways that women were not expected to. Their refusal "to conform" to these expectations is precisely what makes them such strong writers, but it is also what keeps them on the outskirts of "canonical criticism."

Thus, the "investigation of patriarchal authority" in American literary history begun by Dickinson and Stein and continued by contemporary women poets such as Howe takes place in terms of the form of discourse as well as its content. The innovative and difficult forms of writing these women produce are therefore a crucial dimension of their investigations and not merely eccentric ways they "dress up" what they have to say. For Howe, Dickinson in particular serves as a precursor in this investigation: "In prose and poetry she explored the implications of breaking the law just short of breaking off communication with a reader" (1985, 11). This assessment strikes me as being equally true of Howe's poetry. Both Dickinson and Howe stretch the boundaries of the laws of normative grammar and syntax to such a great extent that they are often accused of being unintelligible. Yet if we see the difficulty of their work as an integral part of their respective feminist projects, then those difficulties can rightly be seen as very significant contributions to the "investigation of patriarchal authority" that is so central in virtually all forms of contemporary feminism. As Keller succinctly puts it, "Howe's practice suggests we have been blinded by the clumping together of words into systems, into apparently cohesive images whose validity is difficult to challenge. Pondering words wrenched apart from narrative, from syntax, from speakers, we may see more clearly the ways in which words woven into language have formed a fabric perpetuating women's oppression" (232–33).

So when Howe writes that a "poet is never just a woman or a man" or that "Poetry leads past possession of self to transfiguration beyond gender," it would be misguided to assume that she is indifferent to issues of gender. But what exactly do her remarks suggest? An answer to this question is not simple, for Howe, much like Benjamin, holds in place historicist and theological linguistic registers that may seem contradictory. Her talk of transfiguration and transcendence puts her at odds with most forms of historical materialism. But perhaps, as Keller contends, the "greatest achievement" of Howe's poetry "is in its transcendence . . . of the merely individual, the temporally specific, the singly gendered" (188). What Howe may be signaling in her embrace of seemingly contradictory linguistic registers is that gender is not the essential category by which humans are defined.[4] It is certainly a category but not the category. In this respect, Howe's point is similar to the point made by many post-Marxists, including Laclau and Mouffe, that there is no single determinative category but a series of categories—race, class, and gender among them.

Since many versions of feminism do see gender as the essential category, one way to clarify Howe's position is to draw on the work of a feminist who does not see gender as such an essence. In Gender Trouble, Judith Butler contends that "If one 'is' a woman, that is surely not all one is: the term fails to be exhaustive, not because a pregendered 'person' transcends the specific paraphernalia of its gender, but because gender is not always constituted coherently or consistently in different historical contexts, and because gender intersects with racial, class, ethnic, sexual, and regional modalities of discursively constituted identities" (3). The important point here is that gender is not the essential category because some other "pregendered" category takes precedence; the point is that there is no "exhaustive" essential category. And because gender "intersects" with other determinative categories such as race and class, and because those intersections vary according to differing historical contexts, gender is not an invariable category, which is why it is "not always constituted coherently or consistently." If Butler is correct, then gender is not a stable category, and "if a stable notion of gender no longer proves to be the foundational premise of feminist politics, perhaps a new sort of feminist politics is now desirable to contest the very reifications of gender and identity, one that will take the variable construction of identity as both a methodological and normative prerequisite, if not a political goal" (5).

In both her prose and poetry, Howe does indeed contest the "reifications of gender and identity" that underwrite the patriarchal, racist, and imperialist tendencies in American history in general and American literary history in particular—tendencies that deploy a "positivist efficiency" to uproot Native Americans from their land and consign women writers to the margins of recognition. And both the form and content of Howe's poetry and prose enact an instance of the "new sort of feminist politics" Butler calls for. In this respect, we can see Howe in much the same light as she sees Dickinson—as a poet who "sings the sound of the imagination as learner and founder, sings of liberation in an order beyond gender" (1985, 13). For Howe, that "order" is attained through and in the poetic use of language; it is the poetic that "leads past possession of self to transfiguration beyond gender." I certainly do not believe that Howe would claim that only poetry can lead "beyond" the categories of gender or race or class. But for her, that is the path the "scout" takes in her work because the "poet is an intermediary hunting form beyond form, truth beyond theme through woods of words tangled and tremendous" (1985, 79–80).

Where we are, then, in Howe's poetic investigations, is in these "woods of words tangled and tremendous"—woods filled with "voices that are anonymous, slighted." Throughout her poetry and prose, Howe investigates various forms of writing history poetically in order to articulate those voices silenced in traditional historical accounts. Her investigation takes place on the field of discourse in enactments of poetic form that use parataxis, fractured and fragmented syntax, archaic spellings, multiple voices, and collage techniques, to name a few of the more prominent tactics in her hunting arsenal. In addition, writing history poetically in this manner unsettles our received notions of authorship. "To portray thoughts of a culture," Howe asks, "do you suppress individual dialogue under a controlling discourse, or do you depend entirely on direct quotations?" (Beckett, 24) Walter Benjamin asked a similar question and chose the latter position, claiming that in his Arcades project he would "need say nothing. Only exhibit" (1989, 47). Although Howe's answer to this question leans in much the same direction as Benjamin's, she recognizes that the "selection of particular examples from a large group is always a social act" (1993, 45); consequently, the author always "says" something. I suspect Benjamin eventually came to a similar realization, which may be one reason he struggled to find a satisfactory form for his Arcades manuscript. We should not, however, read either Benjamin's or Howe's unsettling of received notions of history and authorship as either destructive or nihilistic moves; on the contrary, these moves make room for the silenced other of history to enter the cultural dialogue. "If history is a record of survivors," as Howe asserts, then "Poetry shelters other voices" (1993, 47).

We are aware of the fact that the changes of our present history are the unseen moments of a massive transformation in civilization, which is the passage from the all-encompassing world of cultural Sameness, effectively imposed by the West, to a pattern of fragmented Diversity, achieved in a no less creative way by the peoples who have today seized their rightful place in the world.

—Edouard Glissant

2. Nathaniel Mackey
The "Mired Sublime"

Edouard Glissant's incisive sentence—which inaugurates a series of essays, first published in 1981, devoted to the possibilities and difficulties of a cross-cultural poetics—registers the rhetorical-political shift from sameness to diversity that structures so many of the current debates over multiculturalism. Although the Martinican poet and critic raises a familiar charge against the West, that it imposed rather than proposed sameness, I want to draw attention to the curative, utopian dimension of Glissant's diagnosis. Diversity, while fundamentally fragmented, can be "achieved in a no less creative way" than sameness. And it is this curative dimension that opens up one possibility for a cross-cultural poetry and poetics: the representation of the moment, enacted in a text, when traditions cross paths, and sameness yields to diversity to achieve a more rather than less creative encounter.

For the last fifteen years, Nathaniel Mackey, an African-American writer intent on exploring both sides of the hyphen, has investigated a remarkably wide range of subjects and forms. He has published two full-length volumes of poetry, *Eroding Witness* and *School of Udhra*, as well as *Strick: Song of the Andoumboulou 16–25*, a compact disc recording of his poetry set to music; two volumes of an ongoing work of epistolary fiction, *Bedouin Hornbook* and *Djbot Baghostus's Run*; a major collection of essays, *Discrepant Engagement*; numerous articles on music, literature, and culture; and he has coedited *Moment's Notice*, an anthology of poetry and prose inspired by jazz. Mackey is also the founding editor of the literary journal *Hambone,* which Eliot Weinberger rightly calls "the main meeting-place for Third World, American minority and white avant-gardists" (232). Yet despite the wide range of subjects and forms his writing undertakes, Mackey's work almost always gathers around the fact of song. The essays deal with Baraka and the blues, Creeley and jazz; the epistolary fiction is comprised of letters from "N," a member of a jazz band, the Mystic Horn Society; and many of the poems are dedicated to musicians such as John Coltrane, Don Cherry, Jimi Hendrix, Pharoah Sanders, and Cecil Taylor. In this chapter I concentrate on the ways in which Mackey's serial poem, *Song of the Andoumboulou,* and his two volumes of epistolary fiction generate diverse forms of writing history poetically in order to investigate poetically the possibilities of the cross-cultural encounter Glissant calls for. I will begin with *Song of the Andoumboulou.*

American literature in this century has witnessed its own series of attempts to produce a cross-cultural epic poem capable of telling the "tale of the tribe"[1]—a tale including not only American but world history as well. This series of "world-poems" begins with the *Cantos* of Ezra Pound and continues in Louis Zukofsky's *"A,"* H. D.'s *Trilogy* and *Helen in Egypt,* Robert Duncan's *Passages,* and, I contend, Nathaniel Mackey's *Song of the Andoumboulou.* Each of these works, in its own distinct way, holds out the possibility of a utopian vision created in and by poetry. Yet not all of these poems enact the passage from sameness to diversity that marks Glissant's definition of cross-cultural poetry. Pound's declaration in *The Spirit of Romance* that "all ages are contemporaneous" (1968b, 6) has the unfortunate effect of reducing diversity to a transcendent sameness in the service of an all-encompassing view of world history, an effect all too evident in parts of the *Cantos.* As Mackey argues in his study of the twentieth-century American world-poem, *Gassire's Lute: Robert Duncan's Vietnam War Poems,* these poems allow for more diversity as we move closer to the present and as they begin to admit the impossibility of composing an all-encompassing tale of the human tribe, a tale that does not seek to cover up the holes in history. This admission, however, does not close the door on the possibility of a world-poem; on the contrary, it opens the door for the kind of creative encounter between cultures that Glissant calls for—an encounter based on the recognition of the irreducible diversity of the disparate cultures that populate the world. Nathaniel Mackey achieves just such an encounter in his world-poem *Song of the Andoumboulou.*

For Mackey, song, which includes poetry, creates the possibility of what he terms a "discrepant engagement" between cultures. The phrase serves as a title for his recent book of essays and a description of his reading of the cross-cultural moment. Mackey defines the term in relation to

> the name the Dogon of West Africa give their weaving block, the base on which the loom they weave upon sits. They call it the "creaking of the word." It is the noise upon which the word is based, the discrepant foundation of all coherence and articulation, of the purchase upon the world fabrication affords. Discrepant engagement, rather than suppressing or seeking to silence that noise, acknowledges it. In its antifoundational acknowledgment of founding noise, discrepant engagement sings "bass," voicing reminders of the axiomatic exclusions upon which positings of identity and meaning depend. (1993c, 19)

Discrepant engagement, then, not only denotes a theory of cross-culturality; it enacts one in the structure of its definition. The crossing traditions of Dogon and Western cosmologies and philosophies of language allow Mackey to present a second crossing, one in which traditions of sense and nonsense, noise and word, encounter one and other. Mackey uncovers in this second opposition the cross-cultural moment shared by both traditions, although the judgment concerning that moment's value is clearly not shared. This opposition animates most of Mackey's writing and generates the cross-cultural recognition embodied in the moment of song.

Mackey's *Song of the Andoumboulou* presents this illusive and allusive moment, this discrepant engagement, when two traditions of poetic cosmology—the Dogon tradition of West Africa and the American tradition of the world-poem—cross paths and articulate one another.[2] For Mackey, the cultural judgment concerning the value of song coincides with the way a given culture reacts to the opposition between noise and word, with how much "creaking" a culture tolerates in its words. If we recall Mackey's contention that the "founding noise" of language also serves to remind us of a tradition's "axiomatic exclusions," then it follows that a culture's definitions of and judgments about noise have political as well as aesthetic implications.

Glissant offers a useful interpretation of the politics of noise he finds at work in the "jumbled rush" of sound that composes Martinican Creole. "This is how the dispossessed man organizes his speech by weaving it into the apparently meaningless texture of extreme noise," Glissant contends. "So the meaning of a sentence is sometimes hidden in the accelerated nonsense created by scrambled sounds. But this nonsense does convey real meaning to which the master's ear cannot have access" (124). The "scrambled sounds" of Creole hide meaning from the master; the dispossessed find a form of subversion in the noise ignored by those who possess, and they hide meaning most often in song. In Mackey's work, song inhabits this ambiguous ground. In the words of "N," Mackey's "namesake" correspondent in his epistolary fiction, "Did song imply a forfeiture of speech or was it speech's fulfillment?" (1993b, 160) As we will see, Mackey's poetry and poetics offer a deliberately ambivalent answer to this question.

In *Gassire's Lute,* Mackey describes the world-poem in light of Duncan's understanding of Pound's, H. D.'s, and Charles Olson's initial attempts to produce such a poem.

> The world-poem is a global, multiphasic work in which various times and various places interpenetrate. It is no accident, as Duncan sees it, that this sort of work began to appear during the period of the two World Wars, a time when national divisions and hostilities were at the forefront. What he puts forth is a sense of the world-poem as a dialectical, oppositional response to the outright disunity of a world at war. (1991b, 151–52)

The world-poem, then, is by design a cross-cultural work. It seeks to represent in collage or serial form the "luminous moments," to use Pound's phrase, that transcend temporal and cultural boundaries in order to overcome the nationalistic tendencies that led to two world wars. Yet both the world-poem in particular and the practice of collage in general raise significant questions concerning the relation of the author to the material appropriated from other cultures. Does the author necessarily underwrite the values of all the sources on which he or she draws? Is the author claiming "mastery" over these sources, or does he or she attempt to set up a more dialogic relationship with them? And given the often unwritten strictures against overly discursive language in these genres, how does the author make his or her relation to the source texts evident? I am not suggesting that Mackey answers all of these questions directly in his version of the world-poem. There are potential incongruities between the material he borrows from Dogon cosmology and his own position as author: for instance, incongruities between the Dogon treatment of gender and sexuality and Mackey's treatment that are not fully addressed or worked out in the poetry.[3] Nevertheless, Mackey's concept of a "discrepant engagement" between cultures allows room for such unresolved incongruities without undermining the worth of his project.

Furthermore, Mackey does address in *Gassire's Lute* the general problem of authorship and inspiration in a way that sheds light on his understanding of the possible dangers involved in the authorship of a world-poem. Mackey's book investigates the ways in which the story of Gassire's lute provides a connection between previous instances of the world-poem and brings the subjects of war and poetry face to face with each other. But, more significantly, it also investigates the ways in which that story announces the cross-cultural moment in at least three of those poems — Pound's *Cantos,* Olson's *Maximus Poems,* and Duncan's *Passages* — and the ways in which the modernist aesthetic governing the world-poem comes under fire. As Mackey informs us, Pound found the story in Leo Frobenius's and Douglas Fox's *African Genesis* and incorporated it in Canto 74, so the story brings African culture directly into the mix of the American world-poem. Frobenius first heard the story when he was working with the Soninke of Mali, who inhabit the same region of West Africa as the Dogon (1990, 86–89). Gassire, the son of the king of the mythical city of Wagadu, following a fierce battle, hears a partridge singing the Dausi, an African epic song, and determines to trade his role as military leader for that of singer. He orders a special lute to be made but is warned by the craftsman that the lute will only sing if its wood is stained with the blood of Gassire's sons. He is so entranced with the song of the Dausi that he willingly accepts this price, which leads to the death of his eight sons and the destruction of Wagadu.

For Mackey, the story of Gassire's lute becomes a parable about the dangers of song and poetry, about the dangers of placing oneself in the path of daimonic inspiration at the expense of human life. "Taken seriously, the notion [of inspiration] complicates and unsettles what we mean by 'human,' since if we're subject to such invasions our susceptibility has to be a factor of what being human means" (1990, 96). Throughout *Gassire's Lute,* Mackey interrogates the possibility that the poets producing the various world-poems under consideration may in fact be susceptible to just such a danger. In particular, he cites Duncan's analysis of "Pound's refusal to look at the possibility that the ideal might be a party to what betrays it, 'that the sublime is complicit, involved in a total structure, with the obscene — what goes on backstage'" (1991b, 160). According to this line of argument, Pound trusted his muse too much; he refused to question the source of his inspiration and, as a result, was unable or unwilling to see the ways in which the sublime may be intertwined with the political horrors he sought to denounce in the *Cantos.*

Mackey contends that Duncan avoids this trap because his poetry exhibits a "willingness to question or corrupt its own inspiration" (1991a, 159). I want to extend this argument to Mackey's *Song of the Andoumboulou* and argue that he, like Duncan, courts a muse that makes this questioning an integral part of inspiration—a questioning that intentionally leaves both the poet and reader enmeshed in a "mired sublime" (1993a, 18). However, unlike a number of postmodern poets and theorists, Mackey does not unequivocally dismiss the possibility of transcendence through, among other things, song. He contends that song can embody "a simultaneous mystic thrust. Immanence and transcendence meet, making the music social as well as cosmic, political and metaphysical as well" (1993c, 235). Mackey offers a revised notion of transcendence—a notion that incorporates the social and political realms and that not only protects against dangerous notions of inspiration and the reduction of diversity to sameness but holds out the possibility of a truly curative cross-cultural poetry as well.

Mackey's *Song of the Andoumboulou* begins in his first book of poetry, continues in his second, and new sections have been appearing recently in poetry magazines such as *New American Writing, Sulfur,* and *River City.* Because of the ongoing and open-ended nature of the series, Mackey's poems are not easy to enter, nor are they susceptible to an authoritative reading since they too include a certain amount of "founding noise" in their form as well as their content. This difficulty is augmented by the fact that the Andoumboulou are virtually unknown outside of a small group of West African anthropologists. Even for the interested, information on the Andoumboulou is scarce at best. Mackey is aware of only two instances in which the Andoumboulou are mentioned—in the liner notes to François Di Dio's *Les Dogon,* a recording of Dogon music, and in Marcel Griaule and Germaine Dieterlen's *The Pale Fox*—both of which Mackey cites as epigraphs to Songs 1–7 in *Eroding Witness* and Songs 8–15 in *School of Udhra* respectively. In the first instance, Di Dio reveals that "the Song of the Andoumboulou is addressed to the spirits. For this reason the initiates, crouching in a circle, sing it in a whisper in the deserted village, and only the howling of the dogs and the wind disturb the silence of the night" (1985, 31). In the second instance, Griaule and Dieterlen place the Andoumboulou in the context of Dogon cosmology, wherein the Andoumboulou are the product of the incestuous coupling of the Yeban and reside in the earth's interior. As a result of this coupling, the Andoumboulou "attest to Ogo's failure and his lost twinness" (1993a, 1). As we will see, exploring the possibility of a reconciliation of this "lost twinness" animates the utopian dimension of Mackey's world-poem.

Although these citations might not provide the reader with a great deal of information about the Andoumboulou, they do provide Mackey with enough inspiration to begin his poetic investigations. "What really bore most on my initial senses of what would be active in that sequence was the actual music, the 'Song of the Andoumboulou' on that album, a funereal song whose low, croaking vocality intimates the dead and whose climactic trumpet bursts signal breakthru to another world, another life" (1993e). Admittedly, an author's comments on his or her own work do not provide a privileged interpretation of that work; nevertheless, Mackey's gloss of his world-poem brings to the fore two issues that prove crucial for an understanding of the work: the centrality of song and the possibility of transcendence through song. First, note that the music rather than the mythology of the Dogon initially sparks his interest and that it is the blurring of the boundaries between song and noise, the "croaking vocality," that catches his attention in particular. Second, note that this particular kind of song opens the poet up not only to the possibility of encountering the past (the "dead") but to the possibility of encountering "another world, another life." Mackey's conception of transcendence should not be confused with either a Judeo-Christian or a symbolist conception; nevertheless, the possibility of transcendence animates his cross-cultural poetic project.

Although Mackey's understanding of transcendence will unfold more fully as my argument develops, his desire to leave open the possibility of temporal or historical transcendence suggests ways in which his treatment of the Andoumboulou moves beyond a mere antiquarian interest in Dogon mythology. According to Mackey,

> it wasn't until I read *The Pale Fox* in the course of writing *School of Udhra* that I found out the Andoumboulou are specifically the spirits of an earlier, flawed or failed form of human being—what, given the Dogon emphasis on signs, traces, drawings, etc. and the "graphicity" noted above, I tend to think of as a rough draft of human being. I'm lately fond of saying that the Andoumboulou are in fact us, that we're the rough draft. (1993e)

Nathaniel Mackey: The "Mired Sublime" 77

For Mackey, the song of the Andoumboulou is also potentially "our" song—the song of a form of humanity that is not quite finished, that is still in the process of becoming more than it presently is. The reconciliation of the "lost twinness" mentioned above becomes a central preoccupation of Mackey's world-poem, and that reconciliation may suggest a way in which humanity might move beyond the "rough draft" stage of development. Thus, Mackey's remarks on his world-poem not only raise important questions concerning our access to history and tradition; they also suggest the ways in which his series of poems may develop the kind of curative dimension Glissant calls for since they hold out the possibility of humanity going through another "draft" or revision—a revision that recognizes rather than reduces diversity.

The original "Song of the Andoumboulou," as Mackey points out, is a dirge sung by the elders of the Dogon. His world-poem opens with this moment of lament:

> The song says the
> dead will not
> ascend without song.
>
> That because if
> we lure them their names get
> our throats, the
> word sticks.
>
> (1985, 33)

First, what are we to make of the verb in the opening line? If we listen to the version of the "Song of the Andoumboulou" recorded by Di Dio, the song does not "say" anything if we construe that term strictly. The song seems to explore the pre- or post-articulate terrain of chant and groan, whisper and sigh rather than a definite ground of meaning or direct communication. Yet the mood or tone of the song is unmistakably that of a funereal chant; I doubt many listeners, even those unfamiliar with African music, would take the song to be part of a festive occasion.

Both the recording of the "Song of the Andoumboulou" and the first two stanzas of Mackey's poem bring the listener and reader up against the opposition between word and noise that figures prominently in his notion of a discrepant engagement. So the initial cross-cultural engagement between the Dogon song and his own embryonic poem takes place on the contested terrain between word and noise. "There's something, for me at least, particularly 'graphic' about recourse to that strained, straining register, the scratchy tonalities [of the Dogon singers] to which the lines 'their names get / our throats, the / word sticks' allude" (1993e). The direct connection Mackey makes here between the Dogon song and the lines from the second stanza of his first "Song" hinges on the hesitant if not inhibited act of expression. Nevertheless, while the "word sticks" in the singer's throat, the "founding noise" of the song "says" something that both precedes and exceeds that word and which, furthermore, precedes and exceeds the singer as well. Perhaps, then, we can extend Glissant's contention that the noise or "jumbled rush" of sound in Creole speech deliberately conceals meaning from the master to include the contention that the noise inherent in both versions of the "Song of the Andoumboulou" deliberately conceals meaning from an equally domineering master—the master of meaning who demands that all linguistic sounds make rational sense.

This extension of Glissant's argument brings us face to face with the mystical element inherent in Dogon cosmology and in Mackey's poetry and poetics. The term "mysticism," like the equally troublesome term "transcendence," is, for contemporary Western readers in particular, often overwhelmed by its Judeo-Christian connotations, and, as a result, the term needs to be used in a carefully qualified manner. W. T. Jones defines mysticism as the "view that reality is ineffable and transcendent; that it is known, therefore, by some special, nonrational means; that knowledge of it is communicable, if at all, only in poetic imagery and metaphor" (424). I want to add song to Jones's list of the means by which nonrational knowledge may be communicable since the mystical moment in Dogon cosmology and Mackey's poetry transpires in song as well as in imagery and metaphor. Furthermore, nonrational knowledge of the transcendent and ineffable nature of reality may not be communicable at all. Song, imagery, and metaphor can suggest or intimate that knowledge, but they cannot make it explicit or absolute. Yet song, imagery, and metaphor can make explicit their own limits and, via negativa, draw attention to that which transcends those limits. Thus, the encounter between word and noise that comprises the discrepant engagement occurring between the Dogons' "Song of the Andoumboulou" and Mackey's is best understood as part of a movement that simultaneously reveals and conceals a reality that transcends any attempt to represent it in a strictly rational mode of communication. This understanding of the relation between word and noise mitigates against hubristic assumptions about the possibility of an all-encompassing tale of the tribe. Yet it also leaves unresolved—perhaps

Nathaniel Mackey: The "Mired Sublime" 79

intentionally, perhaps not—the potential incongruities between the author's stance and those of the cultural materials on which he or she draws.

Song, imagery, and metaphor, for Mackey, come together in the tradition of lyric poetry—a tradition with close ties to Western romanticism and the claims for transcendence that accompany it. Yet Mackey's understanding of the transcendent moment in lyric poetry cannot simply be equated with romanticism. The transcendent moment for a romantic such as Samuel Taylor Coleridge, for instance, allows access to the "infinite I Am" of the Judeo-Christian tradition (263). In Coleridge's poetics, lyric poetry is one of the primary means by which one can transcend the finite, material world of the senses and move into the infinite, immaterial world of God's presence. For Mackey, on the other hand, the transcendental tradition of lyric poetry allows access to "modes of being prior to *one's own* experience," to "records of experience that are part of the communal and collective inheritance that we have access to even though we have not personally experienced those things" (Foster, 48). Mackey's conception of transcendence, then, is best understood in a sociological or historical rather than theological or metaphysical sense—as a human-to-human rather than a human-to-divine encounter. In short, Mackey offers a "horizontal" rather than "vertical" notion of transcendence. For Mackey, language is one of the primary means of attaining this moment of transcendence since "in language we inherit the voices of the dead. Language is passed on to us by people who are now in their graves and brings with it access to history, tradition, times and places that are not at all immediate to our own immediate and particular occasion whether we look at it individually and personally or whether we look at it in a more collective way and talk about a specific community" (Foster, 54). Yet language is only one means of transcendence, and, due to the "founding noise" inherent in the word, it does not hold out the possibility of absolute transcendence.

An equally important means of transcendence for Mackey is found in human sexuality. In "Song of the Andoumboulou: 1," we are told that "the dead don't want / us bled, but to be / sung. // And she said the same, / a thin wisp of soul, / *But I want the meat of / my body sounded*" (1985, 35). I read the lines in italics as pertaining to that which both "she" and the "dead" desire: to be "sounded" in song, not as disembodied entities but as beings composed of flesh. Thus, two themes that are truly cross-cultural, sex and death, meet in the act of song—an act that purports to take the singer and the listener beyond the limits of their own experience but not out of their own bodies in order to share the sacred common ground of generation and degeneration. As we move through Mackey's poems, both of these themes take on mythological proportions to such a great extent that in "Song of the Andoumboulou: 7" "N," the same "N" who is the protagonist in Mackey's fiction, admits to having "been accused of upwardly displacing sex" (1985, 54). Understanding how this "upward" displacement functions in the poems helps shed light on the possibility of reconciling the "lost twinness" through the potential transcendence in sexuality.

"Song of the Andoumboulou: 3" is an extended instance of this "upward displacement," and, as such, it deserves close attention. The following passage is from the poem's first section.

> What song there
> was delivered up to
> above where sound leaves off,
>
> though whatever place words talk us
> into'd be like hers,
> who'd only speak
> to herself . . .
>
> (A hill, down thru
> its hole only ants
> where this
> was. The mud
>
> hut was her body.)
>
> Embraced, but
> on the edge of speech
> though she spoke
>
> without words,
> as in a dream.
>
> The loincloth, he
> said, is tight,
> which is so that it conceals
> the woman's sacred parts.
> But that in him
> this worked a longing
> to unveil what's underneath,
>
> the Word the Nommo

> put inside the fabric's
> woven secret,
>
>   the Book wherein
> the wet of kisses
>   keeps.
>
>   (1985, 39–40)

The first two stanzas set the scene of transcendence, which transpires in song and in the space between silence, "where sound leaves off," and signification, the "place words talk us / into," a place likened to "her." Following a parenthetical element, "she" appears "on the edge of speech," speaking "without words"—a condition reminiscent of the paradoxical way the song "says" in the first poem of the series. This passage implicitly articulates the issues of language, song, transcendence, and sexuality, but to understand how these concerns are explicitly connected, we need to consult what is perhaps the primary source for the study of Dogon cosmology, Marcel Griaule's *Conversations with Ogotemmêli*.

Griaule's book records his unique discussions with Ogotemmêli, a blind Dogon sage, which took place in 1946 and which still stand as the most intimate and authoritative account of Dogon cosmology available. Mackey signals the importance of these conversations for his way of writing history poetically by prefacing the first poem with an epigraph from the book. Yet not until "Song of the Andoumboulou: 3" does the full impact of Ogotemmêli's narrative become evident. In his commentary on the symbolic import of the Dogon women's clothing, Ogotemmêli tells Griaule that " 'The loin-cloth is tight . . . to conceal the woman's sex, but it stimulates a desire to see what is underneath. This is because of the Word, which the Nummo put in the fabric. That word is every woman's secret, and is what attracts the man. A woman must have secret parts to inspire desire" (Griaule, 82). The last four stanzas of the section from "Song of the Andoumboulou: 3" cited above are a poetic paraphrase of Ogotemmêli, and the common thread that runs between the two passages concerns the essential role concealment plays in desire. But this concealment provokes hermeneutical as well as sexual desire since what is longed for "underneath" the loincloth is "the Word." According to Ogotemmêli, Amma, the originary God in Dogon lore, created the earth from a lump of clay and, after fashioning female genitalia in the form of an ant hill, proceeded to have sex with his creation—an act Ogotemmêli calls "the primordial blunder of God" (Griaule, 17). This act eventually led to the birth of twin spirits, called Nummo (spelled "Nommo" in Mackey's version), who determined to bring speech to their speechless mother, the earth. "The Nummo accordingly came down to earth, bringing with them fibres pulled from plants already created in the heavenly regions" and formed a loincloth for their mother. But "the purpose of this garment was not merely modesty": the "coiled fringes of the skirt were therefore the chosen vehicle for the words which the Spirit desired to reveal to the earth" (Griaule, 19–20).

To the extent that mystical discourse simultaneously reveals and conceals the reality that exceeds rational understanding, the connection between language and sexuality as potential media of transcendence becomes more apparent if we explore not only the role the image of the loincloth plays in Dogon cosmology but the image of weaving as well. For the Dogon, as Griaule points out, "weaving is a form of speech, which is imparted to the fabric by the to-and-fro of the shuttle on the warp" (Griaule, 77). As Ogotemmêli explains, "The weaver, representing a dead man, is also the male who opens and closes the womb of the woman, represented by the heddle. The stretched threads represent the act of procreation"; and the "Word . . . is in the sound of the block and the shuttle. The name of the block means 'creaking of the word.'. . . It is interwoven with the threads: it fills the interstices in the fabric" (Griaule, 73). Thus, the image of weaving brings us in contact with the primary elements of Dogon cosmology and Mackey's poetics. The word and its creaking (the "founding noise" upon which the word is based) are essential parts of the procreative craft that produces the clothing that provokes the desire "to unveil what's underneath"—a desire never fully satisfied in and by song or poetry.

As I argued earlier, the form of the world-poem raises troublesome questions concerning the author's relation to the cultural materials on which he or she draws, and Mackey's use of Dogon cosmology here is a case in point: by granting the essentialist notions of gender and sexuality implicit in Dogon cosmology such a prominent place in his world-poem, Mackey risks an unsavory equation of Dogon notions of gender and sexuality with his own. The all too familiar representation of woman as the passive provoker of desire and of man as the aggressive unveiler of truth is not one with which I suspect Mackey identifies. And although Mackey does not address this issue directly in *Song of the Andoumboulou* in a manner that draws a clear distinction between his views on this matter and the Dogons', he does, particularly in the recently published sections of the series, explore notions that are consonant with a more contemporary understanding of gender and sexuality. I will return to this issue later; for now, let me suggest that the reconciliation of "lost twinness" will prove to be bound up with a less essentialist understanding of gender and sexuality.

To return to the connection between language and sexuality depicted in Ogotemmêli's account, this sexualized image of the origin of language has strong implications for the notion of poetic inspiration that underlies Mackey's world-poem. Recall his argument in *Gassire's Lute* concerning the dangers of an unquestioned allegiance to the all-encompassing claims of a transcendent source of inspiration and the ways in which such claims can blind a poet to the possible complicity between poetry and politics. "Song of the Andoumboulou: 5," which carries the significant subtitle "gassire's lute," opens with "she"—whom I take to be the same "she" encountered in Songs 1 and 3—warning the poet to "'beware the / burnt odor of blood you / say we ask of you" (1985, 44). The demand for blood clearly alludes to the story of Gassire's lute, but the important point here is that those that "she" represents, the "we" of the third line, do not necessarily make the demand that "you," which I take to be the poet, say they do. This subtle qualification situates the origin of the demand in the human realm of the poet rather than in the realm of "she" and "we." Is it possible, then, that the poet can be accused of "upwardly displacing" the demand for blood in much the same way as he admits to "upwardly displacing sex"? Read this way, Mackey's poem enacts the kind of questioning of the source of inspiration that he finds in Duncan's poetry—a questioning that becomes increasingly prominent in the sections of *Song of the Andoumboulou* that appear in Mackey's most recent book of poetry, *School of Udhra*.

The sections of Mackey's world-poem included in his second book continue to investigate the poetic possibilities of transcendence, but the poems take on a more personal tone as they turn their attention to love as a potential means of transcendence, and, as a result, a reconciliation of "lost twinness." The site of the investigation is also more personal in these poems since they take place, for the most part, in the liminal space between sleeping and waking:

> Not yet asleep I'm no longer
> awake,   lie awaiting what
> stalks the unanswered air,
>   still

> awaiting what blunts the running
> > flood
> or what carries, all Our Mistress's
> > whispers . . .
> > (1993a, 3)

With one foot in the realm of waking reality and one in the realm of dream, the poet awaits the whispered message that will allow him to ascend into the latter realm—a moment that occurs in "Song of the Andoumboulou: 10."

In this poem the poet is again awaiting sleep as he sits "up reading drafts / of a dead friend's poem" (1993a, 5). As sleep arrives, the poet envisions himself with

> > > Legs ascending
> > some unlit stairway, saw myself
> > escorted thru a gate of
> > unrest. The bed my boat, her look
> > > lowers me
> > down, I rise from sleep,
> > > my waking puts
> > a wreath around the sun.
> > > (1993a, 5)

The image of the stairway appears earlier in "Song of the Andoumboulou: 5," when "she" informs the poet "that all ascent moves up / a stairway of shattered / light" (1985, 44). In the passage cited above, "she" also plays a crucial role, although one that cuts against the grain of traditional expectations. Rather than being the vehicle of the poet's ascent—which, for example, is the role Beatrice plays in Dante's epic—it is "her look" that brings the poet back down into waking reality, an act that results in his celebratory gesture toward the sun. Thus, "she" appears to lead the poet toward an earthly rather than otherworldly experience of transcendence.

I suggest this earth-bound transcendence is love: "And what love had to do with it / stuttered, bit its tongue" (1993a, 9). Love, like song, testifies to the dimensions of reality that exceed articulation, that can only be hinted at in a form of discourse that draws attention to its own limitations. Much like the phenomenon of stammering in Susan Howe's work, the phenomenon of stuttering in Mackey's work stands as just such a form. In

"Sound and Sentiment, Sound and Symbol," his major critical piece concerning the transcendent possibilities of music and their representation in literature, Mackey argues that the "stutter is a two-way witness that on one hand symbolizes a need to go beyond the confines of an exclusionary order, while on the other confessing to its at best only limited success at doing so. The impediments to the passage it seeks are acknowledged if not annulled, attested to by exactly the gesture that would overcome them if it could" (1993c, 249). This interpretation aligns stuttering with mystical discourse, which, like stuttering, simultaneously eludes and alludes to that which exceeds articulation and transcends the "exclusionary order" of rational discourse.

"Song of the Andoumboulou: 14" (1993a, 12–14) offers the most complete rendition in the series of the connection between love, transcendence, mysticism, and the limits of language. In this poem, the poet confronts "what speaks of speaking," which is "Boxed in but at its edge alludes / to movement . . ." Self-reflexive language, while "boxed in," can nevertheless point beyond itself to the "needle of light" the poet "laid hands on." Confronting this light, which I take to be the same as that found at the top of the "shattered stairway" mentioned earlier, puts the poet in a position in which, although "move[d] to speak," he finds his "mouth / wired shut":

>   Mute lure, blind mystic
>   light,
>   lost aura.   Erased itself,
>   stuttered,   wouldn't say
>   what

Although the elliptical grammar creates a certain amount of "founding noise" in this passage and makes any reading tentative, the subject of the verbs seems to be the light encountered by the poet. Read this way, the light effaces itself and leaves only a stuttering trace of its presence. Again, stuttering should not be seen as merely a sign of a failure to communicate but as a "two-way witness" to that which exceeds communication. Thus, both the transcendent experience and its object prove to be evanescent, which does not necessarily mean they are illusory; the fact that they do not endure does not mean that they never occurred. It does imply, however, that any representation of either the experience or the object of that experience as stable or eternal falsifies both.

As the poem comes to a close, the poet's encounter with the "mystic light" causes a similar reaction on his part.

> Saw by light so abrupt I stuttered.
>   Tenuous
>   angel I took it for. Took it
>   for lips, an incendiary kiss,
>   momentary madonna. Took it for
>   bread,
>   condolences, cure . . .
>   (1993a, 14)

The first line signals the moment of transcendence in which the subject and the object, the poet and the light, share the experience of stuttering—one that is transitory at best. Note that the light is figured here in feminine form, as an angelic "madonna" whose message comes as a kiss that is "tenuous" and "momentary" rather than authoritative and eternal. Yet despite the evanescent quality of the kiss, it provides, among other things, a curative experience for the poet, an experience that reaches its apogee in "Song of the Andoumboulou: 15," the last in the series published in *School of Udhra.*

At the beginning of this poem the poet moves "Back down the steps" (1993a, 15) of what I read as the "shattered stairway of light," yet this movement does not necessarily indicate a movement from one world to another. As I argued earlier, Mackey's notion of transcendence is best understood in physical rather than metaphysical terms. His reading of the moment of transcendence in Duncan's poetry provides an equally revealing insight into the same moment in his poetry. According to Mackey, the point of Duncan's poetry and poetics "is that we live in a world whose limits we make up and that those limits are therefore subject to unmaking. The 'irreality' the poem refers to is not so much a stepping outside as an extending of reality. This is the meaning of the cosmic impulse or aspiration, the cosmic mediumship to which the poem lays claim" (1992, 194). For Mackey, song and love, both of which are anchored in the material realm of the body, are two of the means by which such an extension of reality occurs:

> The rough body
>   of love at last gifted with
>   wings, at

last bounded on all but one
impenetrable side by the promise
of heartbeats heard on high,
wrought
promise of lips one dreamt of aimlessly
kissing,
throated rift. . .

(1993a, 15)

Unlike a traditional Christian conception of utopia, wherein the soul gets its "wings" only after leaving the body behind, the wings in this poem, which serve as a figure for the means by which the experience of reality is extended, are given to the "rough body / of love." Note also that this body is bounded by the promise rather than fulfillment of transcendence. Furthermore, this promise confronts an "impenetrable" element that, much like the "founding noise" inherent in language, curbs any claims for an unalloyed experience of transcendence and leaves a "rift" in the promise that cannot, and perhaps should not, be overcome.

This scene of provisional transcendence is as close as Mackey comes to a reconciliation of the "lost twinness" that may move humanity beyond the "rough draft" stage of the Andoumboulou. And it also marks the point at which Mackey's own notions of gender and sexuality may move beyond the essentialist notions of Dogon cosmology discussed earlier. Throughout the recently published sections of *Song of the Andoumboulou*, the distinctions between "he" and "she" merge into a "we" that

would include, not reduce to us . . .
He to him, she to her, they to them,
opaque
pronouns, "persons" whether or not we
knew who they were . . .

(1993d, 14)

This "we" does not reduce to either "he" or "she" but to an inclusive notion of humanity that suggests an understanding of gender that views men and women as having their essence in collective rather than gender-specific pronouns. I am not claiming that this invocation of a collective understanding of gender resolves all of the problems raised by Mackey's appropriation of Dogon cosmology in his world-poem; it does, however, point in the direction I suspect Mackey will continue to explore as his on-going world-poem develops and works its way toward a reconciliation of the "lost twinness" that marks the "rough draft" of a form of humanity still in process.

The curative dimension of Mackey's world-poem, then, occurs as it extends our conception of reality beyond the "exclusionary order" of rational discourse—an order that has based its exclusions on essentialist notions of race and gender. What Mackey's *Song of the Andoumboulou* attempts to cure us of is the desire to reduce the representation of diversity and difference to the kind of all-encompassing sameness that compromises some of the initial instances of the American world-poem. As Mackey argues, a troubling measure of American imperialism is implicit in the very idea of a world-poem, which may indeed "reflect a distinctly American sense of privilege, the American feeling of being entitled to everything the world has to offer[.] It may well be the aesthetic arm of an American sensibility of which CIA-arranged coups, multinational corporations and overseas military bases are more obvious extensions" (1991b, 160). The fact that Mackey's poetry conceals as much as it reveals, like the loincloth in Dogon cosmology, serves as one of his principal poetic tactics designed to quell the appetite of such an omnivorous genre, an attempt that situates us in a "mired sublime," a sublime that offers us "no way out / if not thru" (1993a, 18).

Yet this result is no more to be overcome than deplored since, as Mackey contends, the "saving grace of poetry is not a return to an Edenic world, but an ambidextrous, even duplicit capacity for counterpoint, the weaving of a music which harmonizes contending terms" (1992, 199). Mackey's use of the musical metaphor of counterpoint here resonates with Edward Said's use of it in *Culture and Imperialism* to figure his understanding of the dynamics of a truly cross-cultural encounter between peoples and texts. "In counterpoint," Said points out, "various themes play off one another, with only a provisional privilege being given to any particular one; yet in the resulting polyphony there is concert and order, an organized interplay that derives from the themes, not from a rigorous melodic or formal principle outside the work"—a counterpoint that "should be modelled not . . . on a symphony but rather on an atonal ensemble" (51, 318). It is in this sense that the counterpoint in Mackey's poetry between "founding noise" and articulate word and between African and American poetic traditions opens the way for the kind of creative cross-cultural encounter that Edouard Glissant contends marks the "massive transformation" that is shaping our present history. And we can literally hear this "founding noise" of counterpoint on Mackey's *Strick: Song of the Andoumboulou 16–25,* a compact disc recording of ten new installments of his serial poem with Royal Hartigan and Hafez Modirzadeh.

It is a commonplace that poetry and music both originate in the pre-articulate soundings of human beings. Yet, particularly in modern poetry, this common point of origin has been more a matter of analogy than fact. In *Strick,* Mackey, Hartigan, and Modirzadeh bring poetry and music together in an enactment of shared origins that is as unique as it is challenging. The original music composed by Hartigan and Modirzadeh for the poems brings the "croaking vocality" that Mackey hears in the original "Song of the Andoumboulou" into the present by blending the ceremonial sounds of world-music with post-bebop jazz in a way that makes the original ours in a truly cross-cultural sense. The word *strick* refers primarily to pieces of fiber or hemp before they are made into rope. "But I hear in the word more than that," Mackey says. "I hear the word *stick,* I hear the word *strike,* I hear the word *struck,* and I hear the word *strict.* I hear those words which are not really pronounced in that word, but there are overtones or undertones of those words, harmonics of those words. The word *strick,* then, is like a musical chord in which those words which are otherwise not present are present" (1994b). Both the primary meaning of the word and the overtones Mackey hears suggest a process of articulating the materials of poetry, sound and sense, into a weave of words and music that resonates with rather than reconciles the multiple possibilities out of which it is made.

Strick, like much of Mackey's work, brings together the traditions of African-American music, Caribbean and Arabic poetry, and West African mythology, among others, with the Western traditions of philosophy, poetry, and music. Although a mix of such disparate materials could result in a multicultural patchwork, Mackey weaves these traditions together into a taut rope united by the fact of song. He does not, however, gather these traditions together for a celebration of universal sameness or harmony; rather, he introduces into this cross-cultural encounter "a discrepant note meant to call attention to the problematics of rubric-making, a caveat meant to make the act of categorization creak" (1993c, 21). That note signals the discrepancy with which many of the traditions Mackey engages have been treated by the dominant and dominating traditions of the West and causes the categories that authorize that treatment — categories such as "civilized" and "primitive," "Christian" and "heathen" — to creak under the weight of a song "Steeped in memory, bedrock / mischief, misanthropy" in which the "Cries of thousands / cut in on the music" and bear witness to the brutality that more often than not underwrites those categories (1995).

And Hartigan and Modirzadeh bring this discrepant note into the heart of their music. Both are graduates of the music department at Wesleyan University, and both have played in Fred Ho's Afro-Asian Music Ensemble since the late 1980s, performing on the band's two most recent recordings, *We Refuse to Be Used and Abused* (Soul Note Records, 1988) and *The Underground Railroad to My Heart* (Soul Note Records, 1994). In addition to leading his own quartet, Hartigan is a member of Talking Drums, the David Bindman-Tyrone Henderson Project, Liu Qi Chao's American Chinese Quintet, and has worked with Archie Shepp, Reggie Workman, Max Roach, and Ed Blackwell, among others. Modirzadeh's first album, *In Chromodal Discourse,* was released on Asian Improv Records in 1993, and he has worked with Peter Apfelbaum's Hieroglyphics Ensemble, Francis Wong, and others.

Listen to Modirzadeh's vocalized screams into his saxophone on "Song of the Andoumboulou: 16" or Hartigan's "low grumbling of drums" on "Song of the Andoumboulou: 24," and you will hear this discrepant note sounding "Some / ecstatic elsewhere's / advocacy strummed, / unsung" — until now (1995). Or listen to the last few minutes of "Song of the Andoumboulou: 23" as Hartigan's insistent trap drumming and Modirzadeh's snake-charmer sax weave their way around and through Mackey's invocation of a

> Beginningless book thought to've
> unrolled endlessly, more scroll
> than book, talismanic strum.
> As if all want were in this holding
> a note   only a half-beat
> longer . . .
> (1995)

That talismanic strum, held a half-beat longer, combined with Mackey's "Raw-throated / singer beating time with a / dry stick" (1995) results in a cross-cultural, cross-media collaboration unsurpassed by any spoken-word recording produced to date. In *Strick: Song of the Andoumboulou 16–25,* Mackey, Hartigan, and Modirzadeh offer a stunning performance that gestures toward a "we [that] would include, not reduce to us" (1995).

If *Strick* realizes Mackey's engagement with song in a unique form, his ongoing series of prose works, *From a Broken Bottle Traces of Perfume Still Emanate,* realizes that engagement in an equally unique form—epistolary fiction. Just as Susan Howe conducts poetic investigations outside of verse in her critical book *My Emily Dickinson* and her collection of essays on American literature, *The Birth-mark,* Mackey investigates the poetic possibilities of writing history poetically in prose in *Bedouin Hornbook* and *Djbot Baghostus's Run,* the first two volumes of *From a Broken Bottle Traces of Perfume Still Emanate.*

Both *Bedouin Hornbook* and *Djbot Baghostus's Run* consist of letters written to the "Angel of Dust" by "N"—a composer and multi-instrumentalist in the Deconstructive Woodwind Chorus, which soon changes its name to the Mystic Horn Society and consists of three men—N, Lambert, and Penguin—and two women—Aunt Nancy and Djamilaa. The fact that the first two letters appear within "Song of the Andoumboulou: 6 and 7" reveals their poetic origins. As Mackey tells Christopher Funkhouser, "The letters got started from an actual correspondence. A friend of mine to whom I'd sent a couple of poems or something wrote back with some questions. By way of talking about or addressing those questions I wrote it out in the form of a letter which began 'Dear Angel of Dust' and made a copy and sent it to this friend." He goes on to say that he "didn't know how to think of [the letters], whether they were prose poems or what. In any case, a couple of the few first that came occurred in the context of poems and are included in *Eroding Witness.* So it started off being meditational/manifesto type assertions which were making certain propositions about poetics that were related to the poems that they occurred in the context of" (Funkhouser, 328). The letters, then, roam in the terrain shared by verse, prose poetry, and poetics; thus, to limit our explorations of Mackey's work to his verse leaves out a significant dimension of his poetic investigations.

In "Song of the Andoumboulou: 7," N refers to the Angel of Dust as "Nut," the Egyptian sky-goddess, and as the "Bone Goddess," which are two of the few hints about the Angel's gender (1985, 54). I suggest that many of the questions of gender that I earlier claimed are largely unresolved in *Song of the Andoumboulou* are taken up in *From a Broken Bottle*

Traces of Perfume Still Emanate in a manner that illuminates the ways in which Mackey seeks to reconcile the "lost twinness" that results from the incestuous coupling of the Yeban in Dogon cosmology. If N "often en-vision[s] the Angel of Dust as Nut," perhaps he envisions himself as Ra, the Egyptian sky-god and husband of Nut. N and the Angel, then, be-come metaphoric equivalents of another primordial couple who, like the Yeban, produce incestuous offspring, since Nut and Ra's sons, Osiris and Set, marry their sisters, Isis and Nephythys (Jackson, 126–27). Thus, the two modes of transcendence discussed earlier, music and sex, continue to be dominant concerns in Mackey's epistolary fiction, and, as in his verse, these modes of transcendence point toward the utopian recovery, never completely realized, of the "lost twinness" that generates the oppositions between male and female, presence and absence, light and dark, song and silence that haunt human culture throughout history.

In his first letter, which comprises "Song of the Andoumboulou: 6" in *Eroding Witness*, N responds to the Angel's earlier letter, which, like all of her letters, we never see:

Dear Angel of Dust,

In one of your earlier letters, the one you wrote in response to *Song of the Andoumboulou: 3*, you spoke of sorting out "what speaks of speaking of something, and what (more valuably) speaks *from* something, i.e., where the source is available, becomes a re-source rather than some-thing evasive, elusive, sought after." Well, what I wanted to say was this: We not only can but should speak of "loss" or, to avoid, quotation marks notwithstanding, any such inkling of self-pity, speak of *absence* as unavoidably an inherence in the texture of things (dreamseed, ha-bitual cloth). You really do seem to believe in, to hold out for some first or final gist underlying it all, but my preoccupation with origins and ends is exactly that: a pre- (equally post-, I suppose) occupation. (1985, 50)

Recall that "Song of the Andoumboulou: 3" presents the Dogon myth of the origin of the Word as Nommo, which, as Ogotemmêli tells Griaule, "is every woman's secret, and is what attracts the man" (Griaule, 82). Thus, the issue of where language comes from and where one speaks from are conceived in terms of gender. And clearly "she," the Angel, has a much different take on that issue than N does, who interprets her response to the poem as an expression of the desire for a "source" of language that comes out of or from "something," a ground that is "available" in its presence. For N, that "source" can never be experienced apart from the absence that is inherent in the very "texture of things." The opposition between presence and absence, then, is a figurative parallel for the opposition between female and male. In short, "she" believes in an origin "underlying it all" that can serve as a present "re-source" for an understanding of language, of "speaking"; "he," on the other hand, has no such belief. Furthermore, "he" contends that "What was wanted least but now comes to be missed *is* that very absence, an unlikely Other whose inconceivable occupancy glimpses of ocean beg access to" (1985, 50).

This debate, only one side of which we hear directly, is taken up in the first letter of *Bedouin Hornbook.* After relating a dream in which he plays the solo on Archie Shepp's version of John Coltrane's "Naima" with plumbing fixtures that resemble a bass clarinet, N brings up Wilson Harris's notion that "There are musics which haunt us like a phantom limb" (1997, 7). This notion becomes an image for absence throughout *From a Broken Bottle Traces of Perfume Still Emanate.* As Harryette Mullen points out, "The accumulated images of castration/amputation in *Bedouin Hornbook* are related to the persistent association of African Americans with both coerced silence and strategic inarticulateness, although what Mackey investigates is the relative stress placed on either articulation or disarticulation as oppositional values within and between cultures" (37). The phantom limb is one such image, and it suggests how something that is literally absent, the amputated limb, can still be sensed as present in much the same way disarticulation ("founding noise") can be sensed in articulation ("song"). These exfoliating oppositions are therefore inextricably intertwined with each other, which leads N to end this letter with the observation that "this dialogue of ours seems hopelessly enmeshed in the very 'ontology of loss' of which you've insisted I disburden myself" (1997, 9). Tracing these oppositions in selected passages of *Bedouin Hornbook* and *Djbot Baghostus's Run* shows how Mackey investigates the "mired sublime" in prose as well as verse in order to write history poetically.

In the second letter of *Bedouin Hornbook,* N describes to the Angel of Dust one of his new compositions for the Mystic Horn Society titled "Third Leg of the Sun":

> It actually grew out of a passage I'd read in Maya Deren's *voudun,* a passage I might as well quote for you. "Legba," she writes, "who knows the divine language and through whom one might seek recourse from des-

tiny, is himself the destined answer to the riddle of the Sphinx: he was once the new-born infant sun, lived through the fertile prime of his noon, and is now the old sun, walking with a cane—the 'third leg'—into the afternoon of his life." (1997, 11–12).

As Kamau Brathwaite notes, Legba "is the Dahomean/Haitian god of the gateway. He is the crucial link between man and the other gods and, as such, is often the first to be invoked at a ceremony. A celebrant possessed by Legba assumes an aged, limping form and uses a crutch" (1973, 273). The figure of Legba draws together African and Caribbean cosmology in order to reconnect that which the "Middle Passage" tore asunder or "amputated." For N, the image of Legba generates a series of questions that suggest to him an even more detailed historical-cosmological connection:

> Couldn't *Ba* have cut itself off from *Legba* and made the journey back to Egypt, have hidden out there like Stesichorus's Helen, a phantom limb calling itself "Ram" and at other times "Soul"? Couldn't *Leg* have followed suit, have introduced itself as "Thigh," the Great Bear of the northern heavens, then almost immediately have left Egypt for Guatemala, calling itself Huracan, and have come to be known there as "Heart of Heaven"? Couldn't the memory of *Leg* have merged with that of Set back in Egypt, Horus having wounded Set in the thigh when he swallowed the moon? (1997, 12)

N's etymological amputation of *Ba* from *Leg* parallels the historical amputation that took place in Africa. The poetic history N traces moves from Africa to Egypt to the Caribbean, leaving each of its parts as a "phantom limb"—an absence felt as present and a presence felt as absent. If we recall that N implicitly refers to himself as "Ra" to the Angel's "Nut" in "Song of the Andoumboulou: 6," then we may see a layer of personal as well as global history at work here. We may also see another opposition generated in this etymological amputation: soul (*Ba*) and body (*Leg* or *Thigh*). Both *Leg* and *Ba* will appear again in *Bedouin Hornbook* and *Djbot Baghostus's Run,* as will the oppositions they signify—body and soul. Yet whether these oppositions are reunited, or whether that is even desirable, is open to doubt since N tends "to pursue resonance rather than resolution" (1997, 23).

N is particularly concerned that his efforts with the band not be seen as an attempt to resolve the oppositions in history in order to get "outside" history. Responding to the Angel of Dust's critique of his new composition, "The Slave's Day Off," he chides her for sounding "like one of those critics who seem to fear that anything any of us do could somehow escape being 'history'" (1997, 82). Rather, he claims that the work he and the Mystic Horn Society explore is "hyperhistorical," which I take to mean that they are trying to uncover the history that has been ignored or silenced by traditional historical accounts. N's approach here resembles Susan Howe's efforts to uncover from "the dark side of history, voices that are anonymous, slighted—inarticulate." Thus, he takes an interest in movements in musical history such as "scat, where the apparent mangling of articulate speech testifies to an 'unspeakable' history such singers are both vanquishers and victims of" (1997, 83). In "The Slave's Day Off," N hears this "unspeakable" history in "the raspy, non-essentialist quality in Djamilaa's voice," which she creates by singing "with a piece of wax paper about a fourth of an inch in front of her lips," resulting in "a dispersed, ventriloquistic edge" (1997, 83). Djamilaa's muffled voice suggests the muffled voice of the slaves, another instance of "founding noise." Yet there may also be a "hyperhistorical" point being made. The terms "non-essentialist," "dispersed," and "ventriloquistic" suggest a critique of received notions of subjectivity and individuality. N's experience while playing steel drums on the song reinforces this point: "The feeling I had was that I wasn't there, that the 'I' which was was an 'I' which wasn't my own" (1997, 84). Clearly, Western history—modern history in particular, during which the slave trade began—has suppressed such experiences in favor of the experience of a stable, self-contained cogito. If we see jazz in particular and African-American music in general as forms in which the individual and collective resonate with each other, then we need to think in alternative ways about the permeability of the boundaries between the "I" and the "we."

N's experience while sitting in with the "Crossroads Choir" augments this "hyperhistorical" moment. During his bass clarinet solo on the jazz standard "Body and Soul," N recalls a furtive, week-long affair he had years earlier—a case of "love at first sight, proposing impossibly wide horizons and laying claim to only the most unlikely prospects" (1997, 121). As he is playing, the audience begins singing the lyrics to the song—"My life revolves around her, / What earthly good am I without her? / My castle has crumbled, / I'm her's, body and soul"—and N envisions

a ball of light bounced from syllable to syllable as in the sing-along cartoons we saw at the movies when I was a kid. I couldn't help thinking of it as a ball of cabalistic light our week-long courtship had sparked, a promise of one day overcoming division. It was both a ball of cabalistic light and the blank, bouncing check I'd gotten inklings of earlier. I knew I'd come home to the heart. I opened my eyes just in time to see the ball was in fact a balloon the crowd was batting about among themselves, each person tapping it ever so lightly to keep it aloft. It was a white balloon on which, written in black, were the words "Only One." Finally a woman tapped it with a sharp flick of her finger, sending it towards the ceiling. It rose with ever-increasing speed, taking my breath away, only to come down even faster. (1997, 123–24).

The divisions or oppositions this ball promises to overcome are many: between body and soul, male and female, artist and audience, and black and white, all of which are to be, the promise holds out, "Only One." Yet this moment proves to be another instance of the "mired sublime" since the ball comes down just as fast as it rises.

While sitting in the audience prior to his solo with the Crossroads Choir, N experiences the sensation "that numerous bits of broken glass imbedded themselves in my forehead," which "instigate a prolonged, problematic meditation on a theme which up until then had only been tangentially touched upon. Could it be, each and every laserlike sliver of light gave me reason to wonder, that the pinpoint precision of any breakdown of the tribe made for an obsessed, kaleidoscopic rift in sound, the audible harmonic equivalent of a certain impingement or pungency?" (1997, 115, 116) N's solo is, I suggest, an enactment of this "rift," of the "breakdown" of the tribe that once was "Only One" but is now divided. That N's sublime experience with the Crossroads Choir is "mired" in a divided world is evidenced by the fact that he ends up in the hospital shortly after, suffering from dizzy spells "brought on by the bits of glass planted in [his] brow by the Crossroads Choir." He thinks of these pieces of glass, which now "feel more like shattered cowrie shells," "as tightfisted imprints, fossil imprints": "I think of them as a mute but somehow musical motif having to do with thwarted fire, confirming a dizziness intrinsic to the earth but with bedouin roots in the sky" (1997, 125). During these attacks of dizziness, N hears Ornette Coleman's version of "Embraceable You" and his "own heartbeat, amplified and coming from outside. It's as though the heart were a ventriloquist of sorts, throwing its voice at an ever more obtuse angle so as to exact an acoustical shell from the surrounding air" (1997, 126). These attacks accentuate another series of divisions or oppositions—between mute silence and audible music, earth and sky, in-side and outside. Yet note how these divisions emanate from the heart, as do the divisions he experiences during his solo with the Crossroads Choir when he comes "home to the heart."

> The heart's thrown voice, it seems, moves as a mutable window or a "mute" succession of windows, the transparent advance of an elliptical witness to a manytongued yet unmentionable, all the more audacious truth. It appears to elope with each evaporative cranial kiss or breathy phantom caress as with an outrageous, caged or cagey embrace—caught up in the ache or the echoed report of its eventual extinction. It's as if the stolen pulse fed the amputated hand with which one might one day stroke the ribs of a ghost. (1997, 126)

Truth—"many-tongued," "unmentionable," and "audacious"—arrives through the heart's "thrown" or ventriloquized voice and speaks of its own extinction, the "ache" of which feels like the presence of the absent "phantom limb."

This image of the phantom limb returns near the end of *Bedouin Horn-book,* in N's "after-the-fact lecture/libretto," "The Creaking of the Word," a piece that expresses his growing attachment to Djamilaa, the band's vocalist and harmonium player. As N's "namesake" Flaunted Fifth uri-nates in an open field, an act which gets him arrested for "public exposure" of his "private part," N felt a numbness in his "middle leg" or "fifth limb" at the same time that, across town, Djamilaa felt a "phantom" hand that "caressed her right side, eased its way down and a bit to the left to cup the rounded base of her right buttock, squeezed it firmly, then rested there. She turned around to her left to see who it was but saw no one" (1997, 222). The desire for "union" with the other is clearly sexual in this case, but the fact that it is also a desire for union with one of his fellow mu-sicians brings together the two modes of transcendence explored in *Song of the Andoumboulou:* music and sex. Furthermore, these desires emanate from the heart rather than the conscious mind since "Neither [Djamilaa] nor Flaunted Fifth had any way of knowing that the feeling which had fled his hand did so in order to seek out Djamilaa's waist and pantyless rump. It was as if his fanatic, far-reaching net, unbeknown to him, laid claim to the very hand which cast it, to a phantom itch, a fallow eighth-day accent's two-way claw, a need for feeling's numb reciprocal 'catch' " (1997, 222). The desire to scratch that "phantom itch" brings issues of gen-der to the fore—issues taken up at the beginning of *Djbot Baghostus's Run.*

As the second volume of *From a Broken Bottle Traces of Perfume Still Emanate* opens, the Mystic Horn Society is dealing with an issue that arose earlier in *Bedouin Hornbook*—the need for a full-time drummer. Just as the band is about to audition a male drummer named SunStick, Aunt Nancy and Djamilaa stage a wordless "Halve Not, Will Travel" revolt because the male members of the band have not even considered auditioning a woman. Their revolt occurs in the form of a "preemptive recital" in which they get their point across by playing a "Kashmiri drum known as the not" (1993b, 10). As is the case throughout *From a Broken Bottle Traces of Perfume Still Emanate,* communication among the band members takes place through music as often as it does through language. As Mullen notes, "Mackey's work opens up aesthetic space for his own textual improvisations by taking serious liberties with the notion that musicians 'speak' with their instruments; thus words and music become interchangeable as his text performs itself as a verbal composition, an idiosyncratic yet culturally resonant transliteration of the music he loves to hear" (39). Here, N, Lambert, and Penguin do not have to be "told" in order to understand Aunt Nancy and Djamilaa:

> To what extent, one wondered, did the preemptive concert and catechism rolled into one amount to an arraignment, a charge of inequality, a threat of secession? "Halve Not, Will Travel." Each beat was a hoof to one's head, driving home a point. It was more than appropriate, one was made to admit, that the band, on the verge of becoming a sextet, address and take the issue of sexual equality into account. (1993b, 11)

Aunt Nancy and Djamilaa's "preemptive recital" brings to the fore the issue of how one grounds such a critique given its "negative" approach since "the not's clay was a thin crust of nothingness" (1993b, 12). Mackey's play on the word "not" takes us to the heart of what is often called the "postmodern condition":

> There was a sense, of course, in which the music's polemic and its metaphysical insistence were at cross-purposes with one another. If ultimately emptiness and absence reigned, one had reason to ask, on what grounds did one critique and propose an alternative to the brunt of exclusion and the sense of social nothingness one suffered from? . . . It was a question, however, which Aunt Nancy and Djamilaa's contestatory recital casually and with infinite confidence and calm, simply yet cavalierly brushed aside. It proposed a quandary they refused to inhabit

or be inhibited by. . . . "No such problem," the music objected, out-maneuvering the ordeal and desperation which, owing only to the not's and the nay's insistence, began gradually to let me go. (1993b, 13)

Although the argument from absence or emptiness may bring rational solutions to the dilemma of postmodernity to a place of "endless deferral," music "outmaneuvers" the dilemma by a direct appeal to the heart rather than the mind. N, Lambert, and Penguin ultimately hear the emptiness or "loss" in the "contestatory recital" not as the absence of a rational ground but as the presence of deprivation and inequality. Much like a phantom limb, Aunt Nancy and Djamilaa use music to make the men feel the presence of that which is absent—sexual equality in the band. The result of their performance is unequivocal: "Once the music had stopped the two of them simply stared at us in silence. SunStick finally stood up and broke the silence. 'Well, I can take a hint,' he said and began to take his drumset down. Djamilaa, Aunt Nancy, Penguin, Lambert and I all looked at one another. There was no need to say anything more on the matter. It was understood we'd begin looking for a woman drummer" (1933b, 17).

The postmodern fascination with absence or nothingness also haunts N's musings on the self in *Djbot Baghostus's Run,* much as it does in *Bedouin Hornbook.* As he begins to expand his "lecture/Libretto" into a full-scale "Antithetical Opera," N catches himself indulging in reveries about the "shattered I," which bring his work to a halt:

I quickly found myself at a loss as to where to go from there. Not only did words no longer come effortlessly but now they didn't come at all. I found myself put off by and caught up in qualms about the patness of the "shattered I," its apparent endorsement of currently fashionable notions of a nonexistent self, a dead subject and such. My own effortless recourse to some such implication turned me off. That the self gets all the more talked about by way of its widely insisted-upon disappearance turns out to be an irony I'm evidently not able to get beyond. (1993b, 50)

As usual, N's impasse is broken by a mystical experience of music. Immediately following his indictment of "currently fashionable notions of a nonexistent self," N recounts an experience he has after waking up from a dream in which he hears an alto sax playing a tune whose title he cannot recall. On waking he hears the same tune and is shocked to hear it coming out of his own alto sax, "apparently playing itself"—an event which "not only brought the issues of human agency to the fore but brought me more actively into the picture" because N finds himself "trying to correct automatic alto's lapses into awkwardness" (1993b, 52–53). N tries to correct what he takes to be "a beginner's difficulty with the fourth-line D" in the piece it is playing (1993b, 52), which causes N to mime the correct technique. "I could actually feel the weight of the horn pull the strap against the back of my neck, feel the reed against my lower lip, feel the octave key underneath my thumb and so forth. It was as though automatic alto were playing me, as if I were its axe, its instrument" (1993b, 53). With each "mistake," automatic alto "indicted its own suspect effortlessness, but in doing so it implicated a fallible human hand, a broken vessel—namely, in this instance, me. . . . What awkward alto seemed intent on saying was that I was the problem, not the solution" (1993b, 53). By critiquing N's desire for an effortless performance, automatic or awkward alto offers a critique of N's "effortless recourse" to the fashionable notion of the "shattered I" in his Antithetical Opera. This critique allows N to "overcome the impasse" of the postmodern dilemma of absence or emptiness that brought his writing to a halt and results in N's new musical composition, "Robotic Aria for Prepared and Unprepared Alto" (1993b, 55). In short, "phantom" alto makes present that which was absent—a way out of the postmodern dilemma; thus, absence is part of the solution to the very problem it poses.

N's experience with automatic alto returns us to the issue of ventriloquism, of the "heart's thrown voice," that Mackey engages in *Bedouin Hornbook:* whether N throws his voice into automatic alto or vice versa is of less concern than the impasse that act of ventriloquism helps overcome. As we have seen, this phenomenon provides a place where oppositions between absence and presence, body and soul, male and female resonate rather than resolve. Later in *Djbot Baghostus's Run,* another instance of ventriloquism brings to the fore the opposition between black and white in a way that raises issues of racial inequity in much the same way it raises issues of gender inequity. After seeing a performance by the African-American singer Betty Carter, N is struck by the "discrepant play of her precise, near parsimonious delivery against the facial extravagance it's accompanied by" (1993b, 154). Her performance "put [N] in mind of ventriloquism, for every now and then she achieved a throwing or a displacement of her voice" that results in "an elusiveness of source which created an illusion of sourcelessness" (1993b, 155). When he discusses this phenomenon with the band the next day, Lambert is quick to point out the similarities between her performance and that of the minstrel shows that were popular in America during the early part of this century. Lambert sees in her performance

> "a utopian foretaste of sourcelessness." That foretaste, he allowed however, was haunted by contested claims to causation, contentious albeit ambiguous historical debris. . . . He went on to bring up, as an example of historical debris, the minstrel show, making much of what he called "minstrel preemption," the preemption of the black face and voice by derogatory distortions passed off as likenesses. (1993b, 155–56)

The exaggerated imitations of blacks by white performers in minstrel shows generate "a consequent poetics built on suspicion." Thus, when black performers such as Betty Carter resort to "Facial extravagance," they are, according to Lambert, "revel[ing] in distortion to show that it's wise to distortion, immune to presumed equivalence." Lambert's political conclusion is as blunt as it is trenchant: "To steal a person's face," which is what the white performers are doing, "sets the stage for an aesthetic lynching" (1993b, 156).

When black performers "imitate" white imitations of black facial expressions, there is an ambivalent moment in which accommodation and subversion are both in play. If the African Americans living in the times of the minstrel shows were to engage in an outright protest of the overt racism enacted in those shows, they were likely to be lynched, so they were forced to "go along" with those stereotypes and incorporate them in their own performances. Yet those incorporations carried within themselves a critique of those racist imitations. Although some African American musicians—Furry Lewis, for instance—got their start in minstrel and medicine shows and covered their faces with lamp black to please their white audiences, there was usually an implicit and sometimes explicit subversion taking place at the same time as they were accommodating the expectations and prejudices of their audiences. Lewis's recollections of his early days in the minstrel and medicine shows illustrates this point with both clarity and ambiguity:

> We travel in T-model cars, had a big old flatbed truck we go 'round in, that was our stage. We used to crack jokes and tell funny tales and do this and that up on the stage. Sometimes have on pants with a patch on it, everything funny. That's something like a clown, you understand.

Sometimes we wear frocks—that's a coat, long in the back. Wear those kind of hats, derby and all like that. We was all messed up. We work blackface comedian, you know. Just take lamp black, some grease, put it all over your face, like in those vaudeville shows.

I used to sing a song about black, you see, 'cause I have the black on my face. I used to sing a song about black everywhere I went. . . .

> Some people don't like their color.
> Well, I sure do like mine.
> I know I'm black and ugly.
> But I gits along just fine.
> I was going down the street the other day
> Two high browns I did meet,
> Say, "Lord, ain't old Furry black,
> But he sure looks good to me."
> Well, I'm black, I'm black, I'm B-L-A-C-K, black,
> I'm black, but I'm sweet, oh, God.
> I don't wear no diamonds,
> Don't wear no pearls,
> I don't have no hard time
> Coming through this world,
> You can tease, squeeze, just as much as you please.
> I know I'm black, but I ain't unease,
> I'm black, black, B-L-A-C-K, black,
> I'm black, but I'm sweet, oh, God.
>   (McKee and Chisenhall, 106–7)

Although there is no overt critique of white racism in Furry Lewis's recollection—which, given that this interview took place in the early 1970s, would not have been inappropriate or overly dangerous—his affirmation of his race is unmistakable and could have gotten him in a great deal of trouble at the time he sang his song. And there is certainly a covert or "phantom" critique at work here in the sense that the absence of a critique of white racism makes that racism very much present. What we end up with is not, as N warns against, "a simplistic, knee-jerk inversion of minstrel derogation" but an act of "polychromatic permission" that resonates with rather than reconciles the oppositions that haunt it (1993b, 162).

Thus, we find in *Djbot Baghostus's Run,* as we do in *Bedouin Hornbook* and *Song of the Andoumboulou,* a strong measure of dissonance or "founding noise" that carries with it an equally strong measure of political and aesthetic implications. Although Mackey's work deals directly and creatively with issues of gender, issues of race remain central to his cross-cultural poetic investigations. For Mackey, those political and aesthetic implications are inextricably intertwined, for aesthetic works, whether in word or song or other forms, are always already political, particularly for those silenced or left out of traditional history's narrative:

> I think that politics is, among other things, laying claim to one's own authority. And that is obviously something people from socially marginalized groups are not encouraged to do. So simply being an author, and laying claim to one's authority, in that sense, is already fraught with political resonances, especially in the case of African-Americans, who less than 150 years ago were forbidden to read and write. There were laws against African-American literacy for decades and decades in this country. The monopolistic claim to literacy by the dominant white culture is one of the things that the African-American literary tradition has been at odds with and up against from the beginning. (Funkhouser, 329–30)

Any attempt to resolve the racial divisions that mark American and world history—just as any attempt to resolve the divisions between women and men, body and soul, presence and absence—and regain their "lost twinness" are subject to the fact that they obtain within a "mired sublime" that makes such resolution a utopian ideal but a pragmatic impossibility. As I argued earlier, the "rift" between these oppositions not only suggests that they cannot be resolved but that perhaps they should not be resolved, since virtually all of the systems of resolution offered in the Western tradition end up reducing diversity to sameness, to recall Glissant's contention. Even the mystical experiences of a nonrational truth that occur throughout Mackey's work that, like the cabalistic ball N envisions in his encounter with the Crossroads Choir, rise "with ever-increasing speed" and feed our desire for wholeness, still inevitably "come down even faster." This fact should not, however, curb attempts to experience the ways in which these divisions resonate with each other, but it should curb premature proclamations for resolution that all too often end up replicating the divisions they claim to heal. The hope Nathaniel Mackey's form of writing history poetically holds out is that the "massive transformation" from sameness to diversity that Glissant sees as a fundamental change in contemporary culture will be more inclusive without being more reductive, that it will not insist on resolving all the tension involved in a "discrepant engagement" between cultures, and that, as a result, the "rough draft" that we now are will evolve into a form of humanity that lives a life consonant with this diverse world and those embodied in and by it.

> What a history is folded and folded inward and inward again, in the single word I.
>
> —Walt Whitman

3. Lyn Hejinian

Investigating "I"

That single word, that single syllable and letter, has probably claimed more ink than any other sign in contemporary literature, philosophy, and history. Although its place in the Western tradition has been delineated, debated, deconstructed, reconstructed, and refined exhaustively and exhaustingly, many of the central questions raised remain unanswered: What is the "I"? And what is its relation to the other "I"s that accompany it? What power does the "individual" self wield when it is confronted by the influence of those others and the culture in which it finds itself? Can the self overcome those influences? Can it even resist them? Can the exemplary self, the "genius," rise above the level of its surroundings? Does the self contain some "thing," some area or region, sealed off from the claims of culture, and does this "thing" provide the self with the power to shape itself and its culture? Or is the self powerless against the claims of culture? Can it merely react to institutional demands? Is the "I" nothing more than a "blank slate" upon which culture writes its name?

The fact that these questions still arise is not due to a lack of effort or acumen on the part of the many contemporary poets, novelists, historians, philosophers, and social scientists who have investigated the "I." They continue to arise for a simple yet insurmountable reason: the object of the investigation is also the subject conducting the investigation. This situation may seem similar to allowing the police to investigate their own improprieties. The solution in this case is relatively simple: appoint a citizen oversight committee. But what kind of committee can we appoint in the investigation of ourselves? Lyn Hejinian, like many of her contemporaries, has come to grips with the fact that we cannot obtain a position "outside" or "above" ourselves from which to conduct an inquiry about ourselves. Yet, unlike some of those same contemporaries, she does not see this as a reason to abandon such an inquiry. Instead, she makes that fact the guiding principle of her inquiry, the results of which are a poetic history of the "I" that not only folds "inward" as Whitman asserts but "outward" as well to include other selves and culture as fundamental constituents of the self. Because she chooses to focus so closely on the "I," Hejinian investigates her personal history as well as cultural history; thus, she is often the subject of her work to a much greater extent than is the case with Susan Howe or Nathaniel Mackey. In works such as *My Life* and *Oxota,* Hejinian writes a history of the "I" that does not answer the questions raised above because such questions are ultimately unanswerable; rather, she creates a text that illuminates the desire to answer those questions—a text that engages matters personal, philosophical, cultural, and historical.

In order to accomplish this task, Hejinian seeks a form of writing in which the "writer relinquishes total control" over the text "and challenges authority as a principle and control as a motive" (1985, 272). Hejinian sets forth her notion of an open text in her essay, "Rejection of Closure," which bears close scrutiny. The inclusion of the other in her history of the "I," then, is much more than a thematic concern in Hejinian's work; the other plays, as we will see, an important part in the form her compositional practice takes. I will examine shortly just how Hejinian goes about composing such a text, but first I want to consider why she might want to compose such a text—an "open text," as she calls it. By opening up her writing to the influence of the other, Hejinian hopes to account for a "desire" that is more fundamental than the desire to portray the self in a factual, historically and chronologically accurate manner. For Hejinian, "the desire that is stirred by language seems to be located most interestingly within language itself, and hence it is androgynous. It is a desire to say, a desire to create the subject by saying, and even a feeling of doubt very like jealousy that springs from the impossibility of satisfying this desire" (1985, 283). I will discuss the implications of the androgyny of this desire later; for now I want to emphasize that the desire that emanates from within language parallels the desire of the self to portray itself completely and accurately, yet neither of these desires will ever be appeased.

Hejinian's philosophy of composition aligns her work with what has come to be called language writing. Along with Charles Bernstein,

Bruce Andrews, Ron Silliman, and Steve McCaffery, to name a few, Hejinian published her early work in small magazines such as *This*, *Tottle's*, and *Hills* and was a frequent contributor to the influential journal L=A=N=G=U=A=G=E, which appeared in the late 1970s.[1] Much like their predecessors in the modernist tradition of avant-garde poetry, language writers draw attention to the materiality of language as it appears on the page. As the movement gained in maturity during the 1980s and 1990s, it garnered some support and a great deal of criticism within established academic circles. Why? Because language writing, as Jerome McGann argues, "is conceived to reveal the power of writing and the production of meaning as human, social, and limited in exact and articulable ways. Indeed, it is designed to demonstrate and *practice* such a conception" (210).[2] In this respect, language writers in general and Lyn Hejinian in particular should be seen as contemporary continuations of the project of the modernist avant-garde and its attempts to produce a "revolutionary" text.

In "The Rejection of Closure," Hejinian offers an excellent explanation of just what such a revolutionary text might be like. As we have seen, she calls this type of text an "open text" which, as she describes it, "often emphasizes or foregrounds process, either the process of the original composition or of subsequent compositions by readers, and thus resists the cultural tendencies that seek to identify and fix material, turn it into a product; that is, it resists reduction and commodification" (1985, 272). By remaining open to both the process of writing and the process of reading, such a text refuses to become a finished, final product, marked for mass consumption. Which is not to say that an open text rejects or disdains potential readers; on the contrary, the open text, according to Hejinian, "invites participation, rejects the authority of the writer over the reader and thus, by analogy, the authority implicit in other (social, economic, cultural) hierarchies" (1985, 134). Hejinian's open text works to disrupt the authority of the text and those institutions that underwrite that authority, which for Hejinian are the institutions in a capitalist culture that demand products rather than processes. Thus, the reader participates in an open text's authorization in as fundamental a way as the writer does, which means that such a text's meaning is also always in process. The open text, therefore, "speaks for writing that is generative rather than directive" and for writing in which the "writer relinquishes total control" of the composing process, opening the text up to that which exceeds it—to the other (1985, 272).

And because it seeks to include that which exceeds it, the open text disrupts the "I" as author. For Hejinian this disruption or dissonance in the

"I" that makes itself manifest in the open text is produced by "the struggle between language and that which it claims to depict or express"; we, as users of language, as the putative authors of our own lives, want to resolve this struggle and "join words to the world—to close the gap between ourselves and things, and we suffer from doubt and anxiety as to our capacity to do so because of the limits of language itself" (1985, 278, 285). Because this struggle to unite words and the world will never be resolved, it produces doubt and anxiety in the "I" investigating itself. Yet it is just this anxiety that opens the "I" up to that which exceeds it: the signifying process. What Hejinian proposes, then, is a truly revolutionary text since such a text represents the "I" in process: in the process of becoming an "I" in the world, in culture, as well as in the process of becoming an "I" in a text.

To this point, I have used two phrases—"revolutionary text" and "the signifying process"—without much explanation. Both are drawn from Julia Kristeva's *Revolution in Poetic Language,* and an excursus into her book will illuminate Hejinian's work in three ways. First, it will help differentiate her approach to the "I" from many contemporary approaches; second, it will help uncover the generative moment that produces both the "I" and the open text; and third, it will help reveal the ways in which issues of gender are at work in an open text. In a discussion of French feminists such as Luce Irigaray, Hélène Cixous, and Kristeva, Hejinian draws a very strong connection between their explorations of writing and her own:

> the kinds of language that many of these writers advocate seem very close to, if not identical with, what I think of as characteristic of many contemporary avant-garde texts—including interest in syntactic disjunctures and realignments, in montage and pastiche as structural devices, in the fragmentation and explosion of the subject, etc., as well as an antagonism to closed structures of meaning. Yet of the writers from this area whom I have read to date, only Julia Kristeva is exploring this connection. (1985, 283)

For Kristeva, a proper understanding of the signifying process is the key to understanding the connection between the formal and thematic dimensions that characterize the revolutions that have taken place over the last century in poetic language and conceptions of the self—revolutions that, as we will see, greatly affect Hejinian's poetic investigations of the "I."

Kristeva goes to great lengths to distinguish her notions of the self and language from those offered by many of her contemporaries—structuralists and poststructuralists alike. *Revolution in Poetic Language* begins with a critique of modern linguistics, of its "formalism," in particular. Although she clearly accepts many of the principles of structuralism, Kristeva recognizes that something crucial has been left out of the structuralist account of language. For Kristeva that account "lacks a subject or tolerates one only as a *transcendental ego* . . . and defers any interrogation of its (always already dialectical because trans-linguistic) 'externality' " (1984, 21). Kristeva contends that structuralism does not have the tools to deal with the externality of the "I" since this externality is both "dialectical" and "trans-linguistic."[3] According to Kristeva, structuralism does not overcome the "I"; it merely ignores it. As we will see, she lodges a similar complaint against Derrida's grammatology. As John Lechte argues:

> Kristeva seems to go in quite a different direction to that of the grammatologist. For instance, while Derrida had been at pains to point out that "Writing can never be thought under the category of the subject", Kristeva was concerned to develop a theory of the speaking subject aimed at taking account of the nature of language in all its aspects. . . . This project moves the orientation of semiotics away from the study of meaning as a static sign-system, and towards the analysis of meaning as a "signifying process". (98)

Both structuralism and grammatology leave what Kristeva calls the "thetic" moment—the moment the "I" posits itself—out of the account.

Kristeva, like most poststructuralists, argues that the self is constituted in and by the "signifying process." Yet she sees this process as the product of a dialectical encounter between two heterogeneous "modalities of the signifying process"—between the "symbolic" and the "semiotic" modalities (1984, 24). If we understand that the former refers to what we usually call language—the visible and audible signs and sounds we exchange—and that the latter refers to the "trans-linguistic," then it should be clear that Kristeva is not simply reducing the self down to a function of language. In fact, for Kristeva "the *semiotic* precedes the establishment of the sign; it is not, therefore, cognitive in the sense of being assumed by a knowing, already constituted subject" (1984, 27). Kristeva's inclusion of the semiotic modality in her notion of the self not only draws into question the poststructuralist reduction of the self to its linguistic functions; it also draws into question the reduction of the self to its cognitive functions—which is the path most of Western philosophy takes. Since this inclusion of the semiotic modality is so crucial for Kristeva, we should take a closer look at what that modality of the signifying process entails.

Kristeva's understanding of the semiotic owes a great deal, as she readily acknowledges, to Freud's theory of "drives." Because, according to Kristeva, most poststructuralist accounts of language systematically exclude the "thetic" from their interrogation, they conclude that the relation between the signifier and the signified is arbitrary—"unmotivated," to use Saussure's term. However, those that pursue research in semiotics seek "the principle of this motivation in the Freudian notion of the unconscious," in, more specifically, the "drives" and "primary processes" that generate the unconscious (1984, 22). These drives constitute, along with the symbolic systems that comprise language, the "corporeal, linguistic, and social dialectic" that constitutes the "I." The semiotic is, in short, "the structuring *disposition* of drives." According to Kristeva, "Discrete quantities of energy move through the body of the subject who is not yet constituted as such and, in the course of his development, they are arranged according to various constraints imposed on this body—always already involved in a semiotic process—by family and social structures" (1984, 25). She calls this semiotic arrangement of drives a *chora,* "a nonexpressive totality," an "uncertain and indeterminate *articulation*" rather than "a *disposition* that already depends on representation" (1984, 25). This semiotic *chora,* however, is "always already" confronted by the symbolic arrangement of language—a confrontation out of which the signifying process arises.

If we follow the movement of Kristeva's dialectic between the semiotic and symbolic that produces the signifying process, we should also be able to follow the movement that produces the "I" since it, according to Kristeva, is constituted by and in that very signifying process. The semiotic *chora,* for Kristeva, "is no more than the place where the subject is both generated and negated, the place where his unity succumbs before the process of charges and stases that produce" the self (1984, 28). For Kristeva the semiotic *chora* is the "precondition" for what she calls the "thetic," which refers to "the positing of signification" or the moment of "enunciation" that at once unites and separates the self and that which surrounds or exceeds it—that is, "nature and society" (1984, 50, 43). The thetic phase, then, is the moment when the self recognizes that it is at once identical to and different from the other selves it encounters. According to Kristeva, the thetic phase obtains when a "break" or "rupture" occurs in the signifying process—a rupture that is caused by the encounter of the two heterogeneous orders, the semiotic and the symbolic, that constitute that process (1984, 43). Thus, the thetic phase is not only "the precondition for signification, i.e., the precondition for the positing of language," but that it is also "the place of the Other" (1984, 48).

Kristeva emphasizes the thetic phase of the process that produces the self for good reason: it allows her to distinguish her concept of the self from many of the other poststructuralist attempts—from Derrida's in particular. By systematically excluding the "subjective" moment that occurs in the constitution of the self, grammatology is left only with the "objective" or positivist moment of the signifying process that constitutes the self—which is why grammatology ends up portraying the self as nothing more than a function of language, of the symbolic modality, to use Kristeva's term. Derrida's grammatology, therefore, collapses the productive contradiction between the heterogeneous orders of the semiotic and the symbolic, between instinctual drives and symbolic representations, collapses them into a single, homogeneous order. In place of Derrida's grammatology, Kristeva offers a materialist dialectic that brings into contradiction the heterogeneous orders of the semiotic and the symbolic modalities of the signifying process out of which the "I" arises. Thus for Kristeva the self is a "passageway, a non-place, where there is a struggle between conflicting tendencies," between heterogeneous orders (1984, 203). And since these heterogeneous orders never, in Kristeva's dialectic, resolve into a homogeneous whole, the self is not something that is ever completed or finished: negativity, Kristeva contends, "can only produce a subject in process/on trial" (1984, 110–11).

The encounter between the "I" in its thetic phase and the signifying process that exceeds it produces what Kristeva calls "textual experience."

> The thetic—that crucial place on the basis of which the human being constitutes himself as signifying and/or social—is the very place textual experience aims toward. In this sense, textual experience represents one of the most daring explorations the subject can allow himself, one that delves into his constitutive process. But at the same time and as a result, textual experience reaches the very foundations of the social—that which is exploited by sociality but which elaborates and can go beyond it, either destroying or transforming it. (1984, 67)

I assume this experience is open to both the reader and writer of a text, although I suspect Kristeva is ultimately more concerned with the way the writer's experience of the signifying process marks itself in the text. It is also important to note the dual nature of this experience. Not only does it expose the self to its own constitutive process; it exposes the foundations or preconditions of the social—the semiotic *chora*—to the "I." If textual experience does indeed accomplish this, then it truly is a daring exploration.

Certain kinds of texts are, of course, more or less likely to induce such an experience. In fact, Kristeva argues, most texts repress, either intentionally or unintentionally, the very process that produces texts, the signifying process. Furthermore, most texts tend to repress the semiotic more often than the symbolic modality of the process. If, as Kristeva contends, "Our discourse—all discourse—moves with and against the *chora* in the sense that it simultaneously depends upon and refuses it" (1984, 26), then the semiotic, as that which instigates the rupture, would need to be suppressed in order to achieve some level of coherence. There is, however, one kind of text that manages not to "suppress the semiotic *chora* but instead raises the *chora* to the status of a signifier"—the literary text (1984, 57). Above all, Kristeva contends, the literary texts of modern poetry seek to bring the *chora* into the foreground. Because modern poetic language "transgresses grammatical rules, the *positing* of the symbolic . . . finds itself subverted," which means that "poetic language puts the subject in process/on trial" (1984, 57, 58).

The specific historical context of "modern poetic language" for Kristeva begins in late-nineteenth-century France, particularly in the poetry of Comte de Lautreamont and Stéphane Mallarmé, and continues with the modernist experimenters in the early twentieth century. Although she does not mention directly any contemporary examples of modern poetic language, I do not get the impression that Kristeva believes the revolution that takes place in poetic language, which parallels the revolution that takes place in the self, is by any means over, and I contend that this revolution continues in contemporary investigative poetry. Because modern poetic texts bring the self in contact with that which exceeds it, there is a rupture in the self—and that rupture makes itself known in revolutionary texts. Yet if this rupture in both the "I" and the text happens when the semiotic *chora* emerges in the text, and if that *chora* is, by definition, a prelinguistic, prelogical "nonexpressive totality," how is that represented in the text?

At this point in her argument, Kristeva draws an important distinction between two different modalities of a text, a distinction that parallels the one drawn between the semiotic and symbolic modalities of the signifying process. For Kristeva, the *genotext* includes the "semiotic processes but also the advent of the symbolic," while the *phenotext* consists of "language that serves to communicate" (1984, 86, 87). The genotext manifests the "transfers of drive energy" that comprise the semiotic *chora* in such poetic devices as rhythm, repetition, rhyme, and intonation; thus, "even though it can be seen in language, the genotext is not linguistic . . . It is, rather, a *process*" (1984, 86). The genotext represents that which underlies and "precedes" representation: the semiotic *chora*. Using sound as much as sense, poetic language reveals the genotext, which in turn reveals the rupture or break in the signifying process that produces the self. Modern poetic language, therefore, not only transgresses grammatical rules; it transgresses the rules that have traditionally governed the self—that it be autonomous and contained within its consciousness of itself. Because it points beyond itself, toward that which exceeds it, poetic language is ultimately, for Kristeva, "the place of production for a subject who transgresses the thetic by using it as a necessary boundary" (1984, 61). For Kristeva, the genotext acts as a "shifting boundary" that allows the semiotic to transgress the limits of the symbolic, which in turn allows the "I" to transgress its own limits. Poetry, because it welcomes the semiotic, pushes up against "the limits of socially useful discourse and attest[s] to what it represses: the *process* that exceeds the subject and his communicative structures" (1984, 16).

The genotext in modern poetry brings that which is repressed, the semiotic *chora*, to the fore in order to subvert the dominance of the symbolic. It is at this point that, as Toril Moi argues, "the ethics of subversion that dominate Kristeva's linguistic theory here feed into her feminism as well" since "any strengthening of the semiotic, which knows no sexual difference, must therefore lead to a weakening of traditional gender divisions" (163, 165). In much the same way that the semiotic is marginalized by the symbolic, so too is the feminine marginalized by patriarchy. It is important to note that Kristeva's use of the term "feminine" is not restricted to women. According to Rachel Blau DuPlessis, Kristeva "evokes marginality, subversion, dissidence as anti-patriarchal motives beyond all limits. Anything marginalized by patriarchal order is, thus, 'feminine'" (135).

Kristeva's definition of "feminine," as many critics have noted, puts her at odds with many contemporary feminist notions of "women's writing." The issue of "women's writing" has, of course, been the subject of a great deal of debate among feminists and hinges on how one accounts for the difference between men and women and the writing they produce. In "Feminist Criticism in the Wilderness," Elaine Showalter succinctly sums up the current possible explanations for this difference: "Theories of women's writing presently make use of four models of difference: biological, linguistic, psychoanalytic, and cultural." Showalter opts for the latter, since "a theory of culture incorporates ideas about women's body, language, and psyche but interprets them in relation to the social contexts in which they occur" (249, 259). However, a number of feminists have offered an account of gender difference and its effect on writing based on the biological differences between men's and women's bodies; the most compelling of these attempts is Hélène Cixous's "The Laugh of the Medusa." Yet, as Ann Rosalind Jones points out, "Certainly, women's physiology has important meanings for women in various cultures, and it is essential for us to express those meanings rather than to submit to male definitions—that is, appropriations—of our sexuality. But the female body hardly seems the best site to launch an attack on the forces that have alienated us from what our sexuality might become" (368). But why is the body, and the obvious differences between the male and female body, not the "best site" to begin a portrait of the female "I"?

To answer this question properly, we need to draw together what have for the most part been two separate lines of inquiry: feminism and postmodernism. Although these two fields developed at virtually the same time, they have not until recently crossed paths. As Craig Owens pointed out in 1983, the "absence of discussions of sexual difference in writings about postmodernism, as well as the fact that few women have engaged in the modernism/postmodernism debate, suggest that postmodernism may be another masculine invention engineered to exclude women" (61). And even as late as 1986 Andreas Huyssen can still assert, in spite of the emergence in the 1970s and 1980s of many women artists, filmmakers, and theoreticians, that "it is somewhat baffling that feminist criticism has so far largely stayed away from the postmodernism debate which is considered not to be pertinent to feminist concerns" (198). In the last few years, however, a number of feminist critics have taken up the issue of postmodernism and have explored the connections between feminism and postmodernism in ways that allow the insights of each to affect the other.[4] In particular, a number of feminists have taken the postmodern critique of "essentialist" notions of the self and applied that critique to forms of feminism that argue for an "essential" difference between men and women based on physiological differences—a point that takes us back to Jones' contention that the female body is not the "best site" from which to account for the differences between men and women.

As Nancy Fraser and Linda J. Nicholson contend, "appeals to biology to explain social phenomena are essentialist and monocausal," and they "do not allow us to understand the enormous diversity of forms which both gender and sexism assume in different cultures" (28). For feminists such as Fraser, Nicholson, Jones, and Showalter, accounts of gender difference that focus solely on the body end up being not only essentialist but ahistorical, atemporal, and transcultural as well. By treating the body as not only a physiological entity but as a cultural entity as well, these thinkers allow us to include the body within a given self-portrait without resorting to an articulation, to recall Laclau and Mouffe's term, of the "I" based primarily on biological determinants. Fraser and Nicholson describe what a postmodern-feminist alternative to these essentialist, biologistic accounts of gender difference would entail. For them, a "postmodern-feminist theory would be inflected by temporality, with historically specific institutional categories like the modern restricted, maleheaded, nuclear family taking precedence over ahistorical, functionalist categories like reproduction and mothering"; furthermore, "postmodernfeminist theory would be nonuniversalist" and "would replace unitary notions of woman and feminine gender identity with plural and complexly constructed conceptions of social identity, treating gender as one relevant strand among others, attending also to class, race, ethnicity, age, and sexual orientation" (34–35).

A revolutionary text, then, can be seen as "feminine" without necessarily being an instance of "women's writing" as well as an instance of a nonessentialist understanding of gender differences, and I propose that Lyn Hejinian's notion of the open text and her approach to issues of gender are best seen in this light. Although a number of feminists have identified this desire directly with the search for a form of language that would portray a female self in all of its difference and distinctness, Hejinian finds such a search to be highly problematic. I believe she would concur with Kristeva's claim that "the very dichotomy man/woman as an opposition between two rival entities may be understood as belonging to *metaphysics*." And once metaphysics has been drawn into question, Kristeva asks, "What can 'identity', even 'sexual identity', mean in a new theoretical and scientific space where the very notion of identity is challenged?" (1986, 209).

As we will now see, Hejinian does indeed challenge the concept of identity that the essentialist account of gender difference presupposes. Although Hejinian is certainly concerned with the psychological, social, and political implications of gender difference, she concentrates her attention on the creation or construction of the self in and by language as an almost androgynous entity. As she writes in *My Life*, "As such, a person on paper, I am androgynous" (1987, 105). Rather than represent the "I" as being either essentially male or female, Hejinian concentrates on the processes that produce both women and men instead of the differences between men and women. And for Hejinian perhaps the single most important process in the production of the self is the signifying process — the process whereby language at once forms the "I" and allows the "I" to reflect on and participate in that formation in a text. In the sense that Laclau and Mouffe use the term, Hejinian articulates or joins together the two modalities of the signifying process that Kristeva identifies, the semiotic and the symbolic, in order to produce an open text that articulates the "I" in a "revolutionary" way. In the pages that follow, I will discuss two of Hejinian's texts — *My Life*, which is a poem composed in prose paragraphs, and *Oxota*, which is, as its subtitle indicates, "A Short Russian Novel" composed in fourteen line stanzas — in order to illuminate the ways in which her investigating "I" investigates itself. I will begin with *My Life*.[5]

One of the ways an open text diminishes or "rejects" the author-ity of the writer is by including, in the composition process, seemingly arbitrary structural principles. An "inorganic" element, then, plays a part in the realization of the text. Although a number of other contemporary poets have used mathematical or aleatoric procedures as heuristic devices — Ron Silliman and Jackson Mac Low, for instance — Hejinian has, in my opinion, connected this inorganic element with an equally strong organic element: her own "growth" as a human being. For Hejinian, number acts as a structural tactic — which, on the one hand, is impersonal, arbitrary, inorganic, but, on the other hand, is personal, necessary, and organic since the number corresponds to the number of years she has "had" a life. Each section of *My Life* contains the same number of sentences, the number corresponding to the age of the author, and the book as a whole has an equivalent number of sections. And Hejinian's text is very much a text in progress. The first edition, published in 1980, the poet's thirty-seventh year, contains thirty-seven sections, each with thirty-seven sentences; the second edition, published in 1987, contains eight new sections and eight new sentences in each of the first edition's sections. Furthermore, Hejinian's text is still in process. Sections from *My Life in the Early Nineties* have appeared in *Lingo* and *River City*. Thus, in the 1987 edition, there are forty-five sections with forty-five sentences in each, for a poet in her forty-fifth year.

This numerical heuristic is just one of many structural tactics Hejinian uses to diminish the role the author plays in the production of an open text. Hejinian, in composing her open text, concerns herself with such structural devices as "arrangement and, particularly, rearrangement within a work," as well as with repetition (1985, 272). What all these devices do, in effect, is allow what Kristeva calls the genotext to play a direct role in the composition process.

The best way to see how Hejinian's open text works is by looking closely at one section of *My Life* in its entirety. The sixteenth section of the 1987 edition serves as an excellent instance of Hejinian's technique.

She showed the left profile, the good one A man is tall, a mountain is high, the sky's the limit. The spare was flat. The filled valleys made shorter hills which we crested on snow shoes on snow over fences. It seemed that we had hardly begun and we were already there. [5] Personal, oblige, running down. At the time, I saw my life as a struggle against my fate, that is, my personality. She was trapped in the elevator panting in plenty of air. Wounded by gossip's rat-a-tattle. More than horse work on worse hills. [10] On a scroll in the case the sequence of plump wrestlers resembled stages in the development of the blooms on the snapdragons. They were driven indoors by bees. Each time we entered the Metro in Paris I read the small sign which reserved the large facing double seats nearest the door for soldiers and veterans crippled by war, and it was just that small sign that realized for me the place-name and its history. Writing maybe held it, separated, there to see. When you open a letter do you hope for a check. [15] A pause, a rose, something on paper. Duck eggs taste "eggier." One form of shyness is characterized by the fear of making someone else feel awkward or embarrassed, a kind of heightened sensitivity or extreme empathy. Religion is a vague lowing. I often felt "jittery" and took long walks, trying to get a long way from what I actually felt. [20] Ring, plunge, reappear. Bucephalus, Traveller, creatures carrying history. Just offshore she saw seven whales, and then ten, leaping from the water and rolling into it again. As for we who "love to be astonished," so do all relationships move. You have to take on the role of pack leader with your dog. [25] Roaring downtown, the lights ahead out of the blue. A tiny red rocking horse, a plaything, bright and sweet. Any photographer will tell you the same. We took along a loaf of Wonder Bread for the ducks. I have learned to be suspicious of those sudden and spontaneous acts of generosity, for it was in such a mood that I gave away the little wicker rocking chair which had been mine throughout my childhood and had belonged to my mother before that, immediately regretting the gesture, so much so that I couldn't bring myself to ask for its return, since I couldn't do so casually and without resentment, a resentment for which I felt guilty, selfish, embarrassed. [30] There is no greater temptation than that of reminiscence. What memory is not a "gripping" thought. She was born with that stubborn temperament, and it has shaped the particular seriousness by virtue of which she has carried out her intentions. A spiral is the shape of a progression of circles. Thus myopia may serve to dispel the pains of chronophobia. [35] The obvious analogy is with music. Thought it through and through. The inaccessibility of the meaning intrigued me all the more, since I couldn't read the single letters, if that is what they were, the little marks which constitute Persian. Mother dimension; sex. She observed that detail minutely, as if it were botanical. [40] As if words could unite an ardent intellect with the external material world. Listen to the drips. The limits of personality. It's in the nature of language to encourage, and in part to justify, such Faustian longings. Break them up into uncounted continuous and voluminous digressions. [45] The very word "diary" depresses me. (1987, 45–46)[6]

Hejinian's text appears in prose format, with a justified right-hand margin, so how do we know it is poetry? Well, for one, she tells us that it is: "Of course, this is a poem, that model of inquiry" (1987, 105). Beyond the obvious, however, Hejinian's text is poetic because repetition plays such an important role in its composition—as do sound and syntax, metonymy and metaphor, all elements that manifest the semiotic *chora*. So *My Life* is perhaps best termed a prose poem—closer to a novel than to a romantic lyric. "A healthy dialectic between poetry and prose," then, comprises Hejinian's investigation of the "I" (1987, 64). But what of the italicized phrase, floating alone in the upper left-hand margin? I assume it serves as an epigraph for the section, as do the phrases occupying the same space in each section. Almost all of these epigraphs eventually reappear as sentences or parts of sentences in various sections throughout the book. The epigraph for section 16, for instance, reappears in sections 17, 19, 23, 30, and 41. In fact, eight of the forty-five sentences in section 16 appear earlier in *My Life* as epigraphs. The fourth sentence of section 16 appears as the third section's epigraph; the fifteenth sentence appears as the first section's epigraph; the eighteenth sentence appears as the thirteenth section's epigraph; the nineteenth sentence appears as the tenth section's epigraph; the twenty-third sentence appears as the second section's epigraph; the twenty-seventh sentence appears as the fourteenth section's epigraph; the thirty-first sentence appears as the ninth section's epigraph; and the thirty-fifth sentence appears as the sixth section's epigraph. Although these phrases reappear throughout the text, they are not always identical to the initial version, and in some cases the variations advance an intersectional dialogue or pattern of images.

Take the fifteenth sentence of section 16, for example, which appears as the first section's epigraph in *My Life:* "*A pause, a rose, something on paper*" (1987, 7). In the third section, the phrase becomes "A pause, a rose, something on paper, in a nature scrapbook"; in the seventh section it becomes "I found myself dependent on a pause, a rose, something on paper"; in the fourteenth, "A pause, a rose, something on paper implicit in the fragmentary text"; in the twentieth, "There is a pause, a rose, something on paper"; in the twenty-fourth, "A pause, a rose, something on paper—an example of parascription"; in the twenty-fifth, "A pause, a rose, something on paper, of true organic spirals we have no lack"; in the thirty-seventh, "A time slowed down, and a distance brought forward—the wave given pause, a rose, something on paper"; and finally in the thirty-ninth section, one of the sections added on to the second edition, "Things are different but not separate, thoughts are discontinuous but not unmotivated (like a rose without pause)." And even when the phrase appears in its initial form, the context in which it appears is different. As Hejinian puts it, "Because of their recurrence, what had originally seemed merely details of atmosphere became, in time, thematic" (1987, 13). By the seventeenth section, all of the previous sixteen epigraphs have reappeared at least once in the text.

Yet the repetition in *My Life* is not merely intersectional and grammatical, it is intrasectional and semantic as well. In section 16, consider the repetition of certain key words. Like the repetition of phrases across sections, these words are not identical in each usage. For example, a number of nouns are used in a general sense in one sentence and in a specific sense in another. Note how the word "personality" is used in sentences 6 and 42; or how "history" is used in sentences 12 and 21; how "mother" is used in sentences 29 and 38; and how "word(s)" is used in sentences 40 and 45. Hejinian also uses the same word as both a noun and a verb—the word "thought" in sentences 31 and 36 and the word "shape" in sentences 32 and 33—or as a noun and an adjective—the word "duck(s)" in sentences

16 and 28 and the word "horse" in sentences 9 and 26. "Here I refer to irrelevance," Hejinian writes, "that rigidity which never intrudes. Hence, repetitions, free from all ambition" (1987, 7).

But doesn't this numerical fixation and this emphasis on repetition take the reader's attention away from the text's meaning, from its themes? Doesn't it, by focusing attention on the arbitrary, inorganic elements in a text's composition, disrupt the articulation of the "I" that is supposedly the subject of *My Life?* What, after all, have we learned about her life? The thirteenth sentence in section 16 provides one possible answer: "Writing maybe held it, separated, there to see." What, though, does writing hold? Her life—the process of her life, to be more exact. "I was eventually to become one person, gathered up maybe, during a pause, at a comma" (1987, 25). By drawing attention to the process of the text's composition, by drawing attention to the language, the material out of which and in which it is composed, Hejinian draws attention to the process that composes the "I" —to that which is both outside and inside the self, the signifying process. The tactic of repetition in *My Life,* then, is part of Hejinian's larger project: to investigate the "I" as it "breaks through" its own boundaries and finds itself enmeshed in the context that surrounds it, in the material contradictions that constitute that context as a world of social relations. In short, Hejinian's textual strategies open the "I" up to that which exceeds it. As Michael Davidson argues, Hejinian's attempt "to materialize language by exposing its arbitrary, systemic nature has obvious precedents in modernists like Williams and Stein." But Hejinian adds a different dimension: her text "has an additional critical function in exploring the interdependencies of that material world and the 'self' that is produced therefrom" (214).

Furthermore, Hejinian sees the poetic text arising out of "the interplay between two areas of fruitful conflict or struggle." She does, however, focus on two particular struggles that take place in the production of a text. The first struggle occurs when "a natural impulse toward closure" conflicts with an "equal impulse toward a necessarily open-ended and continuous response to what's perceived as the 'world,' unfinished and incomplete." The second struggle is a struggle between "literary form" and "writing's material." For Hejinian, the first struggle "involves the poet with his or her subjective position; the second objectifies the poem in the context of ideas and of language itself" (1984, 134). Although Hejinian does not call these struggles dialectical, it does seem clear that she expects the outcome of these struggles to be "fruitful." And what they produce, in the case of *My Life,* is an articulation of the "I" in which the concept of the self, a concept produced by the first struggle, becomes embodied in the material form in which it appears—a form produced by the second struggle. Hejinian's use of numerical constraints and her strategies of repetition, therefore, do not detract from the text's content or themes; on the contrary, they enact that content in the interplay of these two struggles. Thus, the "I" in *My Life* appears in the nexus between the form and content of her text, and neither should be left out of an analysis of her book—a point which brings us to a discussion of that content.

"It is impossible to return to the state of mind in which these sentences originated," Hejinian writes; "one can run through the holes in memory" (1987, 30). In terms of the content of *My Life*, Hejinian's concern with the inability of language to represent accurately the past in the present act of writing is perhaps most prominent. The inaccuracy of memory, the holes we find in it and in history, coupled with the inherent limits of language, make it "impossible" to recall and articulate completely the events that produce the "I" that is the subject of *My Life*. For one thing, humans typically forget a great deal of what happens to them, creating gaps in their accounts of themselves; for another, the context in which the past is being remembered, the time in which the account is composed, exerts a selective pressure on memory. "*That* morning, this morning" (1987, 8). But rather than lament this situation, she embraces it: there will always be an element of untruth, of fiction, in the investigation of any "I," yet this realization has a "fruitful" effect. As she suggests in the epigraph to section 19, "*Such displacements alter illusions, which is all-to-the-good*" (1987, 52). I suspect Hejinian believes this particular displacement—the displacement of the illusion that a completely accurate, nonfictive portrait of the self is possible—is fruitful precisely because it reveals the "I" as an articulation of fictive and nonfictive elements.

To illustrate her point, Hejinian recalls how her "old aunt entertained [her family] with her lie, a story about an event in her girlhood, a catastrophe in a sailboat that never occurred, but she was blameless, unaccountable, since, in the course of the telling, she had come to believe the lie herself" (1987, 13). Any representation of a life, particularly a self-representation, whether in the telling or the writing, acquires a fictive edge that becomes a boundary between the event remembered and the event as it "originally" occurred. The memory that makes up the self, that constitutes what Hejinian calls a life, is not, then, a repository for a factual account of the sequence of events that have occurred to that self. "What follows a strict chronology," Hejinian claims, "has no memory" (1987, 13). For her, the important thing is "To speak of the 'self' and improve it from memory" (1987, 89). Just what she means by "improve" here is fruitfully ambiguous. Does it mean that, by re-collecting our memories, we improve the accuracy with which we speak about ourselves? Or does it mean that we improve the way we appear in our own memories by telling the kind of "lies" told by Hejinian's aunt?

Clearly, what it means to have a life and to tell or write about that life is, for Hejinian, quite different from what it means for someone like Descartes or Hegel. Hejinian questions and ultimately rejects the rational and logical foundations of both Descartes's and Hegel's versions of the "I." For her, logic and reason are themselves fictive constructs; as she puts it in the epigraph to the twenty-second section of *My Life*, "*Reason looks for two, then arranges it from there*" (1987, 59). This act of "arrangement" is neither as disinterested nor as univocal as it appears, nor is it as immutable. For Hejinian, the arrangements of reason and logic are merely some of the ways the self orders its experience of its own processes. Yet these arrangements tend to represent the self as a finished product rather than as an unfinished process. *My Life,* by drawing attention to the limits of language, draws attention to the limits of logic and, more significantly, to the fictive element in the process that produces both language and logic—the signifying process.

Hejinian, then, uses language in order to point out language's own limits in order to articulate the self as an entity in the process of creating a life in the world as well as in the text, in, to be specific, an open text such as *My Life*. One tactic for drawing attention to the limits of language is by deliberately using words and phrases ambiguously to invoke multiple meanings. We can see this tactic at work by looking at some of the different ways the title phrase gets used in *My Life*. First, recall how the phrase "my life" is used in the sixth sentence of section 16, cited above. "At the time, I saw my life as a struggle against my fate, that is, my personality." Here, the phrase has mostly psychological connotations; it is a comment about the struggle to gain a "personality." But look how Hejinian employs the phrase in section 32: "Now I am adding to my life an account of Arctic inquiry, in which the cold drops in folds composed of brilliant rays of light . . . scarcely and timely" (1987, 80). Her "my life" seems to be more of a fictional than a psychological project—something that can be added to, like Hejinian's own book. As I mentioned, *My Life* is still very much in process, and she has not hesitated to revise the life she had already presented, "rewriting [it] in an unstable text" (1987, 113). Hejinian, though, in the first new section of the second edition of *My Life,* section 38, uses the title phrase in still another way: "My life is a permeable constructedness" (1987, 93). In this case, the phrase seems to be the subject of an ontological claim. The "I" is a construct, a fiction, that is not self-contained or immutable. Again, although here it is an ontological claim, the point is that the self is open to revision since it is still in process. There is, however, one more use of the title phrase I want to point out. In section 39, Hejinian observes "My Lives on a shelf by Trotsky, George Sand" (1987, 96). She uses the plural here because, I suspect, the phrase refers to a number of first edition copies of *My Life* sitting on a shelf. If the first use has psychological connotations and the second had fictional and the third ontological connotations, then this fourth use clearly has materialist connotations: "my life" literally is a text.

For Hejinian, then, "A person is a bit of space that has gotten itself in moments" (1987, 114), and those moments compose an open-ended process out of which the "I" arises. Given that "my life" can signify a number of different "selves"—the self as ego, the self as fiction, the self as being, the self as text—we can, nevertheless, find one similarity among them: they all attempt to catch the moment of the "I" in process. Thus, the signifying process becomes the context in which the dialogue between selves takes place, and it makes possible the dialogue that takes place between the self and the other, a dialogue that Hejinian explores in a most "fruitful" manner in *My Life.* Because Hejinian's poem has a more fully developed autobiographical dimension to it than any of the works examined so far in this book, she is able to present in a more concrete and detailed way the "I" as it unfolds in the cultural context in which that "I" has a life. I do not want to suggest that *My Life* fits the pattern of a traditional autobiography or that it attempts to represent that life chronologically. As Juliana Spahr argues, "*My Life*'s refusal to reflect a single image of the autobiographical subject encourages readers to take on agency and to question changes in perception, knowledge, and thinking they undergo in this autobiographical encounter" (147). Thus, we can see how Hejinian's notion of an open text brings the reader directly into the construction of "her" life. Nevertheless, we do get a sense of the process by which Hejinian's "I" collects a life, a process we can follow by noting the way the relation between the self and the other changes throughout the course of the poem.

In the fourth section of *My Life* the relation between the self and the other is depicted in an almost Cartesian manner. "If, for example, you say,

'I always prefer being by myself,' and, then, one afternoon, you want to telephone a friend, maybe you feel you have betrayed your ideals" (1987, 14). Here, contact with the other seems to imply both a breach of an ethics of independence as well as an adulteration of what the "I" perceives to be an authentic mode of being: a self-contained solitude. The "I" recognizes, in the tenth section, the limitations of this attitude, which creates an opportunity to recognize the importance of the other. "An other is a possibility, isn't it. I have been spoiled with privacy, permitted the luxury of solitude" (1987, 31). Yet the "I" is, at this point, either unable or unwilling to move beyond that attitude: "You are not different from your friend, but with your friend you are different from yourself, and recognizing that, I withdrew, wanting to protect my honesty, because I had defined integrity on two dimensions" (1987, 32). Although the "I" is unwilling to give up the perceived need for self-sufficiency, the relation between the self and other is recognized; the "I" realizes both the identity with and difference from the other, and that contact with the other produces a different self, one in relation rather than solitude.

As we move through the sections of *My Life* that could be considered to correspond to the self's adolescent years, we find that sense of autonomy beginning to waver. "I felt self-sufficient except with regard to my feelings, to which I was always vulnerable, always in relation to someone else" (1987, 39). The exception noted in this sentence seems to include more than it excludes, as the relation to the other seems to be taking over the self's sense of identity, which is becoming more "vulnerable" and less "self-sufficient." Two passages in the seventeenth section portray the self trying to come to grips with this vulnerability in ways that can only be described as adolescent escapism. In the first, the "I" hopes that "The experience of a great passion, a great love, would remove me, elevate me, enable me at last to be both special and ignorant of the other people around me, so that I would be free at last from the necessity of appealing to them, responding to them" (1987, 47). Rather than sealing the self off from the other in order to "be free" from its gaze, the "I" imposes some last-ditch half-measures; perhaps by allowing one specific other, a "great love," access to the self that self can create a breakwater to hold back the waves of other selves clamoring for the attention of the "I." In the second passage, the self works through what is a fairly typical adolescent desire to become someone else. "I suppose I had always hoped that, through an act of will and the effort of practice, I might be someone else, might alter my personality and even my appearance, that I might in fact create myself, but instead

I found myself trapped in the very character which made such a thought possible and such a wish mine" (1987, 47–48). The last clause is perhaps the most significant since the "I" begins to understand the self-reflective nature of the self and that this understanding occurs within the context of a recognition of the other—an other the "I" wants to be—and this understanding leads to the self's desire, near the end of the seventeenth section, to "Let someone from the other lane in" (1987, 48).

As the "I" in *My Life* moves from adolescence to adulthood, the relation between the self and the other becomes less oppositional and more complementary. "We looked at the apartment and took it" (1987, 56). I suspect the "we" in this sentence refers to Hejinian and her husband as they move in together. In this stage of Hejinian's "life" the "I" marries and becomes a mother, a stage in which the others in the self's life become as prominent as the self. And the result of this change: "I rebelled against worlds of my own construction and withdrew into the empirical world surrounding me" (1987, 66). Rather than the supposedly self-sufficient "I" of childhood and adolescence, the "I" now finds identity and fulfillment in the relation between self and the other, in the relation of mother and child in particular. The importance becomes evident when the "I" remarks that "I'm seldom in my dreams without my children" (1987, 74). The process of change the self undergoes is so complete that the "I" becomes "a stranger to the little girl I was, and more—more strange" (1987, 75).

Thus, the "I" in *My Life* cannot be seen as an autonomous, self-contained entity; it is not, as Descartes thought, complete in itself but finds itself in its relation with others. And because the self is a "permeable constructedness" and is always in process, it is never complete: the "I" is an unfinished project, a fragment. "I am a shard, signifying isolation—here I am thinking aloud of my affinity for the separate fragment taken under scrutiny" (1987, 52). We can only expect, then, a partial rendition of the "I" under investigation. Yet Hejinian does not lament this situation since "Only fragments are accurate," and a "fragment is not a fraction but a whole piece" (1987, 55, 82). Any claims for completeness or conclusiveness in an articulation of the "I," therefore, come at the expense of an understanding of the process that generates the self and its relations to other selves. Such claims should, to cite the fragment that ends Hejinian's book, create "Reluctance such that it can't be filled" (1987, 115). Or finished.

In *Oxota,* Hejinian's desire to transgress the boundaries between the "I" and the "you" and between the writer and the reader takes a distinctly cross-cultural turn.[7] The result of her extensive travels in Russia, *Oxota* is a "novel" composed of 270 chapters that draws its formal inspiration from Alexander Pushkin's *Evgeny Onegin,* which is also a novel written in fourteen-line stanzas. Perhaps an even more important source of inspiration is the Dragomoschenko family. Hejinian met Arkadii Dragomoschenko, an avant-garde Russian poet, in 1983, and the two have been involved in a cross-cultural poetic dialogue ever since, translating each other's work and introducing each other to many of the important contemporary poets in their respective cultures. Much of Hejinian's "Short Russian Novel," which is *Oxota*'s subtitle, takes place in the period when she was staying with the Dragomoschenko family in Leningrad; the book is dedicated to Zina Dragomoschenko, Arkadii's wife, and most of the "characters" in the work are members of the immediate or extended family.

Familiarity with the historical context in which her book was written is also necessary to understand both the form and content of the work. Hejinian indicates that *Oxota* was composed between December 18, 1989, and February 18, 1991—a time of great change and turmoil in Russia. Mikhail Gorbachev's policies of *glasnost* and perestroika had precipitated the dissolution rather than reconstruction of the Soviet empire. While Hejinian was writing *Oxota,* Gorbachev received the Nobel Peace Prize, the communist party officially lost its monopoly on power, Boris Yeltsin was elected president, and Eduard Shevardnadze, Gorbachev's foreign minister, resigned in protest against Gorbachev's increasingly conservative attempts to keep the Soviet Union from splitting apart. The months following the composition of *Oxota* saw a failed coup against Gorbachev that ultimately led to his resignation and Yeltsin's rise to power, and to the breakup of the Soviet Union. These events are rarely alluded to directly in *Oxota,* but they do create the conditions in which such a book could be written. The intent of Gorbachev's policy of *glasnost*—which literally means "publicity" or "public voice" but also took on the metaphoric meaning of "opening up"—was to give the public back its voice, which had been suppressed by the restrictive censorship policies of the Communist Party, in order to generate the kind of constructive criticism that would allow the political and economic reforms of perestroika to take place. *Glasnost* also made easier the kind of cross-cultural investigation of poetry conducted by Hejinian and Dragomoschenko, which resulted in an "opening up" of Hejinian's poetry to the influence of Dragomoschenko's and vice versa. As Hejinian puts it, "someone had developed the *glasnost* metaphor: open and / let something out"—or "in," as the case may be

(1991, 236). *Oxota,* then, is a compelling instance of a cross-cultural "open text" designed to bring in to view the personal, political, linguistic, and aesthetic hierarchies and divisions that have separated the Russian and American people for most of this century.

Although Hejinian considers *Oxota* a novel in verse, we should not expect to find a linear narrative governing the book any more than we should expect a linear account of her autobiography in *My Life.* As we will see, certain themes and images recur throughout the work, but these do not constitute a "plot" in any conventional sense; there are "characters," but their development or progress does not seem central to the intent of *Oxota;* and the book is divided into "chapters," each of which consists of fourteen lines, but those chapters do not unfold a strict, temporal sequence of events. I suggest that the plot and progress of the book are found in the activity of writing it. As in *My Life,* Hejinian's concern is to discover a way of writing that gives form to her perception of "the world as vast and overwhelming; each moment stands under an enormous vertical and horizontal pressure of information, potent with ambiguity, meaning-full, unfixed, and certainly incomplete" (1985, 271). And this form must not reduce that perception of ambiguity and uncertainty to the univocity and simplicity of a traditional "closed" text, in "which all the elements of the work are directed toward a single reading of the work" (1985, 270). "What this means in practice," as Marjorie Perloff suggests, "is that ideas, sensations, overheard remarks, and so on are seen from a particular perspective but these perspectives never wholly cohere into anything like a fixed identity or self" (1992, 193). For Hejinian, then, the question is "Can form make chaos (i.e., raw material, unorganized information, uncertainty, incompleteness, vastness) articulate without depriving it of its potency, its generativity? Can form go even further than that and actually generate the potency of uncertainty, incompleteness, vastness, etc.?" And for her, "the answer to this is yes, that this is in fact the function of form in art, that form is not a fixture but an activity" (1985, 275). Form is not, therefore, a static "container" into which one pours content. Form is dynamic and generative because it is an activity that fits the contours of the experience of this "vast and overwhelming" world rather than an atemporal and ahistorical template or set of rules. Thus, the chapters that comprise *Oxota* are not governed by the traditional strictures of set line lengths or patterns of rhyme, and, on a few occasions, they do not even adhere to the fourteen-line requirement. I suggest that Hejinian enacts a poetic policy of *glasnost* toward the form she is working in. She creates an "open" form that resists closure in order to remain true to the uncertainty and ambiguity in her perception and experience of the "vast and overwhelming" world—a world whose dominant geopolitical opposition between Russia and America was itself breaking out of a "closed" form of conflict.

A look at the first chapter in *Oxota* will help illustrate my point:

Chapter One

This time we are both
The old thaw is inert, everything set again in snow
At insomnia, at apathy
We must learn to endure the insecurity as we read
The felt need for a love intrigue
There is no person—he or she was appeased and withdrawn
There is relationship but it lacks simplicity
People are very aggressive and every week more so
The Soviet colonel appearing in such of our stories
He is sentimental and duckfooted
He is held fast, he is in his principles
But here is a small piece of the truth—I am glad to greet you
There, just with a few simple words it is possible to say the truth
It is so because often men and women have their sense of honor

(1991, 11)

First, note the absence of any terminal punctuation; like all the chapters in the book, there are no periods that close one line off from the lines before and after it. There are occasional question marks and exclamation points in *Oxota*, but those serve more as markers of mood than of "completion" of thought. As the fourth line tells us, we need to come to grips with the "insecurity" that this kind of open text breeds. That insecurity pertains to the absence of clear demarcations between and within lines, but it also pertains to the insecurity that arises from the absence of a motivated plot, a "love intrigue"—for instance—or a central narrative voice since "There is no person" gathering the lines together under a controlling perspective. One character does appear, a "Soviet colonel," and he reappears frequently in the book; but he functions more as an image of rigidity, of someone "held fast" by "principles," than as an agent of action in a traditional novel. Hejinian's series of chapters does not, however, strand us in a world without value. There is a notion of "truth" at work throughout the book, although we need to accept the insecurity that comes when we receive only a "small piece" of it here and there. And the first "piece" we receive is indicative of all of Hejinian's work: "I am glad to greet you." Again, as in *My Life,* the dialogue between writer and reader is constitutive of the truth that arises in *Oxota*—a truth that is provisional and open-ended rather than universal and closed off to change and revision. Furthermore, that truth does proceed from a significant source of value: a "sense of honor" among men and women.

In one sense, then, there is a serious and sustained "hunt," which is the English translation of the Russian word *oxota,* for truth throughout the book—a hunt that is open to uncertainty, ambiguity, and incompleteness in both its form and content. This image of the hunt recurs frequently in the book, and a look at a few of those occurrences will give us a sense of the kind of poetic investigation Hejinian enacts in *Oxota.* The word first occurs in the ninth line of the second chapter.

> In the evenings particularly we made notes and took dictation
> > in anticipation of writing a short Russian novel, something
> > neither invented nor constructed but moving through
> > that time as I experienced it unable to take part
> > personally in the hunting
>
> > > > (1991, 12)

First, we should note that the indentations are a printing convention to indicate that this is one line but that the page is not wide enough to "contain" it, so we can see right away that Hejinian's line is not governed by a set number of "feet." In this line Hejinian announces that the formal activity that generates her novel in verse is governed by her temporal experience of her stay in Russia rather than by an invented or constructed plot. I also think we need to understand her claim that she is "unable to take part personally" in the hunt in the context of her earlier remark that "There is no person" overseeing the process. As she writes later in *Oxota,* the hunt "pursues the impersonal narrative—here, our endless it" (1991, 83). Although there is no "person" orchestrating the hunt, "The hunter knows the resource / The hunter resorts / She doesn't think and then decide / She follows word to word in words' design" (1991, 277). The resource, then, is not the "I" or the self but language; nevertheless, "the hunt is intelligible" because her poetic investigation "puts grammar to the hunt" (1991, 170, 69).

As I have suggested, the truths this hunt uncovers are not atemporal,

ahistorical, or immutable. In two chapters of *Oxota,* both titled "Truth,"
Hejinian takes us on a poetic tour of her understanding of truth.

Chapter Seventy-one: Truth

Truth is not precision but evidence
Body and truth at the thought
Crazy who says no longer and is quickly repeated
To hover and hum at the truth (so much longer to love)
To hush
Over ground under cloud as expedient as expands
Nothing had—no moral outrage, no self-righteousness,
     no indignation
Just residue
An all-over corporeal stamina
There isn't really room for the truth—gray birches in full
context—but room for both
As always, as ambient, and as bound
Just as blue, the procedure, reflects
The truth that is halted is squandered
Even the lull is dependent

(1991, 82)

Here, Hejinian allows language to guide the investigation from "word to
word" by associations both aural and conceptual. In lines 4 and 5, the consonants *h* and *l* move the inquiry forward as do the vowels *a, o,* and *u* in
lines 11 and 12. On the conceptual level, we move from a notion of truth as
evidence, "as expedient" and expansive, "as ambient, and as bound," and
as that which is not "halted" and is "dependent." Thus, truth is not a universal property independent of the world of particulars, the "gray birches
in full / context"; "body and truth" fit together in an epistemology that
makes "room for both." Truth, then, is a matter of establishing provisional
connections between events and objects as they occur in experience. But,
as we discover in the second chapter titled "Truth," chapter 261, "Truth
is not a likeness," so "What truths there are in detail have divisions into /
circumstance," and since those circumstances change and are perceived
differently at different times, the truths we find in the hunt are "in actuali-
ties, truths left by practice / The truth to be as we remember it" (1991, 281).
   Hejinian's claim that "Truth is not a likeness" leads to a suspicion of

metaphor as a grounding trope of an "open" poetic investigation. For her, "Metaphor hides the paranoia of writing" because it subsumes difference as a way of gaining closure and coherence at the expense of particularity; thus, "comparisons frequently separate what's identifiable" (1991, 103, 243). Being true to experience entails being true to the differences perceived among events and objects, for "difference has no exceptions / It is true to the irrational particulars to come" (1991, 285). Hejinian's investigation, then, relies more on metonymy than metaphor as a governing trope. Although the differences between metaphor and metonymy have occasioned great debate, it seems safe to say that metaphor generally sets up a relation of identity across categories; in many metaphors, this relation is between an abstract "idea" and a particular "object." When we say "love is a rose," for instance, an abstraction, "love," is perceived to be identical to a particular, a "rose." In short, metaphor relies on the discernment of a figurative "essence" shared by two or more items. "In Metonymy," according to Hayden White,

> phenomena are implicitly apprehended as bearing relationships to one another in the modality of part-part relationships, on the basis of which one can effect a reduction of one of the parts to the status of an aspect or function of the other. To apprehend any given set of phenomena in the modality of part-part relationships (not, as in Metaphor, object-object relationships) is to set thought the task of distinguishing between those parts which are representative of the whole and those which are simply aspects of it. . . . By Metonymy, then, one can simultaneously distinguish between two phenomena and reduce one to the status of a manifestation of the other. (35)

Rather than compare one "object" with another as metaphor does, metonymy distinguishes between the "parts" of an object or event; thus, the former is a trope of identity, while the latter is a trope of difference. To employ a spatial image, metaphor creates a "vertical" transference between a "higher" category (abstract thought) and a "lower" one (sensuous particulars); metonymy, on the other hand, creates a "horizontal" substitution of one particular for another. So if "Metaphor hides the paranoia of writing" by positing identity between an abstract realm of thought and the sensuous world of particulars, "The metonym reduces the monument" to an identity that governs much of Western thought and poetry (1991, 103). When Hejinian writes that the hunter "follows word to word in words' design," she is, I suggest, advocating a metonymic mode of composition, one that moves associatively from one linguistic element to the next by way of a "horizontal" path leading from one particular to the next without a "vertical" leap to a realm of abstraction separated from the realm of particulars. As a result, "Everything really happens and its metonyms happen as well" because "We are among things on which reality has been slowly settling and is then dusted away" (1991, 261, 22).

"Reality," for Hejinian, is also conceived as being provisional, mutable, and open to revision. And if truth is a matter of establishing equally provisional metonymic associations between events and objects as they occur in reality, then many of the hierarchic oppositions that govern Western logic and aesthetics begin to break down as well and are "reduced" metonymically to "parts" of each other rather than distinct "objects" made identical by the force of metaphor. There "are no opposites," Hejinian writes (1991, 20), and, as we move through *Oxota,* she challenges many traditional oppositions because "There is disintegrity in polarities as such" (1991, 100). The following are just a few instances: "Neither art nor life is opposite / Opposition is a stupid government in power to misunderstand" (1991, 49); "So I must oppose the opposition of poetry to prose" (1991, 93); "The false opposition between inside and out" (1991, 252). Of all these oppositions, though, the one she seems most intent on reducing and thereby revising in all her work is the one between self and other: "There's such impertinence in subjectivity / But what could one predict from the syntax of desire to / surpass the opposition between 'me' and 'you'" (1991, 75). As she does in *My Life,* Hejinian consistently returns to the division between the self and the other in order to discover that which we all share—the experience of reality. This is not to say we all experience reality in the same way and as the same "thing." Like the open text, reality is a collaborative event since "reality is the matter mediated" so that "we conspired a novel with reality" (1991, 52, 284). What we share, then, is not the experience of a world stable in its essence but the experience of the absence of an immutable essence, an experience of the open text of reality:

> Our experiences achieve pathos when they force us to
> > acknowledge that the significances and meanings of
> > things—things we've known, it would seem, forever, and
> > certainly since childhood—have changed—or
> > rather, when we are forced to absorb the memory of being
> > utterly unable to catch or trace or name the moment of
> > transition when one meaning changed to another—the

> moment of interruption in the course of our knowing
> such things
>
> (1991, 53)

As I mentioned at the beginning of this chapter, Hejinian, in contrast to many of her contemporaries, does not abandon her investigation of the "I" because a complete and conclusive articulation of that "I" is not possible. And, as I also mentioned, Hejinian is frequently and accurately associated with language writing. Yet language writing is often taken as a singular example of the tendency in contemporary thought to abandon just such an investigation. While this judgment may be true of some of the language writers, my accounts of *My Life* and *Oxota* contend that Hejinian should not be saddled with that judgment. Her investigation places the "I" in the world with other selves, in the midst of the cultural context in which it finds itself, and that placement creates a political dimension in her book that belies attempts to make it an instance of the "death of the subject." Most of the language writers, including Hejinian, came of age during the Vietnam War and found themselves at odds with the right-wing faction of American culture that waged and supported the war. A great deal of the work of the language writers emerges out of that political context. As McGann rightly notes, "Oppositional politics are a paramount concern" for these writers (199). Their politics amount to much more than just an opposition to the imperialism of American culture exhibited during the Vietnam War. They are just as concerned with the ways language gets used to make this culture of imperialism and consumption palatable. Perhaps the best way of demonstrating how these oppositional politics help form Hejinian's articulation of an "I" that is neither fully absent nor fully present is by contrasting her version of "language" writing with the most prominent attempt to make that kind of writing an example of the abandonment of the self in contemporary culture.

In *Postmodernism, or The Cultural Logic of Late Capitalism*, Fredric Jameson argues that language writers "have adopted schizophrenic fragmentation as their fundamental aesthetic" and therefore advance a notion of the self as either absent or "depthless" (28). As we have seen, Hejinian does indeed take a fragmentary view of the "I," but does that necessarily mean that "I" is absent or without depth? Jameson is careful to point out that his analysis is a description of the cultural logic of the present rather than a psychological diagnosis of any particular writer, and that, following Jacques Lacan, he is interested in schizophrenia as it manifests itself in language rather than in the ego. Given these caveats, Jameson characterizes "schizophrenia as a breakdown in the signifying chain" and contends that this "breakdown" characterizes the paratactic sentences and fragments of the language writers in general and Bob Perelman in particular (26–30). Again, Jameson is not claiming that Perelman or any of the language writers are schizophrenic—although, as George Hartley points out, Jameson may well be deploying a "strategic form of guilt by association" (47). He is claiming, however, that this kind of writing typifies the cultural logic of postmodernism—a logic that, according to Jameson, exhibits the same kind of "breakdown" evident in cases of schizophrenia. In short, he uses the Lacanian account of schizophrenia to connect the literary context of language writing with the cultural context in which such writing occurs.

"With the breakdown of the signifying chain," Jameson argues, "the schizophrenic is reduced to an experience of pure material signifiers, or, in other words, a series of pure and unrelated presents in time" (27). Thus, the schizophrenic as well as the reader and writer of language writing experience the text as an ahistorical, atemporal flow of "depthless" signifiers unattached to any signifieds—unattached, in other words, to the cultural context in which such writing is written and read. McGann, on the other hand, interprets the language writers' "preoccupation with non-sense, unmeaning, and fragmentation" as part of a larger project "conceived to reveal the power of writing and the production of meaning as human, social, and limited in exact and articulable ways" (209–10). And Perelman, in his rebuttal of Jameson's argument, makes much the same point as McGann, claiming that the paratactic mode of language writing "encourages attention to the act of writing and to the writer's particular position within larger social frames" (1993, 316). Rather than drawing attention to the "breakdown" (a term that in itself conjures up images of mental illness) of the signifying chain, McGann and Perelman draw attention to the ways in which language writing foregrounds or thematizes the signifying process, which, as Kristeva contends, is not an endless displacement of signifiers unattached to signifieds but a materialist dialectic composed of the semiotic and symbolic modalities. Thus, language writing does not force the reader or writer into an ahistorical or atemporal realm of schizophrenic "depthlessness." On the contrary, language writing places the reader or writer in a distinct sociohistorical context and enacts an equally distinct political agenda that "involves dismantling the ideology . . . that language—which in this context means producing and reproducing texts—is an object, an icon" (McGann, 209).

"But language is restless," Hejinian asserts (1987, 17). Language writers in general and Hejinian in particular use language to draw attention to the restlessness within language and to the ways in which that restlessness is put to use for different purposes—some personal, some political, some commercial, some aesthetic, but social purposes one and all. And these writers draw attention to the ways in which that restlessness manifests itself in the signifying process—not as an aberrational breakdown but as a constitutive activity: an activity revealing that language, like the text and like the self, is an event rather than an object. "Language itself is never at rest," Hejinian argues, and "the experience of using it, which includes the experience of understanding it, either as speech or writing, is inevitably active. I mean both intellectually and emotionally active" (1985, 279). By drawing the reader's attention not only to the "I" as a theme in a text but to the text itself, the reader is thrown back on his or her self—an event that draws attention to that which both share.

"Are your fingers in the margin," Hejinian asks (1987, 10). The "I" that writes and the "I" that reads share the activity, the practice, of having a world, and language is a constitutive presence in that world. I do not mean to suggest that *I* or *you* or *we* share some impalpable, impermeable essence with each other or with those selves that populated the past. I do mean to suggest, however, that we do share activities and practices with each other, and one of those practices we share is the practice of language. More particularly, we share texts and contexts. As Hejinian so aptly puts it, "It is a way of saying, I want you, too, to have this experience, so that we are more alike, so that we are closer, bound together, sharing a point of view" (1987, 21–22). This, then, is the "desire" underwriting the production of an open text: to share in the construction of a world in a way that "invites participation, rejects the authority of the writer over the reader and thus, by analogy, the authority implicit in other (social, economic, cultural) hierarchies" (1985, 134). Again, I am not claiming that a direct "link" exists between the writer and reader of an open text; such a claim presupposes that the link—language, the text—is a transparent medium rather than an interpretive activity. Nevertheless, a dialogue between the reader and writer of an open text occurs amid certain expectations that most readers and writers share. These expectations have less to do with a transcendent essence than with a social consensus and are manifest in the "shared features" Wittgenstein contends underlie our ability to discern "family resemblances" among practices.

Open texts such as *My Life* and *Oxota,* then, transgress the boundary between the "I" that writes and the other that reads, and "After crossing the boundary which distinguishes the work from the rest of the universe, the reader is expected to recross the boundary with something in mind" (1987, 77). Hejinian, then, writes a history of the "I" that folds outward as well as inward, and in this sense her work bears a striking family resemblance less to that of Walt Whitman than to that of another great American writer, William James. "Our fields of experience have no more definite boundaries than have our fields of view. Both are fringed forever by a *more* that continuously develops, and that continuously supersedes them as life proceeds" (1173). Hejinian's open texts conduct poetic investigations of this undefined and undefinable *more* that fringes the indefinite boundaries of the experience of experience that human beings share in history. This yields, of course, only an "imperfect intimacy," to quote James again, but it is an intimacy that allows Hejinian, and us as well, that "small piece of truth—I am glad to greet you" (1991, 11).

An "international" tradition by all means for those who wish it. *But a creole*
culture as well. And a creole way of seeing, first. It is from this stone that we
must begin.
    —Kamau Brathwaite

4. Kamau Brathwaite
Tidalectic Rhythms

Kamau Brathwaite's call—first issued in his 1967 essay "Jazz and the West
Indian Novel" and in the same year he published his first book of poetry,
Rights of Passage—for a "way of seeing" that includes both an international
and creole perspective brings us to the core of his poetic investigation into
the connections between Caribbean, African, and Euro-American culture.
Over the course of thirty years, he has created a way of writing history
poetically that is truly cross-cultural in form and content by mixing the
traditions of Caribbean folk art, African history, British literature, and
American music, to name a few of the major cultural strands that weave
through his work. Yet his work is much more than a pastiche of traditions; rather, it is a "creolization" of those traditions. For Brathwaite, a
creolized culture is one in which "the society concerned is caught up 'in
some kind of colonial arrangement' with a metropolitan European power,
on the one hand, and a plantation arrangement on the other; and where
the society is multiracial but organized for the benefit of a minority of
European origin" (1971, xv). His definition recognizes and highlights the
political, economic, and racial inequities that characterize the countries of
the Caribbean in ways that a pastiche—which, as Fredric Jameson contends, is "a neutral practice of mimicry" that levels out difference—does
not (17). Although Brathwaite's poetry does indeed have an international
dimension, that dimension is grounded in and grows out of the experience of being a member of a creolized culture: "It is from this stone we

must begin." And it is from that "stone" that my account of Brathwaite's work will begin as well.

Near the beginning of *Barabajan Poems*—an autobiographical/historical essay poem, first published in 1994, on the culture of his home island, Barbados—Brathwaite remarks that "for a long time I have been aware that although my work is now read quite widely and has been studied in some place(s), I have never yet seen a critique relating to the obvious: my house my home here my home/land island my Bajan culture" (1994b, 22). Critics, he contends, often treat him as either "an **African-oriented** writer—a person involved mainly with Africa (I lived in Ghana 10 years)" or a proponent "of **Jamaican writing** (with an element of protest & reggae & rasta & urban/herban blues & so on)" (1994b, 22–23), but not as a Barabajan or Barbadian poet. Brathwaite certainly does not intend to deny the African and Jamaican dimensions of his work. His first trilogy, *The Arrivants*, is more than ample evidence that his ten-year stay in Ghana secured the ground of his poetics. But that ground was uncovered earlier in Barbados. And the twenty-five years spent in Jamaica as a professor at the University of the West Indies certainly imbue his work with a Jamaican sound, most evident in *Trench Town Rock*. But Brathwaite wants us to listen for a more originary song, first heard on the shore of Barbados: another "stone's" song as it skips on water.

It began the day I bent down for a pebble to play duck-and-drakes, skidding it along the water . . *skip skip skip skip* . . . along the water . . . with that little *hiss,* as if the pebble had its own life until it like spins in its own little white & disappears

It began the day I picked up this pebble & saw the connection: the grains & feel of sand at my feet: the pebble as a large smooth grain of the sand/the sand as the pebble ground down (ground-down) to its nam: the pebble & sand both from the same continent, the underwater bone of the world, built by the polyp of god into this cosmos of smooth in my hand like the disc of the sun I could feel in the stone in my hand I could feel on my back on the skin in the bone I could feel on my head on my face on the stretching brittle Brown's Beach under my feet

[I was to have this very same or similar xperience & sensation years later—in 1972—at Bathsheba (BASHEEBA)—

when **Mother Poem** was about to happen] & I picked that
pebble up—and skidded it across the water—and it bloomed
into islands

5

This at least was a. this at last was a. start: when God set out
to create the islands of th(e) Caribbean, he skidded a duck-
&-drakes stone from Barbados (let's say) north through
Grenada, St Vincent, St Lucia, Dominica, & on through the
Leewards, Antigua, Barbuda, Anguilla & . . curving as the
stone we skidded . . . Puerto Rico *hiss hiss* Hispaniola . Dominica & Haiti . Cuba . Caymanas & Cat & Guanahani . . .

But that was only the visible part. When God created the
islands of the Caribbean, he also did so with music; he must
have! with sound: the noise that he heard that gave creation
shape. Again, was it Milton's? or Lowell's Nantucket? Bee-
thoven's Fifth Trump? Dvorak's New World? Peter Tosh/In
the Beginning? Gustav Holtz' Planets?

And then I saw or rather heard it: the pebbles of the pan,
the plangent syllables of blue, the on-rolling syncopation,
the rhythmic tidalectics: and it was the islands' own sound,
not taken or borrowed from no where else or if borrowed
borrowed so creatively it becomes our own: & the irksome
wonder/*why so long?* why did it take so long, take me so long
to come to this so natural so obvious so beautiful so easily
our own:

the kaiso

So that when God created Caribbean, he took a pebble,
skidded it along the water w/a sound of our own & this is
how it went: his archipelago: my vision: yr poem

[Singing]
The stone had skidded arc'd and bloomed into islands:
Cuba and San Domingo
Jamaica and Puerto Rico
Grenada Guadeloupe Bonaire
curved stone hissed into reef
wave teeth fanged into clay

> *white splash flashed into spray*
> *Bathsheba Montego Bay*
>
> •
>
> *bloom of the arcing summers*
> (1994b, 117–18)[1]

The lines sung at the end of this passage comprise the opening section of "Calypso"—which appears midway in Brathwaite's first book of poems, *Rights of Passage,* and marks the beginning of his poetic investigations. The setting is Barbados; not New York, London, or Paris, Ghana, Kenya, or Jamaica. The arc of the pebble surely leads out to these cities and countries, as does the arc of Brathwaite's poetry, but both begin in Barbados. The identity between the cosmological and the autobiographical in Brathwaite's account of his call to poetry resembles Walt Whitman's call recorded in "Out of the Cradle Endlessly Rocking." Both poets hear their song and their culture's song arising from nature, from the sounds of the sea in particular; both poets hear that song in the vernacular of their people rather than in the imposed rhythms of British verse; and both poets seek new forms to embody their experiences of the union of cosmology and autobiography. However, where Whitman's sense of the musical structure of his work was, as F. O. Matthiessen and others have shown, essentially operatic, Brathwaite's sense of music derives from calypso, blues, jazz, and reggae. This difference may seem to be merely a matter of taste in music, but there are significant political as well as aesthetic implications lurking in this difference. Whitman selects as his compositional model the "highest" of Western culture's high art forms, but opera's celebration of European hierarchies of order and artifice seems at odds with Whitman's already contradictory mix of American exceptionalism and a democratic "urge to merge" with all people in all cultures. Brathwaite's model is the sound, sight, and insight of a pebble skipping across water—the sound "that gave creation shape," "the plangent syllables of blue," which he also hears in "kaiso" (calypso) music. Calypso, unlike opera, rises from the colonized rather than colonizer, from black skin rather than white.

Brathwaite's metaphor links the natural and the cosmological, but it also links the aesthetic and the political: the pebble sounds out God's act of creation as well as the poet's, but it is also the skipping, unpredictable sound of revolt, the discordant note in calypso, jazz, and blues that undermines the smooth consumption of Caribbean culture required by the tourist trade. It is no romanticized whim, then, that prefaces those lines from "Calypso" with "*[Singing]*"; in performance, Brathwaite sings this poem as a calypso song. And the final stanzas of the poem bring the subversive element of kaiso out from under the pleasant surface of sound:

> perhaps when they come
> with their cameras and straw
> hats: sacred pink tourists from the frozen Nawth
>
> we should get down to those
> white beaches
> where if we don't wear breeches
>
> it becomes an island dance
> *Some people doin' well*
> *while others are catchin' hell*
>
> o the boss gave our Johnny the sack
> though we beg him please
> please to take 'im back
>
> so the boy nigratin' overseas . . .
>
> (1973, 49–50)

The final line and its mordant pun capture the essence of the Caribbean diaspora of late capitalism. As Brathwaite once put it, Caribbeans are the number one export item from the islands, while tourists are the number one import item. The unjust dichotomy expressed in the italicized lines, lilting end-rhyme and all, indicts the whole economic system of colonialism and neocolonialism in which the workers have little recourse other than begging and pleading with "the boss" or "nigratin' overseas."

The neocolonial dispersal of the Caribbean people, which began in earnest in the early 1950s, included a great many of the islands' most prominent and promising artists, writers, and musicians—one of whom was Edward Brathwaite, who was originally Lawson Edward and who would become Edward Kamau and finally Kamau. The power of giving, taking, and imposing names is of great concern to Brathwaite. The changes in his own name reflect periods of rejection, of compromise, followed by a rejection of that initial rejection and an affirmation of a name given with his consent: "I own now & use the name **Kamau** in preference to the earlier **Edwar(d)**" (1994b, 237). Brathwaite received his African name in a ceremony in Kenya in 1971, which for him was "an important statement of cultural position/commitment/orientation, as it were . . . to know the **meaning** of that name—yr name—to know that that name—the name has qualities in it which begin to affect you & your outlook" (1994b, 237). Brathwaite follows this account of his affirmative experience with the power of naming in *Barabajan Poems* with a rerun of the scene in the televised version of Alex Haley's *Roots* in which a slave, Kinta Kunte, is tortured until he "accepts" the name, Toby, given by his owner. This is followed in turn by a letter-by-letter gloss of the meaning of the name Kamau, both forward and backward, and his declaration that

name

therefore becomes important and what we name and call ourselves be comes even more important, especially in a colonial or post-colonial situation where we have been named by other people and where it is therefore our responsibility to rename & redefine ourselves. (1994b, 240–41)

For Brathwaite, this redefinition is accomplished by creating "our own sense of self of hope of history" and "our own-own true-true poems" that rise from the sights and sounds of nature and culture and from the knowledge that, "like the hurricane, our seas don't usually speak in pentameters" (1994b, 116, 115). Thus, a new name needs a new measure consonant with a new self-definition.

The iambic pentameter line becomes for Brathwaite a synecdoche of the various colonial practices that impose not only names but laws, values, and standards, aesthetic as well as moral, on the colonized. Its regular, staccato rhythms remind him of the marching of imperial soldiers rather than the sound of that pebble as it plays on the sea and in the wind. In "History of the Voice" Brathwaite contends that in terms of Anglo-American poetry, the "pentameter prevails" from Chaucer to the present. "Over in the New World, the Americans—Walt Whitman—tried to bridge or break the pentameter through a cosmic movement, a large movement of sound. Cummings tried to fragment it. And Marianne Moore attacked it with syllabics. But basically the pentameter remained, and it carries with it a certain kind of experience, which is not the experience of a hurricane" (1993b, 265).[2] Like the imposition of the English language on the slaves brought to the Caribbean by way of the Middle Passage, the imposition of the iambic line on Caribbean poets by the British education system implanted in their culture forced the African languages and rhythms to "submerge" themselves in clandestine and disguised practices.

As these practices begin to emerge from the shadows in the 1960s and become the cause of investigation and celebration, Brathwaite conducts his investigation and celebration of what he calls "nation language," which, he contends, "largely ignores the pentameter" (1993b, 265). Nation language arises when the English language is infiltrated by the linguistic "noise" that signals the remnants of African cultures. Nation language is not a dialect, which, Brathwaite argues, "has a long history coming from the plantation where people's dignity was distorted through their languages and their descriptions that the dialect gave them. Nation language, on the other hand, is the submerged area of that dialect that is much more closely allied to the African aspect of experience in the Caribbean. It may be in English, but often it is an English which is like a howl, or a shout, or a machine-gun, or the wind, or a wave. It is also like the blues" (1993b, 266). In short, nation language is subversive; dialect is submissive. As it takes the form of poetry, then, nation language emerges from the refusal to submit to the rule of the iambic pentameter. Nation language is one of Brathwaite's primary tactics to disrupt or negate that rule, but it also announces and affirms the African element in Caribbean culture.

For Brathwaite, that subversive element first became apparent in music. Back in Barbados, before he left the island first for England and then for Ghana, he began his own jazz collection, "although since jazz, and especially the new dissonant, 'flattened fifth' bebop of Bird, Monk & Dizzy Gillespie was considered *unmusic* & even *subversive* by the then ruling Establishments, including the Bajan, I had a hard time, as I was saying, with it; though at the same time this very appreciation of 'subversive' was opening me up to possibilities & alternatives (**alter/natives**) within not only our developing Caribbean literature, but within 'English' literature as a whole" (1994b, 34). The outward arc of Brathwaite's thought here resembles the outward arc of the pebble in his cosmological account of the creation of the Caribbean islands and their music. He begins by placing himself within his own Bajan culture as one who listened to another's dissonant song and heard his own return. Brathwaite, in other words, listened to jazz *from* somewhere, which, although very different from the primary scenes of bebop staged in New York, played to a similar need for the subversive sound of the flattened fifth. For Brathwaite, the implications of that sound arc out from the local (Barabajan literature) to the regional (Caribbean literature) to the colonial (English literature) to a global aesthetic that reaches Africa and returns home on the harmattan winds and the coastal tides.

Brathwaite, then, sees his work and his world in terms of a *tidalectic* rather than *dialectic* pattern of movement—"the pebbles of the pan, the plangent syllables of blue, the on-rolling syncopation, the rhythmic tidalectics." Brathwaite's neologism nicely weaves together the naturalistic and political strands of his poetry and poetics. But it also helps understand how he views the movement between and among his so-called trilogies— *The Arrivants,* which consists of *Rights of Passage, Masks,* and *Islands; The Ancestors,* which consists of *Mother Poem, Sun Poem,* and *X/Self;* and a third, unnamed set, *Shar, The Zea Mexican Diary,* and *Trench Town Rock.* As Brathwaite explains:

> I started off with a plan saying I would like to do three trilogies, and it turned out that I wrote *Rights of Passage, Masks* and *Islands.* I could see that very clearly as a program, but after that although I went on talking about these trilogies, although there are certain things that are still in threes, there were other shapes that were taking place in my mind. The one that rules me more than others is the rejection of the notion of dialectic, which is three—the resolution in the third. Now I go for a concept I call "tide-alectic" which is the ripple and the two tide movement. So that the whole shape has changed because of that notion. (1995)

In this passage from an interview conducted in 1995, Brathwaite makes a conscious break not only with Hegelian dialectics but with his own earlier understanding of his trilogies. In an interview with Nathaniel Mackey, conducted in 1990, he is still thinking about the first two trilogies in Hegelian terms. *The Arrivants* "was really a matter of raising an issue, replying to that issue and trying to create a synthesis. . . . And the same thing happens in the second trilogy" (1991, 43). Perhaps the tragic subject matter of the third trilogy— *The Zea Mexican Diary* is about the death of his wife; *Shar* is about the hurricane that destroyed his house; and *Trench Town Rock* is about being shot and robbed in Jamaica—does not allow him to think in terms of a synthesis, or perhaps he has come to see the limits of dialectics. Either or both answers may be correct, but I suggest that we look at his trilogies in terms of "the ripple and the two tide movement." This image allows us to see these works in terms of a going out and a return without imposing a "resolution" on that movement.

In this chapter I investigate this tidalectic movement in the first two trilogies in order to chart the changes in Brathwaite's poetry.[3] These changes are formal as well as thematic, and both of these dimensions of his poetry can be seen by focusing on the Barabajan "origin" of his work, the "stone [from which] we must begin," and the crucial part played by music throughout the trilogies. I will also refer to *Barabajan Poems* throughout this chapter, both for the information it provides but also because that book shows Brathwaite writing history poetically in a form other than verse. Thus, Brathwaite's work clearly poses a distinct challenge to those who see poetic forms as politically neutral containers of content. I contend that Brathwaite moves closer and closer to his notion of nation language as his work develops—a development paralleled by the changes in his name as he moves toward a deeper understanding of his "nam," which Brathwaite defines as "not only the soul/atom but *indestructible self/sense of culture under crisis*" (1987, 127).

During the mid- to late sixties, while Brathwaite was writing the poems that became *The Arrivants,* he was also writing his most important early essay, "Jazz and the West Indian Novel." Early in that essay he argues that "there is no West Indian jazz. The urban, emancipated Negro musical forms in the West Indies, where they appear at all—the calypso in Trinidad, the ska in Jamaica, and the similar, related forms in some of the Spanish and French islands—are concerned with protest only incidentally. . . . There is no suggestion of alienation, no note of chaos in calypso" (1993b, 59). By contrasting the smooth sounds of calypso with the more jagged, dissonant sounds of jazz, Brathwaite again brings to the fore the subversive force of art, jazz in this case, and argues that truly emancipatory art must be subversive in both its form and content. Accordingly, the "post-emancipation protest" music of the Caribbean "has achieved little or no liberating, self-creative expression. . . . the development here has been mainly literary: in the words, the lyrics, not in the impulse of the music itself" (1993b, 60). We need to recall that this essay was first published in 1967, before reggae music was in full flower. In a footnote added to the essay in 1983, he acknowledges that the situation has changed in fifteen years: "Jamaican reggae, emerging out of the cultural revolution of the 60s, especially under the aegis of its ikon, Bob Marley, has transformed Caribbean musical expression & nativized it in form, content and symbolization. Similar, if less dramatic developments also took place in the calypso, not only in the nature of the lyrics, but in the intensification of musical form" (1993b, 59). It was during those fifteen years, years in which reggae became an indigenous form of political art as revolutionary in its sounds as in its lyrics, that Brathwaite began work on his three trilogies. In the 1995 interview, Brathwaite speaks of the origin and development of that work in terms that recall the arc and return of that pebble skipping on the sea off the coast of Barbados.

> When I started, I was concerned with trying to write a syncopative narrative, a narrative of broken chain, broken islands, broken slavery, and therefore, the lines of the poetry in a technical sense of poetics were very thin lines, like Miles Davis' trumpet. That was the idea. But as I became more confident—I think this is what happened—I came back into the Caribbean and I discovered that jazz was a trigger. But because I recognized that jazz was still not native to us, increasingly the folk music of the Caribbean took over for jazz. It was the cayso and then the kumina. I found that the poetics began to follow. (1995)

This movement from a somewhat hesitant "syncopative narrative" of lines broken like a Miles Davis solo to a confident embrace of his own culture's music as a model for his poetry underlies the often radical changes in content, form, and typography that occur across the range of his three trilogies. Yet those changes, radical as they may be, are consistently in the service of Brathwaite's principal project: the development of nation language and a poetry consonant with it.

Given this developmental claim, we should start where Brathwaite starts:

> Drum skin whip
> lash, master sun's
> cutting edge of
> heat, taut
> surfaces of things
> I sing
> I shout
> I groan
> I dream
> about
>
> (1973, 4)

These lines open "Prelude," the first poem in the first section, significantly titled "Work Song and Blues," of the first book, *Rights of Passage,* of *The Arrivants.* From the beginning, then, Brathwaite confronts the reader with that syncopated, broken narrative that tells of "broken chain, broken islands, broken slavery." The image of the drum, as we will see, runs throughout Brathwaite's poetry, and it often signifies the origin of song and dance, of community and communication, of subversion and rebellion, so it is fitting that it be the first word in his first trilogy. The second word elicits multiple possible readings and initiates the tactic of ambiguity that permeates this broken or fragmented poetic history: "skin" can refer to the surface of the drum or to the surface of a human, a slave, being whipped. And the break between the first two lines separates, but only briefly, the implement of the action, the whip, from its consequence, the lash across the skin. The comma in the second line creates another ambiguity. Is the "master," who may be seen as the agent of the whipping action, the slave owner or the sun, whose "cutting edge / of heat" resembles the "cutting edge" of the whip in line 1? This second ambiguity sets up one of the central questions of *The Arrivants:* was the enslavement of many Africans caused by a cosmological judgment levied by angry or spurned gods (the "master sun"), or was it caused by a more mundane agent, cultural imperialism (the "master" as marauding slave trader)? No wonder the "I" of this passage reacts to this scene with such a disparate display of emotion—singing, shouting, groaning, and dreaming.

"Prelude" then moves through a very elemental and highly compressed poetic history of the migration of African peoples prior to the invasion of European slave traders. We witness the "hot / wheel'd caravan's / carcases / rot" as that migration progresses from east to west to a place where "cool / dew falls / in the evening"—a place where those people are enjoined to

> Build now
> the new
> villages, you
> must mix spittle
> with dirt, dung
> to saliva and
> sweat: round
> mud walls will rise
> in the dawn
> walled cities
> arise
> from savanna and
> rock river bed:

O Kano Bamako
Gao
(1973, 4–5)

The need to combine earth and water, fire and air together to form a culture requires not only skill and ingenuity but, it seems, the cooperation of the gods. In charting the "fall" of this emergent civilization in *The Arrivants,* Nathaniel Mackey traces the effects of "the necessary failure of the gods" to protect West Africans from themselves and the imminent invaders from Europe, which, as Mackey shows, is a theme that runs throughout the three books of Brathwaite's first trilogy (1993c, 140). Immediately following the passage commanding the construction of the civilization, we learn that "populations of flies / arise from the cattle / towns," and, as a result, "Milk / curdles in / udder" (1973, 5–6). These lines suggest that civilization may be the cause of its own demise: domesticating animals creates "cattle," which create flies and the consequent diseases they carry—diseases that affect both humans and animals, causing milk to spoil in the udder. Whether these cultural conditions are explained as the fruits of the betrayal of the gods or whether the betrayal of the gods is a narrative created to explain the cultural conditions is left unresolved in *The Arrivants.* And we find a similar lack of resolution when the issue of the arrival of European slave traders is raised: are the gods agents of the action, or are they explanatory surrogates for the real agent, imperialism?

This lack of resolution or ambivalence finds its central image near the end of "Prelude":

> Flame
> that red idol, is our power's
> founder: flames fashion wood; with powder,
> iron. Long iron
> runs to swords,
> to spears, to burnished points
> that stall the wild, the eyes, the whinneyings.
>
> Flame is our god, our last defence, our peril.
>
> Flame burns the village down.
>
> (1973, 8)

In the elemental world of ancient West Africa, fire is both founder, defender, and destroyer of this emergent civilization. The image of flame invokes Ogun, the Yoruba god of fire, and, as Mackey asserts, "the technological motive or imperative he thus embodies" (1993c, 142)—an imperative that creates tools of agriculture as well as weapons of war.

Yet fire is also used to make musical instruments. In "The Making of the Drum," the second poem in *Masks,* the second book of the first trilogy, Brathwaite recounts the ritual process of making an instrument that is not primarily a source of entertainment but a means of communicating with the gods. "First the goat / must be killed / and the skin / stretched" in order "to make a thin / voice that will reach // further than hope / further than heaven" (1973, 94). The theme of sacrifice continues in the poem's second section, in which the barrel of the drum is cut from the "*tweneduru* tree." This cut unleashes the voice of nature—the "wounds / of the forest," the "vowels of reed- / lips, pebbles / of consonants" (1973, 95). Then the wood is subject to the shaping flame:

> You dumb *adom* wood
> will be bent,
> will be solemnly bent, belly
> rounded with fire, wound-
> ed with tools
>
> that will shape you.
> You will bleed,
> cedar dark,
> when we cut you;
> speak, when we touch you.
>   (1973, 95)

Here, Brathwaite subtly emphasizes the agency of the human rather than divine, the "we" of the people rather than the "they" of the gods: it is this "we" that makes the drum speak. Brathwaite carries this movement from the divine to the human to its conclusion in the final section of "The Making of the Drum":

> God is dumb
> until the drum
> speaks.

The drum
is dumb
until the gong-gong leads

it. Man made,
the gong-gong's
iron eyes

of music
walk us through the humble
dead to meet

the dumb
blind drum
where Odomankoma speaks:
                    (1973, 97)

"God," then, gains voice through the drum, and the drum gains voice
through the "Man made" gong, whose "iron eyes // of music" are forged
in fire.

The colon in the final line of "The Making of the Drum" leads directly
into the next poem, "Atumpan," the talking drum through which Odomankoma, the Sky-God-Creator of the Ashanti people, both speaks and
is addressed. In "Note(s) on Caribbean Cosmology," Brathwaite defines
atumpan as "**(drum & more recently pan) (integration vibration—
man's voice of god etc—that links the sacred & secular into a cosmology of kinesis that interweaves & does not separate the two**" (1996,
2). The poem "Atumpan" captures this interweaving of the sacred and the
secular with its percussive, syncopated lines, beaten out in Ashanti—"*Kon
kon kon kon / kun kun kun kun*"—and in its dialogic message from and to
Odomankoma:

The Great Drummer of Odomankoma says
The Great Drummer of Odomankoma says

that he has come from sleep
that he has come from sleep
and is arising
and is arising

like *akoko* the cock
like *akoko* the cock who clucks

Kamau Brathwaite: Tidalectic Rhythms 151

who crows in the morning
who crows in the morning

we are addressing you
ye re kyere wo

we are addressing you
ye re kyere wo

listen
let us succeed

listen
may we succeed . . .

(1973, 98–99)

For the Ashanti, success entails the journey to and construction of Kumasi, "city of gold / paved with silver, / ivory altars / tables of horn" (1973, 138). For Brathwaite, success entails a similar journey and construction.

"Atumpan," like most of the poems in his first trilogy, grows out of Brathwaite's sojourn in Ghana. "In the ten years that I lived in the Gold Coast/Ghana, was I able 'slowly, slowly, ever so slowly to understand—to begin to glimpse/to understand, something of where we had come from—as I moved slowly towards, let us call it, Kumasi, City of Gold, at the ?start & centre—in a sense, at the *interior* of my journey" (1994b, 75). Kumasi was the ancestral seat of power of the Ashanti nation, and it is also, for Brathwaite, the utopian image of a unified African civilization to which he staged a pilgrimage during his stay in Ghana and sought an audience with Nana, the "Prempeh" or leader of the city. Brathwaite and his friend were denied an audience and, as a result, received their own lesson in history: "we—Citizens of the World and now would-be Africans and Diasporans—did not know that it was the West India Regiment, hurriedly summoned from its Caribbean stations in 1895 or thereabouts [this info was supplied, after imprecations as to why we could not meet w/ Nana, by his okyeame] that had brought about the defeat of the nation & th(e) banishmant of Prempeh to the Seychelles in 1896 at what the history books claim to be 'the hands of the British.' " It was only after learning "this mikkle of our history" that Brathwaite began "the real what I have called *interior journey* into the history & culture of our *selves*" (1994b, 77). As the "drum [of Kumasi] grows / in the moon- / light," then, the journey from the "interior" of Africa and the self begins, for Brathwaite, to arc out toward his own history in the Caribbean, which is the subject of *Islands,* the third book of his first trilogy.

And it is the image of the talking drum that Brathwaite uses to articulate or connect the histories of Africa and the Caribbean. As he points out, the power of Atumpan was not lost on those who sought to control the victims of the Middle Passage:

> In 1740 in the English-speaking Caribbean, and a little later in the Spanish and French Caribbean, the drum was banned because "they" recognized that there was some connection, the planters said, between rebellion and lion and drum. What they didn't recognize is that there is also a connection between drum and rebellion and culture—and, as I've said over & over again now, they are all cosmo/logically connected So that even though dem ban the drum, they couldn't kill/silence it, since we turn to hum and hannclap and footstamp, voice vibration . . . (1996, 17)

The "cosmo/logical" connection between the cultures begins in Africa and sounds itself through the drum and, despite the ban, into the Caribbean. In "Shepherd," Brathwaite rediscovers the drum's voice in the rites and rituals that result from the mix of African and Christian ceremonies: "Dumb / dumb / dumb // the drum trembles / the knocking wakes its sound / the tambourine tinkles // and my feet have found / the calling clear" (1973, 186). As in "The Making of the Drum," "God is dumb / until the drum / speaks"; here, however, it is the gods rather than the single god Odomankoma, "but the gods still have their places; / they can walk up out of the sea / into our houses . . . Every tree praises them / every ambition that aspires; / the drum praises them // and the rope that loosens the tongue of the steeple; / they speak to us with the voices of crickets, / with the shatter of leaves" (1973, 190). The mix of animistic and Christian images in Caribbean poetry in general and Brathwaite's in particular highlights the conflict between a history that colonialism almost successfully effaced and one it almost successfully imposed.

This conflict is beautifully expressed in "Tizzic," which is the name of a man who "prefer the booze / an' women" (1973, 260). In the poem's second part, which I will quote in full, we find Tizzic celebrating Carnival:

> For he was a slave
> to drums, to flutes, brave

brass and rhythm; the jump-up saved
him from the thought of holes, damp,

rain through the roof of his have-
nothing cottage; kele, kalinda-stamp,

the limbo, calypso-season camp,
these he loved best of all; the road-march tramp

down Princess Street, round Mar-
aval; Kitch, Sparrow, Dougla, these were the stars

of his melodic heaven. Their little winking songs carried him back to days of green unhur-

ried growing. The Car-
nival's apotheosis blazed for two nights

without fear or sorrow, colour bar
or anyone to question or restrain his height-

ened, borrowed glory. He walked so far
on stilts of song, of masqueraded story; stars

were near. Doors of St. Peter's heaven were ajar.
Mary, Christ's Christmas mother was there

too, her sweet inclined compassion
in full view. In such bright swinging company

he could no longer feel the cramp
of poverty's confinement, spirit's damp;

he could have all he wished, he ever
wanted. But the good stilts splinter-

ed, wood legs broke, calypso steel pan
rhythm faltered. The midnight church

bell fell across the glow, the lurch-
ing cardboard crosses. Behind the masks, grave

Lenten sorrows waited: Ash-
Wednesday, ashes, darkness, death.

After the *bambalula bambulai*
he was a slave again.

(1973, 261–62)

Tizzic, then, is a slave in two senses: to his passion for music and dissi-
pation and to the poverty imposed by the form of colonialism that hides
behind the "mask" of Christianity. Although the first form of slavery—
to the drums, flutes, and brass of calypso music—can free him from the
second form of slavery, that freedom is only good for "two nights / without fear or sorrow" brought on by the "colour bar" of colonialism. Once
that brief time has passed, the "Doors of St. Peter's heaven" slam shut,
and Mary's "sweet inclined compassion" fades as the masks are removed,
revealing "ashes, darkness, death."

Although for Tizzic Carnival is ultimately a disguised ritual of submis-
sion, it can also be a ritual of subversion, a time when nation language can
make itself known. Brathwaite connects Carnival—which, on its surface,
is the Christian ritual signifying the beginning of Lent—with the African
ritual of *konnu*, which serves to ward off the terrible effects of the harmattan winds in West Africa. Like the drum, this ritual was banned because
the plantation masters saw it as a form of rebellion. But an element of
the konnu/carnival ritual was permitted—the part of "*carnival* that took
place before light, before dawn, i.e **in the dark**—*jouvert, (jouver, jou'vert,
jour ouvert*—the(e) beginning of the day . . . Here were and are the masks
(& masques) that re/membered (and re/enacted) the dismembered & dis-
remembered *lwa* African gods African forms that would be allowed to
process during only the hours of early darkness." Participants in *jouvert*
cover themselves in mud and molasses, which is a symbolic way of "pro-
pitiating and appropriating the something you are supposed to be—mad,
mud, African and ugly." In one sense, this ritual seems fairly demean-
ing, but in another sense, it subverts the colonialist attempts to wipe out
all traces of African culture in the Caribbean. Thus, *jouvert* "becomes
tremor, count-er-tenor, counter-trauma—productive reinvestment (in the
sense of clothing & later *possession*) in the destitution which is now revealed
as apparent only—the mud & molasses revealing themselves not as insults
or self-insults, but as living, darkly glistenin(g), human ital masks—and
look. *subtle but significant in that mud & molasses*—the symbols of vege-
tation, birth, rebirth, regeneration: grass & straw & green (another *mki issi*
from the 'vert' in *jouvert*) & glitter" (1996, 13). Beneath what appears to be a

Christianized ritual, we find a celebration of African culture that subverts concentrated attempts to wipe it out and cover over the holes in history those acts of colonial aggression create. It is no accident, then, that the final poem in *The Arrivants* is titled "Jou'vert":

> So
>
> *bambalula bambulai*
> *bambalula bambulai*
>
> stretch the drum
> tight hips will sway
>
> stretch the back
> tight whips will flay
>
> *bambalula bambulai*
> *bambalula bambulai*
>
> kink the gong gong
> loop and play
>
> ashes come
> and Christ will pray
>
> Christ will pray
> to Odomankoma .
>
> (1973, 267)

From the sounds of the drum and whip we hear of the ultimate act of subversion: the God of the Christians bows down to the God of the Africans—Christ prays to Odomankoma. In the ritual of *jouvert* the sorrows of enslavement "burn to ashes // grey rocks / melt to pools // of lashes' / sweat and flowers // bloom along the way // *bambalula bambulai* / *bambalula bambulai* // flowers bloom / their tom tom sun // heads raising / little steel pan // petals to the music's / doom" (1973, 268–69). As the sun's drum beats and dawn rises over "shattered homes" and "musty ghettos," the participants in *jouvert* watch

> in the Lent
>
> en morning
> hurts for-

gotten, hearts
no longer bound

to black and bitter
ashes in the ground

now waking
making

making
with their

rhythms some-
thing torn

and new
                    (1973, 269–70)

In one sense, Brathwaite's first trilogy ends where it began, with the rhythms of Atumpan, the talking drum. Yet the three books of *The Arrivants* bring us back to that beginning informed by a poetic history that, like the arc of the pebble Brathwaite cast as a child across the waves breaking on Brown's Beach, take us from that beach in Barbados over to Africa and back again to feel in the tidalectic rhythms of his poetry "some- / thing torn // and new"—a new vision of the Middle Passage that subverts, through the poetic tactic of nation language, a vision of that catastrophic event that would see it as either an unfortunate moment in the march of Western progress or as the complete destruction of the people and culture that were the victims of it.

Brathwaite's second trilogy, *The Ancestors,* traces a similar arc. *Mother Poem, Sun Poem,* and *X/Self* begin in Barbados, move out to the Caribbean as a whole, then toward a global history of the conflict between colonizers and colonized, and finally return back to Barbados. *The Ancestors,* however, is not a simple repetition of *The Arrivants.* Brathwaite's second trilogy presents a more detailed poetic history of Barbados, particularly in *Mother Poem* and *Sun Poem,* and of the interaction between races in the modern world, particularly in *X/Self.* The second trilogy also presents a much more personal poetic history; the "I" in *Mother Poem* and *Sun Poem* is less representative and more autobiographical than in *The Arrivants.* Like the first trilogy, the second one answers a series of questions:

"Where were you born? The nature of your landscape? *Mother Poem:* the mother, the coral, limestone. Then, is that your only source of influence, power, aura? The answer was no, there was a male element as well, your father. *Sun Poem:* light, air, in addition to water and ocean. And then the third movement, the resolution into myself, into *X/Self* " (1991, 43). And in the second trilogy we find that, as Mackey concludes, "nation-language itself assumes a much more prominent, pervasive role in the second trilogy than in the first" (1994c, 737). The fractured words, ana-grams, neologisms, and "calibanisms"—Brathwaite's term for his tactical combinations of English and nation language words—"question the very notion of proper speech" as a way of "decolonizing the word" (1994c, 734). Yet these poetic tactics also signal the emergence of the African elements in Caribbean culture.

In *Mother Poem,* these elements emerge almost against the will of the book's geologic, cultural, and personal protagonist: the mother. In the book's preface, Brathwaite explains that "This poem is about porous lime-stone: my mother, Barbados: most English of West Indian islands, but at the same time nearest, as the slaves fly, to Africa. Hence the protestant pentecostalism of its language, interleaved with Catholic bells and ku-mina" (1977, no page number). The "mother" is both Brathwaite's island and the woman who gave birth to him, and the book takes up the issue of the mixture of Christian and African rituals that produce the "protestant pentecostalism" of nation language. Thus, "The poem is also about slavery (which brought us here) and its effect on the manscape. So we find my mother having to define her home as plot of ground—the little she can win and own—and the precious seedling children planted for the future. But that plot and plan is limited and constantly threatened or destroyed by the plantation and the fact that the males of her life have become creatures, often agents, of the owner-merchant" (1977, no page number). Brathwaite's calibanism, *manscape,* articulates the connection between the geologic "landscape" of Barbados and the plight of the humans that were brought there. More pointedly, the book traces the effects of slavery on the women of the island, so "mother" refers as well to all Caribbean women of African ancestry. *Mother Poem* is Brathwaite's most extended poetic investigation of gender issues as they intertwine with issues of race and class, and much of the book explores the ways in which his island and its women deal with the effects of slavery on men as they become co-opted by the very system that oppresses them.

Particularly in "Nightwash," the book's second section, Brathwaite writes of the many degrading things African-Caribbean women must do to keep their "body and soul-seam together." In "Miss Own," we find women "Selling calico cloth on the mercantile shame- / rock" and "half-sole shoes in the leather / department" (1977, 35–36); in "Horse weebles" a woman is "sellin biscut an sawlfish in de plantation shop" (1977, 38). Ultimately, these women are "forced into a series of expedients, ending in prostitution, love-loss, and abortion; though it is at this very moment of *extremis* that she discovers her underground resources (her *nam*)" (1977, no page number). This moment of discovery in which those underground resources make themselves known is the moment when the remnant of African culture in the Caribbean emerges. I mentioned earlier that this remnant emerges almost against the will of the mother, so this moment of discovery in *Mother Poem* is a highly ambivalent experience and often occurs in scenes of glossolalia, which, in Brathwaite's poetry, figure as reluctant expressions of the repressed in the eruption of nation language. This experience of glossolalia is at the heart of the "protestant pentecostalism" that characterizes the language of *Mother Poem*. Yet his use of the term "protestant" has its subversive angle, since the book is largely a protest against the imposition of Christianity on the victims of the Middle Passage and their descendants. As was the case in the American South, the women of Barbados and the Caribbean were the backbone of the Christian church, and, as a result, the emergence of the underground resource that comes from Africa would mostly likely encounter more resistance from women than men. As we read through *Mother Poem,* we find the protagonist in all her guises moving from an unquestioned acceptance of Christianity to an almost complete rejection of it. I say almost because the expression of that rejection comes from somewhere other than the will of the mother. In "Angel / Engine" in particular, we witness a scene of glossolalia in which a stammering, stuttering rejection and replacement of Christianity occurs while the mother is "possessed." Before turning to that key poem, however, we need to trace the path that leads from acceptance to rejection.

In the book's first poem, "Alpha," Brathwaite sets up two of the many meanings of "mother," the first of which is geological:

The ancient watercourses of my island
echo of river, trickle, worn stone,
the sunken voice of glitter inching its pattern to the sea,

> memory of foam, fossil, erased beaches high above the eaten
>   boulders of st philip
>
> my mother is a pool

(1977, 3)

Most primally, the mother is water and the father, as we will see in the second book of *The Ancestors,* is the sun; she "rains upon the island with her loud voices" (1977, 3). Yet *Mother Poem* is full of images of dryness, which suggest that the "original" source of water, that which remains underground, has been blocked. In the poem's second section, an "I" depicts a domestic scene where we are introduced to a father who works in a sugar "warehouse" and has "gone out to the world columbus found / to the world raleigh raided / to the plantation ground // while my mother sits and calls on jesus name // she waits for his return" (1977, 4). I suggest the mother here is a representative figure for those women in the Caribbean who found perhaps their only solace in the promises of Christianity. Yet that solace has made her passive; her only activity in this poem is waiting for "his" return, which may refer to either the father or Jesus. Another voice emerges in the third and final section of the poem; here, we encounter the language of Christian spirituals with four repetitions of the phrase *"when the roll is called up yonder,"* followed by the affirmative conclusion of the whole statement, *"when the roll is called up yonder i'll be there"* (1977, 5). That this section is all in italics is significant since Brathwaite often uses italics in *Mother Poem* to signal that a cultural rather than individual "voice" is speaking. In this case, it is the cultural voice of Christianity, but in a later poem, "Prayer," that cultural voice begins to recede as another begins to emerge.

In "Prayer" the congregation of a church is going through the motions of reciting the Lord's Prayer when the repressed African remnant intrudes: "our father which art in // *kilimanjaro* // hallowed be thy // *nyam*" (1977, 82). Here, nation language is used to dis- and re-locate the divine; rather than locate the father in heaven, he is found in Africa, and his *nyam* is to be revered rather than his name. For Brathwaite, *nyam* is one of the most important terms in nation language. In a note to the poem "Nam" in *X/Self,* he tells us that *nam* "means not only *soul*/atom but *indestructible self/sense of culture under crisis.* Its meaning involves root words from many cultures (meaning 'soul'; but also (for me) *man* in disguise (*man* spelled backwards)); and the *main* or *mane* of *name* after the weak *e* or tail has been eaten by the conquistador; leaving life (*a*/alpha) protected by the boulder consonants *n* and *m*. In its future, *nam* is capable of atomic explosion: *nam . . . dynamo . . . dynamite* and apotheosis: *nam . . . nyam . . . onyame . . .*" (1987, 127). Given these multiple meanings of the term, its insertion into the Lord's Prayer clearly subverts the monologic, monotheistic intent of that prayer, while at the same time it affirms that which steps forward when a culture is in crisis—"maimed" but still in possession of a "nyam" that, although submerged, is capable of exploding in a dynamic moment of apotheosis. As we move through "Prayer," the italicized passages become more and more subversive to the extent that the cultural voice of Christianity, which spoke in italics in "Alpha," is replaced by the cultural voice of nation language—a voice wanting to dismiss rather than accept the solace Christianity offers and beginning to confront Christianity with its complicity in colonialism. Thus, the last two italicized phrases in "Prayer": "*endure thy ministers with righteousness*"; "*o lord save thy king/doom . . .*" And thus, the protagonist begins her own apotheosis in the poem's concluding line: "my mother blazes forth to these from faithless night" (1977, 85).

An important moment in this apotheosis of the mother and, as it turns out, Brathwaite as well, occurs in "Angel/Engine," another poem set in church; but this time the church is a carpenter's shop, and the service has a much more pentecostal flavor. In *Barabajan Poems* Brathwaite recounts the episode that generated the poem. While he was in the process of composing *Mother Poem,* he walked by the carpenter shop one night as "de zion" meeting was in session.

I mean you have the sound of the drums the tambourines. voices in many ranges. the hand*clap* hand*clap*/ a faraway washing/ hand*clash* syncopation/ an underground volcane of voice/ sound & throat/ pulse & naaase & deep *chest/belly* vibe (1994b, 178)

If we recall Brathwaite's description of what happened when the drum was banned in the Caribbean, that the people turned "to hum and hannclap and footstamp, voice vibration," then we can see this service as the descendant of that earlier moment in Caribbean history, although the drum has been reclaimed. When Brathwaite enters the carpenter's shop, he sees a woman "**sinuously moving froward & froward & wheeling & twisting . . . comin(g) into the being of Da Da Damballa the Dahomean loa of movement & healing & rainbow**" (1994b, 179). The woman in this pentecostal service, then, is possessed not by the "Holy Spirit" of Christianity but by the African goddess Damballa. Not only is there a displacement of religion here but a displacement of gender as well: like the other members of the Christian Trinity, the Holy Spirit is assigned a masculine pronoun; thus, in this service "he" is replaced by "she." Witnessing this possession "**drags** [Brathwaite] **tidalectic into this tangled urgent meaning to & fro . like foam . saltless as from the bottom of the sea . dragging our meaning our moaning/song from Calabar along the sea-floor sea-floor with pebble sound & conch & wound & sea-sound moon It could have been Yemanjaa . That night it was Damballa . dancing with that whisper of a sound inside a simple unsuspecting shop in Mile&Q, Barbados**" (1994b, 182). What he has seen, Brathwaite concludes, is the "**transmigration of simple Bajan country worshippers from Christian God to African apotheosis**" (1994b, 184).

Yet the realization of this apotheosis is not as complete for the woman or, it seems, for the rest of the congregation. Once again, Brathwaite uses italics in "Angel/Engine" to signal when a cultural voice is speaking to or through an individual voice. At the beginning of the poem's second section, the woman chants "*praaaze be to god,*" which soon becomes "*praaaze be to gg*" (1977, 98). The stutter suggests the woman's increasing inability to say "god," but by the end of the poem she is also unable to vocalize the replacement: "praaaze be to // *sssssssssshhhhhhh*" (1997, 103). What she is unable to name here is the

> Yoruba/Dahomey god Shango of hammer & axe & electricity & fire & blinding lightning/thunder . . . who, with Ogou his brother/half-brother of metal, xpresses himself in the Americas as among other ikons John Henry the legendary African-American folk hero th(e) rebel hammermann working the railway tracks; as Bob Marley (listen to *Comin in from the cold,* for instance/Marley began life as a Trench Town electrical/welder); as Aretha Franklin = Oya—Shango's wife/sister (really "female interpart"/listen to her *Pullin*)—all these trainsong trainsounds—all those trai(n) spirituals & blues—Jazzversions too—. . . John Coltrane's axe/hammer saxophone / Legba's inverted symbol crutch & Elvin Jones th(e) sweating angel/engine w/ him on *Giant steps, Impressions & Soul Train*

> the long line of worksong fieldhollers . howlinwolf blues gospel & boogie-woogie . . . and the hissing snake/steam Damballa—**gods of the**

Middle Passage—who came over—who arrive—walking on the water of our conscience (1994b, 172–73)

Although Brathwaite is able to decode the underground resource in this moment of glossolalia and trace the transmigration of the African cosmology to the Caribbean and the American South, at this point in *Mother Poem,* the protagonist is unable or unwilling to be completely possessed by this resource. In the poem following "Angel/Engine," we learn that "my mother watches the marshalled angels / brass tinkle gong gong / the shinning trumpets of the damned going forth" (1977, 104).

The final poem in *Mother Poem,* "Driftword," however, suggests that the mother will ultimately allow herself to be possessed by her true heritage. Although the mother still "dreams of michael who will bring a sword" (1977, 112), the poem holds out hope that the very ceremony that keeps her within the confines of Christianity will also be the scene of her transformation:

> let it be hand and clap and tambour
> and she will praise the lord
>
> so that losing her now
> you will slowly restore her silent gutters of word-fall
>
> slipping over her footsteps like grass
> slippering out of her wrinkles like rain
>
> re-echo of the stream and bubble
> re-echo of the cliff and scarface mountain
>
> past the ruinate mill and the plantation stable
> past the bell and the churchwall, the chapel
>
> half-trampled with cordia leaves: the graveyard of slaves
> (1977, 117)

Brathwaite brings together in this passage the different meanings of mother as woman and as the island's source of water so that the restoration of one is the restoration of the other. When both return to their underground resource of African ancestry, the "the ancient watercourses" of Barbados will finally begin "trickling slowly into the coral / travelling inwards under the limestone // widening outwards into the sunlight / towards the breaking of her flesh with foam" (1977, 117).

That movement into sunlight marks the place where the first book of

Brathwaite's second trilogy joins with the second book, *Sun Poem,* which takes up the "male element" figured as light and air. This book begins with "Red Rising," a poem that ties together the creation of the earth with the creation of the ground of Brathwaite's poetry. In this cosmogony, "song" is already present "When the earth was made" and "the son of my song, father-giver, the sun/sum / walks the four corners of the magnet, caught in the wind, blind // in the eye of ihs own hurricane" (1982, 1). The sun, then, is the son of song, and the sun and the earth or mother produce life, but they also produce the *son.* Thus, under the name of "Adam," Brathwaite investigates his own childhood as a representative "son" of the elements on Barbados. *Sun Poem* follows Adam/Brathwaite as he moves with his mother and father from the *"brick brack plantation shack"* (1982, 5) in the middle of the island to their new home next to Brown's Beach in Bridgetown, which lies on the western or "sunset" side of the island. Throughout the book, Brathwaite ties the development of Adam to the interactions of water and light, the mother and father of all. The poem "Orange Origen" takes another look at the scene of Brathwaite's call to poetry; here we see Adam as he wakes up on his first morning in his new home and sees on his bedroom wall the reflection of the sunlight dancing on the waves. "Son" recounts Adam's plunge into the sea when "he saw the white sand coming to meet / him through the huge sun" (1982, 13). And "Yellow Minnin" brings the innocent youth, who observes how "the sun made patterns on the water that gave birth to children," face to face with the dreamless world of work, exploitation, and capitalism as he learns that "the sons of the earth ignore dreamers // faced with bone iron steel" (1982, 19, 37). *Sun Poem* also marks a change in form as Brathwaite begins to mix in passages of prose poetry along with verse, and it is often in these passages of prose poetry that nation language makes its appearance.

Although these early poems are filled with the language of dialect, it is only in "The Crossing" and "Noom" that the shift from dialect to nation language takes place. These two poems enact "the Middle Passage in reverse" (1982, 100), as Adam attends a school excursion to "the island's other shore: at bathsheba and cattlewash: the ragged coasts where the sun came from" (1982, 39). The journey to the eastern or "sunrise" side of Barbados takes Adam to the side of the island that faces Africa. In "The Crossing" we again find italicized passages that signal the cultural voice of Christianity. As the boys board the buses, they hear an *"aaaamen /* to the godspeed prayers in the church" and sing a hymnlike song on the way: *"we're going to a wonderful place"* (1982, 40). And as they drive up Hearse

Hill near the center of the island, the boys become frightened by the ascent and call on God for deliverance: "*is it me o lord? is i is the one? / dear god if it isnt too late to pray lemme pray*" (1982, 44). When the bus reaches the top of the hill, the boys can look down to the sea "so far far below that they gripped their seats was the promised land" (1982, 45). Yet that "promised land" does not initiate Adam into the folds of Christianity but into the underground resource of his African heritage and into the horrific history of the Middle Passage, all of which takes place in "Noom."

Brathwaite recounts in prose poetry Adam's encounter with "the cattle-wash boys" in the poem's second section, an encounter that gives him his first taste of African/Caribbean cosmology:

it had happened a long time ago said the cattlewash boys longer ago than uh nevvah remember when the *loa* came out of the sea the sun shining down and everything peaceful when they lifted themselves loudly heavy and darkly out of the water chasing their dreadren out of the sea . . . as he fled said the cattlewash boys he grew taller and taller pushing the water before him bringing bad weather ashore . . . coming in slowly loudly and legba . . . it took half a day before he could reach the shore [. . .] once he had stopped turned looked back at his home . . . at the sea and the distant thinder of guinea [. . .] and standing there still and looking there longing he would have seen his brothers watching . . . *ga dagomba dogon dahomey* [. . .] so he had roamed said the cattlewash boys raging along the thundery coast tearing the trees uprooting foundations of quietest rock tumbling boulder on boulder until they resembled his anger [. . .] and when his raving was done he had stood on a cliff called hackletons cliff and gazing full at the sun that was beating tormenting drums in his head he had raised his head in a shout so loud it had entered the gullies and rocks and was heard in the hills and howls of that place with the sound of wind in a cavern

it was noon

and his cry grew greater as the pain of the world grew black for him and he staggered and fell slipped staggered and fell down hackletons cliff down past the few bent coconut trees [. . .]

falling full length in the water

he dead where yu stannin now said the cattlewash boys (1982, 51–52)

For Adam/Brathwaite, this is a highly significant encounter and constitutes a second scene of origin for his work: "So that in the same way that on Brown's Beach there was the genesis of islands with my pebble; here now on the other side of the island, another beginning with these great eastern boulders, closest to maroon & slave & heroes & Africa: the god Legba I celebrate here, being the lord of beginnings" (1994b, 230). What emerges from these scenes of origin are two poetic histories of Barbados in particular and the Caribbean in general—one from the "inside" that traces the arc of the pebble on Brown's Beach from Barbados out to the Caribbean and then to Africa, and one from the "outside" that traces the arrival, against their will, of the *loa* or gods from Africa. The other four sections of "Noom" fill out this second history.

In the poem's first section, a ship arrives on Barbados with the first colonists-mercantilists aboard. At first, they try to cultivate Barbados for profit with their own labor, "but the sun was too hot and their waxen flesh / melted like candles of fetish or faith within their wooden churches // they saw their profits recede like hope or mirage" until "their grey folded thoughts turned to africa" (1982, 47–48). Following a compressed history of the assault on Africa in search of slaves, we find a series of instructions for slave owners to help them keep control over their "property": "above all, love / ignore their songs their manimal membranes resounding with the / sounds of their godderel / and don't try to learn their langridge: teach them spanglish / preach them rum" (1982, 49). The prescription here is clear: ignore or suppress the music and language the slaves bring with them; teach them hybrid forms of language that will allow a modicum of communication while keeping slaves illiterate; and keep them drunk— to this day Barbados is one of the world's leading producers of rum. The poem's third section depicts the arrival of the slaves and the prospering of the colonial economy. It also includes a plaintive supplication to the sun:

> sun have you forgotten your brother
> sun have you forgotten my mother
> sun who gave birth to shango my uncle
>   who was fixed in his place by ogoun the master of iron . . .
>
> sun who has clothed arethas voice in dark gospel
>   who works on the railroad tracks
>   who gave jesse owens his engine
>   who blue coltranes crippled train

remember us now in this sweat juiced jail
in this hail of cutlass splinters of cane
in this pale sail of soil

(1982, 53)

As in "angel/Engine" and *Barabajan Poems,* Brathwaite articulates connections between Shango the Yoruba/Dahomey god of thunder and lightning
and the "trainsongs" of black musicians and athletes, but in this poem the
sun is figured as father to them all. The fourth part of the poem chronicles
the 1816 slave revolt, one of the few that occurred on Barbados, led by
Bussa and Washington Franklin. Significantly, this section also marks the
most sustained eruption of nation language to this point in Brathwaite's
work, and, as in *Mother Poem,* the most subversive moments in this account are italicized:

> *we gine block evry blow dem can pelt*
> > *like a stick*
> *man gwine bite dem like*
> > *shaego or shark*
>
> *cause all a man want in dis worl*
> *is de peace a e pipe an a lit*
> *tle tobacco or ganja or snuff*
> *an e umman*
>
> *an de right to walk or ride bout*
> > *dis parish*
> *wid a fair field under de eye*
> *a e foot an no favour*

(1982, 59)

This revolt caught the plantation owners by surprise: "de white / people
vex // dat we fight / in instead a flight // in from dem jess be / cause a dis
man // who couldnt care less / bout defeat: wha name so: // *e mane bussa*"
(1982, 60). The final italicized line takes on even greater significance if
we recall that *mane* is one of the derivations of *nam,* which "means not
only *soul*/atom but *indestructible self/sense of culture under crisis.*" This revolt ultimately failed, and that failure and others like it populate the fifth
and final section of "Noom," for "heroes were in books / and few of our
fathers were heroes // and we their sons learnt mainly to survive / although

a few went out and fought / or spoke brave words from pulpits" (1982, 61). Thus, the sons of the sun in Barbados are left to live in a culture that has no monuments to the furtive heroism of their progenitors—no monuments to those who worked in the "factory of mister massa midas," to "those who built canoes sculls schooners / those who could peel and plane sandpaper cedar / carving out rockers and glimmering banqueting tables and chairs," and to "those headmaster backyard schools / who got up dawn each morn / ing to fuel // a promising scholarship pupil with words / with latin verbs with white hope with the right / rote" (1982, 61–62).

Sun Poem contains many other poems that detail the son's path to manhood. "Clips" finds a number of sons coming to grips with the human frailties of their fathers; "Return of the Son" depicts Adam's initial sexual encounters with women; "Fleches" has Adam reflecting on pictures of his parents' wedding and early pictures of himself; and in "Indigone" he witnesses his grandfather's funeral and his own father's grief. But the discovery of the underground resource of his island's history in "Noom" is the most significant rite of passage in this transitional book. If the second trilogy's third book, *X/Self*, enacts Brathwaite's "resolution into myself," then *Sun Poem* and *Mother Poem* create and then clear the ground for that resolution.

As J. Edward Chamberlin asserts, "*X/Self* tells of a journey home, a journey both geographical (from Africa and Europe to the West Indies) and psychological (from a diminished sense of self to a liberated one), and both linear and cyclical" (190). Yet that journey does not entail a turn toward a simple autobiographical mode of writing history poetically; *X/Self* deploys nation language in a montage style that brings European and Amerindian history into play to a much greater extent than in his earlier work. As a result the "self" in this book is an *X*—a variable determined by the historical and cultural context in a given poem. This formal change in *X/Self* is, according to Brathwaite, a consequence of "my widening sense of history, of the influences that make up not only the biological history of the Caribbean but the personal one, the intellectual history. *X/Self* is a biography of my history, if you can put it that way. It is how the things that influenced my own growing up—not the physical aspect of the growing up—in a sense it is a Calibanization of what I have read, the things that informed my growth in terms of ideas" (1991, 44).

In his notes to *X/Self*, Brathwaite calls the kind of poetry that inhabits the book "magical realism" and "magical montage" (1987, 113, 115). For Brathwaite, magical realism is, as he tells Mackey, "the conversion once

more of the deterioration of images from one thing to another, the transformation of *reality*. . . . It is a kind of surrealism as well, but magical
realism, I think, is nearer to it, because it is the transformation of reality
into this prism of imagination and light" (1991, 50). The connections between magical realism, surrealism, and montage form in *X/Self* resemble
Walter Benjamin's historical project discussed in the introduction, and, as
with Benjamin, we need to see Brathwaite's use of these linguistic tactics
as much more than a change of style: they constitute a critique of traditional approaches to history and of the written forms those approaches
take. As Keith Tuma argues, "What Brathwaite calls 'magical realism' is
constituted not just by a rejection of the content of European history, but
also by a rejection of the form of such history and the ideas of reason, language, teleology, progress, and 'realism' such forms sustain" (93). I have
argued throughout this chapter that Brathwaite's poetry constitutes a critique of both the content and form of received versions of history, but
the intensity of his formal critique reaches a crescendo in *X/Self*. Recall
Benjamin's claim that "Thinking involves not only the flow of thoughts,
but their arrest as well. Where thinking suddenly stops in a configuration pregnant with tensions, it gives the configuration a shock, by which
it crystallizes into a monad" (1968, 263–64), and that the compositional
method of montage is one of the most potent ways of producing this
shock. The tension Brathwaite generates between images from different
historical periods, juxtaposed in ways that simultaneously flatten and accentuate the temporal differences, and the tension he generates between
different language games, between nation language and more traditional
forms of poetic discourse, not only "arrest" the traditional narrative of
progress that underwrites colonialism; they also deliver a stunning shock
to that system, making the holes in history visible.

The first few stanzas of "Julia" illustrate this point:

In that long gown supple marble plinth capital column superb
balustrade of breasts
i see where ceasars young mulatto sister will parade her
formidable chic

we know she knows no hens
ice
picks perhaps
the blue cubes placid in the crusted frost electric gourd

but claudius her husband never is at home
at grapetime tv supper time or when she takes her pills
and now there is terracing of worry underneath her eyes
that all the dark mascara of the evenings cannot hide

would you have married ali when he was mohammet of the blow
by blow? would you have made it on the late late
cosby show? you would sign i know to appear with apollo
but could you boogie boogie on down

with tina and toots at the apollo?

for a long time now there have been rumours at court
montgomery bus boycott stars falling on alabama
now we are the world will the new posse take you along?

(1987, 12)

In the "magical montage" of this poem, Brathwaite juxtaposes at least
three historical periods in which an empire is in a moment of crisis: Rome,
as it begins its decline, America, as it is confronted by the demands of
African-Americans in the late 1960s, and America at the time the poem is
being composed, the mid-1980s when the culture industry "produced" the
simulated presidency of Reagan/Headrest. The figure of Julia cuts across
all three time frames: she is Caesar's sister and Claudius's wife during the
Roman empire; she has the title role in the first prime-time television
show, aired in the late 1960s, to star an African-American; and she is a
potential guest on the most successful television show starring an African-
American, the Cosby show of the mid-1980s. This montage of images
"arrests" the narrative of progress in a number of ways. First, it suggests
that the role of women as window-dressing has changed very little and
that their identity is still determined by their relations with men. Julia is
left with little to do but look good while she worries about her husband.
Second, it suggests that people of mixed race are simultaneously marginalized and exploited by the dominant culture in half-hearted attempts to
redress the problems that cause events like the "montgomery bus boycott."
Third, it suggests that the products of contemporary consumer culture are
merely pacifiers—ice from an "electric gourd" and advertising slogans pro-
moting a capitalist version of multicultural consumption in which "we are
the world." And fourth, the deliberately banal rhymes and rhythms of this
passage—so distinct from the nation language rhythms that characterize
most of Brathwaite's poetry—suggest that mainstream poetry may also

participate in the commodification of culture. Particularly in the fourth stanza, the rhyming of "blow," "show," and "apollo" trivializes the options traditionally offered to someone like Julia.

Brathwaite sustains this critique of capitalist consumer culture throughout *X/Self*. In "X/plosive video tape salesman," the variable self takes on the persona of one who markets a device that literally represents history as a simulated event, which makes him an almost omnipotent manipulator in contemporary culture: "i / can breach your banks // i / can corrupt your citadels // i / am in easy reachings of your / heart your harbours & your clanks // i / can easily enter you through / this likkle ewer of bleeps" (1987, 40). As the poem progresses, this "i" is "trying to say what my name" is (1987, 41) by reciting a series of historical events at which he was present:

> that's me
> winding the clock
> on the remmington rifle
>
> that's me
> slipping the bolt back for the west
> at amoy
>
> & clambering down
> the trap
> doors at troy
>
> that's me
> mopping up the mess
> at thermopylae
>
> that's me
> with the king
>
> that's me
> with the cong
>
> that's me
> with king kong
>
> i
> am locking him
>
> up
> in the mekong delta with

        blondie

        that's me
        at the helm with the poison pen . . .

        that's me
        at the forge
        sledgehammer of cloud

        bellows of hiroshima

        that's me
        walking away
        in the shroud of the flame
                                        (1987, 44–45)

Brathwaite's fast-paced montage simultaneously collapses and heightens
distinctions between mythical and historical wars—Troy and Vietnam;
between minor and major acts of destruction—a single rifle and an atomic
bomb; and between modes of reproduction—writing ("poison pen"), film
(King Kong), and comics (Blondie, "the eternally young, sensible Mrs.
Middle America," as he puts it in his notes to this poem). By the end of the
poem, the "i" partially says his name, and the other interlocutor of this dialogic poem responds: "christ/opher who?" (1987, 47)—which combines a
reference to Christ and Columbus in a dialectical image, to use Benjamin's
term, that suggests that the "X/plosive" video salesman is a metonymy for
the cultural confluence of Christianity, capitalism, and colonialism.

    At the heart of this confluence is, for Brathwaite, the underground re-
source of African-Caribbean cosmology, which is at once a resource of affirmation and resistance, of vision and revision; and at the heart of that resource is the African god whose name could not quite be spoken in *Mother
Poem*—Shango, *loa* of thunder and lightning. In the final poem of *X/Self*,
we find this god as the ultimate variable in the "resolution into myself"
that obtains in the last book of his second trilogy: *Shango* now becomes
Xango. Rather than a repressed moment in an experience of glossolalia,
Xango is not only named but figured as the source of a "new breath" and a
"victory of sparrows" (1987, 107). In the third section of the poem Xango
is seen as an "ikon" surviving in Abomey, ancient capital of Dahomey:

        and all this while he smiles carved terra cotta
            high life/ing in abomey
        he has learned to live with rebellions

book and bribe
bomb
blast and the wrecked village

he is earning his place on the corner
phantom jet flight of angels
computer conjur man

he embraces them all

for there is green at the root of his bullet
michelangelo working away at the roof of his murderous rocket

he anointeth the sun with oil
star.tick.star.tick.crick.et.clock.tick

and his blues will inherit the world

(1987, 109–10)

Despite the efforts of Christianity, capitalism, and colonialism, Xango survives as the remnant of African culture, enduring the Middle Passage and inheriting the New World with "his blues"—"after so many twists / after so many journeys / after so many changes // bop hard bop soul bop funk / new thing marley soul rock shank / *buck johnson is ridin again*" (1987, 110–11). Thus, the apotheosis of Brathwaite's vision in this poem, as it is in virtually all of his work, is catalyzed by the music derived from African origins. Xango "embraces them all" through this music, the ancient rebels as well as the contemporary "computer conjur man."

And it is also through that music—first heard by Brathwaite in those "plangent syllables of blue, the on-rolling syncopation, the rhythmic tidalectics" in Barbados on Brown's Beach—that others may tap into that underground resource that wells up in Xango and "embrace / him." Much more than a simple affirmative utopian gesture, it is highly subversive as well, since "he will shatter outwards to your light and calm and history" to deliver a shock to the configuration of history that presents itself as the univocal march of progress in Western culture in such a way that our "thunder has come home" (1987, 111). The tidalectic rhythms Brathwaite heard as a young boy when he skipped that pebble across the waves return us home to a sense of history that includes that which has been submerged—the underground resource of Africa, carried by the slaves across the Middle Passage into the Caribbean and up into the United States as the sound of an originary song that Western history has only begun to hear.

Female slaves will be provided who, through marriage with the male slaves, will
make the latter less eager for revolt, and the number of runaways will be
reduced to a minimum.

　　　　　　—Ferdinand, king of Spain, to Miguels Pasamonte,
　　　　　　　　treasurer for Hispaniola, April 1514

5. M. Nourbese Philip
"Dis Placing" Him

When M. Nourbese Philip cites King Ferdinand's letter in *"Dis Place
The Space Between,"* she does so to draw attention to the public policy
that determined the essentially conservative role black women were assigned in colonial culture in the Caribbean. "The black woman comes to
the New World with only the body. And the space between. The European buys her not only for her strength, but also to service the black man
sexually—to keep him calm. And to produce new chattels—units of production—for the plantation machine. The black woman. And the space
between her legs," which is also the "'black magic' of the white man's
pleasure," and, thus that space becomes "the fulcrum of the New World
plantation" (1994, 289–90). Black women were brought to the Caribbean
both to serve and conserve plantation culture against their will. Throughout her work, Philip conducts a poetic investigation of the displacement
of "dis place," of the ways black women's bodies, specifically their genitalia, have been treated as the property of men, both black and white, in
order to return "dis place" to black women. Her work brings together two
of the central concerns of this book, race and gender, in a historically informed and aesthetically compelling series of books that range widely in
forms of poetry, fiction, and critical prose.

　　Yet her work also addresses issues of class as well as race and gender.
As Johnetta Cole contends, "women in the Caribbean who work other
than domestic work are mostly self-employed as purveyors of cooked

foods, seamstresses and petty traders"; thus, "it should be emphasised that although there are some black women in the Caribbean (as in the USA) who become professionals, the majority of black women remain at the bottom of the labor-market: ununionized and underpaid and as a group paid less than men for the same job done" (10). For Philip, who was born and grew up in a middle-class family in Tobago, the world Cole describes was the one she and members of her class were trying to transcend. As Philip recounts in "The Absence of Writing or How I Almost Became a Spy," which serves as an introduction to *She Tries Her Tongue, Her Silence Softly Breaks*, "Black and brown middle class people—my family, short on money but long on respectability, belonged to this class—wanted their children to get 'good jobs' and, better yet, go into the professions. Massa day was done and dreams were running high. . . . Education was going to be the salvation of the black middle classes—so we believed—and a profession was the best proof that you had put servitude behind you, and were becoming more like the upper classes" (1989, 10–11). Judging by this standard, Philip's life has been a great success: she took an undergraduate degree in economics from the University of the West Indies, a master's degree in political science from the University of Western Ontario, and became a lawyer and practiced immigration law in Canada for seven years. Yet that very standard contained a silent proscription: "Profession, vocation, career—anything but writer" (1989, 11).

That middle-class proscription cannot simply be attributed to the fact that writers, for the most part, do not make much money and will therefore have great difficulty maintaining middle-class status. For many Caribbeans, writing is the exclusive property of the ruling classes; consequently, Philip "never contemplated that writing would be a profession for me because the black middle classes and even the working classes in the Caribbean never thought of writing as something worthwhile to do. That was something white people did, white men, so there was nothing that I could model myself on" (1996, 23). The proscription against writing encodes elements of race, class, and gender bias since it is seen as an activity of wealthy white men. More important, writing is clearly a subversive activity that seeks to undermine the conservative impulses many Caribbeans inherit from the "plantation machine." For Philip, these impulses can only be uncovered and overturned by a thorough investigation of language, because "only when we understand language and its role in a colonial society can we understand the role of writing and the writer in such a society; only then, perhaps, can we understand why writing was not and still, to a large degree, is not recognized as a career, a profession, or a way of be-ing in the Caribbean and even among Caribbean people resident in Canada" (1989, 11–12). As we saw in the last chapter, language, particularly the standard British English taught in the schools of the Anglophone Caribbean, was and continues to be a means of repressing the African remnant in that culture and replacing it with the traditions and values of Christianity, capitalism, and colonialism. Rather than conserve this legacy, Philip, like Brathwaite, works to subvert what she calls the "father tongue" of the patriarchal, colonial language and recover what she admits is unrecoverable: the "mother tongue" of Africa.

So Philip, like the other four writers discussed in this book, envisions writing as a subversive activity that disrupts or "arrests," to use Walter Benjamin's term, the traditional narrative of Western history. Thus, "The power and threat of the artist, poet or writer lies in this ability to create new i-mages, i-mages that speak to the essential being of the people among whom and for whom the artist creates. If allowed free expression, these i-mages succeed in altering the way a society perceives itself and, eventually, its collective consciousness" (1989, 12). It is important to note that her fracturing of the word *image* into *i-mage* "does not represent the increasingly conventional deconstruction of certain words, but draws on the Rastafarian practice of privileging the 'I' in many words" (1989, 12). Philip's distinction amounts to much more than a simple clarification of word choice since "I" is perhaps the word most often subject to "conventional deconstruction." The critique of essentialist claims for identity has been a crucial issue in much contemporary investigative poetry, yet it is a critique that needs careful consideration when it is applied to marginalized groups and their work. As bell hooks warns in "Postmodern Blackness," "should we not be suspicious of postmodern critiques of the 'subject' when they surface at a historical moment when many subjugated people feel themselves coming to voice for the first time" (28). The danger here is that overgeneralized assertions about the pitfalls of "identity politics" may abrogate, intentionally or unintentionally, the "power and threat" of artists from marginalized groups. "Any critic exploring the radical potential of postmodernism as it relates to racial difference and racial domination," hooks contends, "would need to consider the implications of a critique of identity for oppressed groups" (26).

To avoid forestalling the subversive potential of work such as Philip's, we need to acknowledge that not all assertions of identity can simply be dismissed as reinscriptions of the Western tradition that has been deconstructed. To do so is to mistake *a* language game for *the* language game, to put it in Wittgensteinian terms; in other words, a critique of *a* notion of identity, the notion of identity handed down from Descartes to Kant to Husserl, cannot be taken as a critique of *all* notions of identity. After all, Philip wants "to create new i-mages" of identity, not replicate traditional Western images that prop up the system she intends to subvert. By drawing on "the Rastafarian practice of privileging the 'I,'" Philip ties her notion of identity to a tradition that derives from Africa and takes root in the Caribbean; to apply cavalierly the results of a critique pertaining to the Western tradition to that alternative Rastafarian tradition flirts with a kind of philosophical colonialism by implying that it is impossible to think in terms other than those dictated by the Western tradition. I suggest that if we consider identity as primarily a sociological rather than a metaphysical phenomena, then we will be able to do justice to the claims for identity of marginalized groups without either lapsing into the "metaphysics of presence" or dulling the subversive edge of those claims.

For Philip, privileging the "I" in her "i-mages" is a crucial tactic in the project of "altering the way a society perceives itself," particularly when the "I" has been subjugated in that society and not allowed "free expression." This project not only involves educating white readers about the experience of blacks in the Caribbean—it involves educating blacks as well. According to Philip, "I-mages that comprised the African aesthetic had previously been thought to be primitive, naive, and ugly, and consequently had been dismissed not only by white Westerners, but by the Africans themselves living outside Africa—so far were Africans themselves removed from their power to create, control and even understand their own i-mages" (1989, 13). The proscription against African Caribbeans becoming writers needs to be seen in the context of the devaluation by blacks and whites of the African aesthetic: if there is nothing aesthetically pleasing in their African heritage, then writing may not be "something worthwhile to do"; if Western standards of beauty are all that are available, then indeed writing may best be left to "white men." Affirming the beauty in the African aesthetic is the first step in confronting and overturning the conservative impulse that keeps many blacks in the Caribbean from creating, controlling, and understanding themselves and their place in contemporary culture. Creating "new i-mages," whether in the visual, musical, or linguistic arts, is therefore very much a subversive activity that can indeed alter "the way a society perceives itself." Without this activity, Philip argues, African Caribbeans will not be able to move beyond the image of themselves assigned by Western colonial culture:

> The African in the Caribbean could move away from the experience of slavery in time; she could even acquire some perspective upon it, but the experience, having never been reclaimed and integrated metaphorically through language and so within the psyche, could never be transcended. To reclaim and integrate the experience required autonomous i-mage makers and therefore a language with the emotional, linguistic, and historical resources capable of giving voice to the particular i-mages arising out of the experience. (1989, 15–16)

Here Philip offers a prescription for writing designed to overturn the proscription against writing that prevents African Caribbeans from seeing writing as a legitimate career choice. The question remains, however, whether a language with those "emotional, linguistic, and historical resources" is available to aspiring writers in the Caribbean.

There is no simple, unproblematic answer to this question since, as Philip asserts, "The place African Caribbean writers occupy is one that is unique, and one that forces the writer to operate in a language that was used to brutalize and diminish Africans so that they would come to a profound belief in their own lack of humanity" (1989, 19). Like Brathwaite, Philip is acutely aware that she must use a language imposed on her ancestors by the "plantation machine" that stripped them of their original language and caused them to question their status as human beings. The colonial use of the English language not only denigrated the actual and potential beauty of the African aesthetic; it consigned Africans to the category of "other" than human. If the alleviation of this dilemma was merely a matter of "relearning" African languages, then the solution would be relatively simple. But returning to that "origin" would be to deny what has actually happened in history—the almost complete erasure of that origin. "The challenge, therefore, facing the African Caribbean writer who is at all sensitive to language and to the issues that language generates, is to use the language in such a way that the historical realities are not erased or obliterated, so that English is revealed as the tainted tongue it truly is. Only in so doing will English be redeemed" (1989, 19).

For Philip, this challenge is met by embracing the demotic tradition in the Caribbean—a solution that bears a great resemblance to Brathwaite's embrace of nation language. "In the vortex of New World slavery," she contends, "the African forged new and different words, developed strategies to impress her experience on the language. The formal standard was subverted, turned upside down, inside out, and even sometimes erased. . . . The havoc that the African wreaked upon the English language is, in fact, the metaphorical equivalent of the havoc that coming to the New World represented for the African" (1989, 17–18). Thus, using the demotic not only exacts a modicum of revenge; it also embraces the historical reality of what has happened linguistically in the Caribbean. But to write only in the demotic amounts to a denial of the influence of standard English on the experience of African Caribbeans. To reduce the expression of that experience to an either/or option involves an effacement of historical reality and, therefore, of the subversive potential of such writing. Thus, "to say that the experience can only be expressed in standard English (if there is such a thing) or only in the Caribbean demotic (there *is* such a thing) is, in fact, to limit the experience for the African artist working in the Caribbean demotic. It is *in the continuum of expression* from standard to Caribbean English that the veracity of the experience lies" (1989, 18).

All of Philip's work, whether in verse, fiction, or critical prose, investigates this continuum in a variety of aesthetically and politically stunning ways. Although she has published four books of poetry — *Thorns; Salmon Courage; She Tries Her Tongue, Her Silence Softly Breaks;* and *Looking for Livingstone* — one novel, *Harriet's Daughter* — and a collection of critical essays, *Frontiers: Essays and Writings on Racism and Culture* — her work has been the most overlooked of the five writers discussed in this book. This neglect may be due to several reasons. First, because of the proscription against taking up writing as a career, she only began writing full time in 1982, after she gave up the practice of law. Second, she lives in Canada and publishes with small Canadian presses that gain little notice in the United States. Third, she is a black woman working in innovative rather than conventional forms and consequently does not attract the attention that writers like Maya Angelou, Rita Dove, or Lucille Clifton do. Fourth, the content and form of her work may simply be too radical for many readers to accept. If we recall the conservative role black women in the Caribbean during colonialism were assigned, her work represents a full-scale and often blunt assault on the remnants of that role that are still operative in the Caribbean. In her essay "Trinidad and Tobago Women's Writing, 1929–69," Jennifer Rahim remarks that "the literary output of women in Trinidad between 1929 and 1969 displayed a conservatism in terms of the choice of subject matter, its treatment and the lack of concern for women's issues that reflects the nature of their self-awareness and their absorption into the society's gender definitions" (236). Philip is part of a younger generation that takes that conservatism to task in both the form and content of her work by reclaiming ownership of her body, of "dis place," and by redefining her body on her own terms. She "i-mages" her body as much more than a "thing" used to pacify black men or give pleasure to white men. As Philip notes, "there was a profound eruption of the body into the text of *She Tries Her Tongue*" (1989, 24), and that eruption subverts the conservative expectations foisted on black women in the Caribbean. In this chapter, I will trace this eruption as it occurs in two of Philip's books, *She Tries Her Tongue, Her Silence Softly Breaks* and *Looking for Livingstone,* in order to show that writing history poetically is for her a matter of great political and aesthetic concern.

She Tries Her Tongue, Her Silence Softly Breaks, which won the Casa de las Americas prize in 1988, is a tightly organized book that presents a progression of poems exploring "the continuum of expression" between standard English and Caribbean demotic. The book consists of nine sections, each of which presents a dialogic confrontation between traditional Western and emergent Caribbean values and forms. At the beginning of the book, these confrontations seemed to be dominated by Western terms of engagement, but the "voice" of the Caribbean soon takes over and the relation of domination is almost completely reversed by the end of the book. Yet *She Tries Her Tongue, Her Silence Softly Breaks* does not violate the historical realities of the situation in the Caribbean by depicting a complete "victory" over the oppressor culture; it does, however, articulate the increasing power of "her tongue" to both speak and be silent by choice rather than compulsion.

The book's first section, "And Over Every Land and Sea," uses Ovid's version of the Greek myth of Ceres and Proserpine to frame a Caribbean enactment of a mother's search for her daughter and a daughter's search for her mother. By placing quotations from Ovid in italics above the poems, Philip begins her book by keeping the Western and Caribbean poles of the continuum of expression separate and distinct. The contrast between the classical tones of Ovid and the demotic of many of the poems in this section reinforces that separation. On one level, the poems are a poetic rendering of Philip's "exile" to Canada and her mother's attempt to intervene in that event. On another level, they "i-mage" a daughter's search for her "mother" or African tongue that has been silenced by the "father" tongue of English. The first poem, "Questions! Questions!" is a demotic rendition of the mother's initial panic-stricken response to her daughter's disappearance: "Where she, where she, where she / be, where she gone? / Where high and low meet I search, / find can't, way down the islands' way / I gone—south" (1989, 28). The second poem, "Adoption Bureau," is part demotic, part standard English and depicts the daughter's search for the mother tongue she never knew yet misses: "tell me, do / I smell like her? . . . something / again knows sweat earth / the smell-like of I and she / the perhaps blood lost—// She whom they call mother, I seek" (1989, 29).

In "Clues" and "The Search," the mother learns her daughter may be "up where north marry cold I could find she—/ Stateside, England, Canada" and travels north to find "the how in lost between She / and I, call and response in tongue and / word that buck up strange" (1989, 30, 31). And in "Sightings," the daughter engages in a synesthetic questioning of her memory, wondering

> didn't I once
> see her song, hear her image call
> me by name—my name—another sound, a song,
> the name of me we knew she named
> the sound of song sung long past time,
> as I cracked from her shell—
> the surf of surge
> the song of birth.
>
> (1989, 35)

The daughter's memory of her birth metamorphoses into the mother's memory of the same event in "Adoption Bureau Revisited" (1989, 36), the final poem in this section. Here, the mother follows the "blood-spoored" trail that "follows / me / following her /north." The "i-mage" of blood, of "betrayal and birth-blood / unearthed," suggests the mother's loss as she gives birth and as her daughter is taken from her. There is, then, a dual displacement in "dis place," to recall Philip's term for female genitalia— the displacement of the child from the mother during birth and the displacement of the child during her "exile" in Canada, an exile that parallels Proserpine's sentence to spend four months of the year in Hades. And the mother's loss is at once the object of her daughter's search: "She came, you say, from where / she went—to her loss: / 'the need of your need' / in her groin." That this loss in "dis place" is something that neither the mother nor the daughter can overcome is emphasized by the framing quotation

M. Nourbese Philip: "Dis Placing" Him 181

from Ovid Philip chooses for this poem: "*For behold, the daughter I have sought so long has now at last been found—if you call it 'finding' to be more certain that I have lost her, of if knowing where she is is finding her.*"

"Cyclamen Girl," the book's second section, takes up the "i-mage" of blood and uses it as a metonymy for two other moments of "dis place-ment"—a young woman's first experiences of communion and menstrua-tion, both of which involve an "eruption" of the body. In these poems, however, the Western and Caribbean poles of the continuum of expression are not kept separate and distinct as they are in the first section. The result of that separation in "And Over Every Land and Sea" is a somewhat static relationship between the two poles of the continuum. The intermingling of values and forms in "Cyclamen Girl," however, leads to a "transfigura-tion" of a young woman as she rejects one of those poles and embraces the other. This series of poems presents a grown woman looking at a picture of herself, "black girl white dress," as she prepares to take her first commu-nion in the Anglican Church: "So there, circa 1960, she stands—/ black and white in frozen fluidity . . . caught between / blurred images of / massa and master" (1989, 38). In "Vows," she is pictured in her "White / satin ribbons / White / cotton sox / White / Bata shoes / White / Book of Com-mon Prayer / White / satin-cotton confirmation dress / White / Soul."

> The cyclamen girl
>
> > stood
> >
> > ready
> >
> > to
>
> Promise
>
> > the triple lie
>
> She
>
> > who believed
> >
> > in and on
> >
> > the "triune majesty" —
> >
> > > sunshine
> > >
> > > black skin &
> > >
> > > doubt
>
> (in that order)
>
> > (1989, 41)

Once again, the conflict between black and white, Caribbean and Chris-tian involves displacement. However, rather than being the object of that displacement, the cyclamen girl is the agent. And the direction of the displacement has changed: the Caribbean trinity of "sunshine / black skin & / doubt" replaces the Christian trinity of Father, Son, and Holy Spirit, which reverses the original displacement enforced by colonialism. Note also that the new trinity is gender neutral, which displaces patriarchy as well.

"Transfiguration" (1989, 42–43) subverts one of the most significant epiphanies of Christianity, the moment when Jesus unveils his divinity to his male disciples on Mount Hermon. Philip replaces that epiphany with one in which a girl unveils her womanhood. "In the ceremony of White / The cyclamen girl would answer / To her name." The ambiguity of the phrase "answer to" can be read as either a locution of accountability or of identification, an ambiguity that begins the subversion. The correct answer to the question posed in the "White ceremony" — the gateway to communion, the ritual in which believers consume the blood of Christ — is, of course, Mary, Mother of God. The displacement of her name by first Aphrodite, the Greek goddess of love and beauty, then by Atabey and Oshun, two African goddesses, parallels the displacement of the "answers" and "promises" of the Christian ceremony by "First the drums / Then the women [who] / Called out her name." Again, the ambiguity of the last line is rich: are the women calling out Atabey's name or the cyclamen girl's? This ambiguity suggests that the transfiguration occurring here is from one girl to many women who are one with many names.

As she whirls
Into the circle of grief
For her fleeting childhood
Passed like the blood
Of her first menses
Quick and painful
Name her

Rhythm!
Song!
Drum!

Mahogany-tipped breast catches
The glare of the fires
Women of the moon feast and fast
And feast again

Name her

M. Nourbese Philip: "Dis Placing" Him 183

Aphrodite! Mary! Atebey!
Orehu! Yemoja!
Oshun!

For her newly arrived wound
Name her!
(1989, 42–43)

Philip's communion ceremony exchanges the blood of Christ for the blood of the cyclamen girl's "fist menses": "dis place" has taken "His" place. And her ceremony exchanges the call and response of the Anglican catechism for the call and response of African music. Philip's transfiguration enacts the redemption of the African aesthetic, which has been repressed and denigrated by the Western tradition; as a result, it rather than the Western aesthetic will dominate the continuum of expression in the rest of *She Tries Her Tongue, Her Silence Softly Breaks*. The next two sections of the book take a look at this African aesthetic from the perspective of an African Caribbean woman looking at herself and at the way she and other members of her race are looked at.

"African Majesty" (1989, 48–49) begins with a poetic landscape seemingly from Africa: "Hot breath / death-charred / winds / depth-charged / words: / rainfall / magic / power." But we soon discover the landscape is a simulation, an exhibit in the "mute / muse / museums / of man," the Barbara and Murray Frum Collection in this case. Placing *muse* in between *mute* and *museum* locates the poetic tactic waiting to subvert this simulation. The muse offers "i-mages" of "wanderers / in the centuries of curses / the lost I's." Although the exhibit is "filtered of fear / by light of the au courant of fashion / the wisdomed wood / stripped of reason / restored to 'living / proof' of primitive aesthetics," and although the "lost I" of the poem knows the exhibit "prisons and prisms the real"—that "I" also knows that the real cannot be erased. It is there, in history and in its holes, its presence and absence of equal note, ready "to adorn the word with meaning / to mourn the meaning in loss." As we saw in "And Over Every Land and Sea," loss was at once the daughter's inheritance and clue concerning her "mother tongue"; "African Majesty" takes up that dual role of loss, but it also carries the critique of representation much further. In terms of the poem's form, "African Majesty" uses much more of the page than the poems that come before it. In one sense, Philip critiques one form of writing African Caribbeans are expected to exhibit, the craft of British verse; this poem and many of those that follow it look like they were written by William Carlos Williams or Ezra Pound, not Percy Shelley or Alfred Lord Tennyson. In terms of the poem's content, she critiques the exhibit's simulation of African culture but moves beyond it by imagining a less simulated version of that culture, one that includes the meaning of loss as well as the loss of meaning.

In "Meditations on the Declension of Beauty by the Girl with the Flying Cheek-bones" (1989, 52–53), the book's fourth section, Philip investigates another dimension of the African aesthetic, physical beauty. This is also the poem in which a new "i-mage" of the "I" takes over the book. Embracing "the Rastafarian practice of privileging the 'I'," she interrogates the "owners" of the English language. Philip first asks, "In whose language / Am I I am / If not in yours." The instant shift from ontological question to affirmation in the second line privileges the "I" not as a unitary, autonomous *cogito* but as activity engaging in a process of identification open at once to doubt and certitude, a process registered in the way the questions in the poem, which can be taken as straightforward or rhetorical, are posed. Philip next asks about the standards of beauty encoded in that language. She asks about the "Girl with the flying cheek-bones," the "Woman with the behind that drives men mad," about the "woman with a nose broad / As her strength," and wonders where her place in that language is. The final question of the poem is much more of a declaration than a query: "In whose language / Am I / If not in yours / Beautiful." This moment of affirmation is, however, equally a moment of resignation since it also suggests that there really is no alternative language by which to be judged. Once again, loss is at the core of the daughter's search for a mother tongue to counteract the dominance of the father tongue—the received tongue of patriarchal colonialism. That Philip calls her interrogation of the way black women are looked at a "declension" suggests the extent to which her poetic investigation focuses on the structures of power that underwrite the grammar of displacement. The next three sections of *She Tries Her Tongue, Her Silence Softly Breaks* hone in on the connection between grammar and power in a stunning display of writing history poetically.

For Philip, a change in content means a change in form; radical content means radical form. The next three sections of her book become more radical in both senses. "Discourse on the Logic of Language" begins a series of poems that juxtapose differing accounts of the origin and use of language. Four language-games compete for attention, visually as well as verbally. I treat this four-page poem as two visual events, each composed of the recto and verso of facing pages; this way, all four language-games can be seen at once. Running up the left margin of the left page, turned ninety degrees from "normal," a passage playing the language-game of cosmology offers an account of the origin of language: "WHEN IT WAS BORN, THE MOTHER HELD HER NEWBORN CHILD CLOSE: SHE BEGAN THEN TO LICK IT ALL OVER. THE CHILD WHIM-PERED A LITTLE, BUT AS THE MOTHER'S TONGUE MOVED FASTER AND STRONGER OVER ITS BODY, IT GREW SILENT" (1989, 56). If we follow this voice over to the next page, we learn that the mother "TOUCHES HER TONGUE TO THE CHILD'S TONGUE, AND HOLDING THE TINY MOUTH OPEN, SHE BLOWS INTO IT—HARD. SHE WAS BLOWING WORDS—HER WORDS, HER MOTHER'S WORDS, THOSE OF HER MOTHER'S MOTHER, AND ALL THEIR MOTHERS BEFORE—INTO HER DAUGH-TER'S MOUTH" (1989, 58). The unadorned language of this passage gives it a primal, elemental tone as it renders the ur-myth of the mother tongue. The absence of any images of oppression suggests that the "time" of this passage predates the imposition of patriarchy and colonialism. Here the mother is free to pass language on to her daughter; their bodies are not yet the properties of the "plantation machine," and there is no mention of "him."

On the right-hand pages these two passages face, another language-game occurs in which Western science offers one of its versions of the origin of language. First, there is a synopsis of Broca's theory of the brain: "Dr. Broca believed the size of the brain determined intelligence; he de-voted much of his time to 'proving' that white males of the Caucasian race had larger brains than, and were therefore superior to, women, Blacks and other peoples of colour" (1989, 57). On the next recto page, the language-game of "testing" emerges as the poem takes on the form of multiple-choice questions. Both of these passages present methods that measure intelligence and, therefore, the quantity of humanness a thing possesses. These are just two of the more prominent methods of measuring intelli-gence that have been and continue to be used to assign humans rank ac-cording to race and gender characteristics. In *Mismeasure of Man*, Stephen Jay Gould contends science hides its prejudices under the cloak of objec-tivity: "The mystique of science proclaims that numbers are the ultimate test of objectivity. Surely we can weigh a brain or score an intelligence test without recording our social preferences." Gould goes on to debunk this mystique as it appears in Broca's craniology and Binet's IQ scale, conclud-ing that these "arguments for ranking people according to a single scale of intelligence, no matter how numerically sophisticated, have recorded little more than social prejudice" (26, 28). Philip subverts the binary logic of such tests by making most of the responses correct even though they are not "identical" to each other. For instance, the possible conclusions to the phrase "In man the tongue is," include "(a) the principal organ of taste. / (b) the principal organ of articulate speech. / (c) the principal organ of oppression and exploitation. / (d) all of the above" (1989, 59).

In the space between the languages of myth and science, Philip juxtaposes two more language-games, the political and the personal. In the former, edicts for slave owners appear in italics. In the first, we learn that "*Every owner of slaves shall, wherever possible, ensure that his slaves belong to as many ethnolinguistic groups as possible. If they cannot speak to each other, they cannot then foment rebellion and revolution*" (1989, 56); in the second, that "*Every slave caught speaking his native language shall be severely punished. Where necessary, removal of the tongue is recommended. The offending organ, when removed, should be hung on high in a central place, so that all may see and tremble*" (1989, 58). Running between these edicts and the ur-myth of the mother tongue is a passage that takes the tone of most of the book up to this point, a personal yet almost syllogistic tone. In the first stanza, the "I" proclaims "English / is my mother tongue," in the second, "English is / my father tongue," and in the fourth, "I have no mother tongue," which leads her to conclude "I must therefore be tongue / dumb" (1989, 56). The passage ends with a plea for the mother to "tongue me / mothertongue me" (1989, 58), which articulates this language-game with the language of the ur-myth of the mother tongue. The clamor of these four language-games leaves us in a position similar to the first section of the book, "And Over Every Land and Sea," in which a stasis seems to exist between the language of Ovid and the language of the Caribbean. In "Discourse on the Logic of Language," the language-games do not overlap significantly, which is not the case in "Universal Grammar," the book's sixth section.

In this poem, Philip again juxtaposes four divergent language-games, but the displacement of the dominating discourse of Western rationality is much more explicit. "Universal Grammar" refers to the linguistic theories of Noam Chomsky. Philip includes quotations from Chomsky in the poem, cast in upper-case letters, which set up a contrast with the ur-myth of the mother tongue in the last poem. According to Chomsky, "THE THEORY OF UNIVERSAL GRAMMAR SUGGESTS THE WAY WE LEARN LANGUAGE IS INNATE—THAT THE CON-

SCIOUS MIND IS NOT AS RESPONSIBLE AS WE MIGHT BE-
LIEVE IN THIS PROCESS. OUR CHOICES OF GRAMMATICAL
POSSIBILITIES AND EXPRESSIONS ARE, IN FACT, SEVERELY
LIMITED; IT IS THESE VERY LIMITATIONS THAT ENSURE WE
LEARN LANGUAGE EASILY AND NATURALLY" (1989, 65). I doubt
Philip would agree with Chomsky that the ability to learn language is innate, but I am sure she would not agree with the notion that there is a
"universal" structure of grammar. For her, grammar is contingent on the
particularities of its cultural context, and one of those contexts may be
one in which the pretensions to universality are unmasked by willful sub-
versions of standard English. On the pages opposite the Chomsky quotations, Philip offers what are certainly not universal definitions of the parts
of grammar. These begin with a rather bland definition of parsing: "*the
exercise of telling the part of speech of each work in a sentence*" (1989, 62). On
the page opposite these definitions, directly above a passage from Chomsky, are six italicized lines. The first consists only of the word "*Man,*" the
second of "*Man is*"; each line acquires a word until the sixth line reads
"*The tall, blond, blue-eyed, white-skinned man is,*" and that sentence is repeated directly below the quotation from Chomsky, followed by a third
language-game, a poem presenting an alternative "i-mage" of the grammar of memory.

The first four words of this poem—"the smallest cell / remembers"
(1989, 63)—are the subjects of Philip's definitions. She defines "cell" as a
"*—common noun, neuter gender, singular number, third person, nominative
case governing the intransitive verb, remembers. (Long-term memory im-
proves cell growth in nerve cells),*" and she defines "remembers" as a "*regular
verb, transitive, active voice, indicative mood, present tense, singular number,
third person agreeing with its nominative, cell which remembers and so remembers*" (1989, 62). These definitions veer slightly from the norm, but as
Philip's "i-mage" of the grammar of memory precedes, we learn that what
the cell remembers is

> a secret order
> among syllables
>> Leg/ba
>> O/shun
>> Shan/go
>
> heart races
> blood pounds

remembers
               speech
fragments
             brief
      as Sappho's
tremble of tongue on the brink of
ex/
    (when the passage of sound is completely
     blocked a consonant is called)
plosive
tongue on the brink of
ex/
    (prefix — occurring only before vowels)
odus
orcize
on the brink of
ex/
    (to strip or peel off (the skin) 1547)
coriate

The tall, blond, blue-eyed, white-skinned man is shooting

tongue trembles
on the again and again
of forget
                        (1989, 63, 65)

The "secret" rather than "universal" order of language is the object of Philip's investigation: that which the West has almost successfully concealed—the African dimension of Caribbean culture. In her definitions, Philip glosses "O" as a *"sound of exclamation as in O God! Made by rounding the lips; first syllable of word name of African goddess of the river—O/shun"* (1989, 62). That sound is, for Philip, the remnant of remembered speech, a legacy that erupts from the rounded lips of the body as exclamation. This definition clearly takes a subversive angle, displacing "God" with "O/shun," and those that follow become increasingly subversive. The definition for "ex," for instance: *"—prefix signifying in English and Latin 'out' or 'forth' as in exodus—the departure of the Israelites from the black land, Egypt; 'to remove', 'expel' or 'drive out' as in exorcize by use of a holy name like Legba, Oshun or Shango"* (1989, 64). Adding the adjective "black" to the characterization of Egypt brings the racial element of the Exodus to attention, and then, once again, the Western religious tradition is replace by the African Caribbean as the source of definition.

Next, Philip brings the issue of gender to attention with her gloss on "man": "**man**—*common noun, male gender, singular number, third person nominative case governing the verb, is. And woman*" (1989, 64). Man thus defines and governs all that has being, that is, including "woman." Call this the ur-myth of the father tongue, in which language and that to which it refers, all that is, is considered "property" to be used to "his" ends. As we have seen, the uses of African women in the colonial Caribbean, "dis placed" from their bodies and cultures, were primarily sexual and repro- ductive, although physical labor was clearly part of the script as well. As "Universal Grammar" reaches its end, Philip enacts a very radical and em- bodied displacement of man from the center of the definition process:

> Slip mouth over the syllable; moisten with tongue the word. Suck Slide Play Caress Blow—Love it, but if the word gags, does not nourish, bite it off—at its source—
> Spit it out
> Start again
>
> From *Mother's Recipes on How to Make a Language Yours*
> *or How Not to Get Raped* (1989, 67)

Aside from saying "Ouch," this male critic feels the central image in this passage needs little elaboration. Suffice it to say that the "i-mage" of the self here is radically different from Descartes's. Philip presents an "I" that is embodied, sexual, capable of love and vengeance, and, above all, making a language hers.

"The Question of Language Is the Answer to Power" advances a new "i-mage" of the Word, displacing both the Christian tradition of the Word as God and the patriarchal tradition in poetry in which "his" word is art and "hers" is not. The poem opens with a prose section called "*LESSONS FOR THE VOICE (1)*": "*Vowels are by nature either long or short. In the fol- lowing list the long ones appear in capital letters. These vowels are all shaped predominantly by the lips, though the position and freedom of the blade of the tongue affects their quality*" (1989, 70). We are then given a list of phrases that emphasize the pronunciation of the vowel being learned. The items in this list reappear on the opposing page, intermixed with a poem that reimagines the word:

word it off
speech it off
word in my word
word in your word
I going word my word
                    begin
the in of beginning   *OO as in how did they "lose" a language.*
empires   *oo as in "look" at the spook.*
              erect with new
"Make it new"
              he said
"Make it new"
floundering in the old

                             but I fancy the new—
                                        in everything
                             insist upon it
                             the evidence of newness
                                             is
                                        upon us
OH as in the slaves came   without nigger slave coolie
        by "boat."   the wog of taint
AW as in they were valued the word
        for their "brawn." that in the beginning was
                                             —not his
                             I decree it mine
                                        at centre
                             soft
                             plastic
                             pliable
                                   doing my bid as in
                                             smash
                             the in-the-beginning word
                                        (1989, 71)

Philip's dual assault on Pound's poetic dictum to "make it new" and on the
Christian theological dictum that "In the beginning was the Word" allows
the "I" to "decree" language hers. But the italicized portions recognize
how much of the language and the power it carries have been determined

by "him." By placing language-games like these and those in the previous two poems side by side, Philip generates what Benjamin would call dialectical images, which arrest the narrative of history as progress and expose the contingent rather than universal foundations of that narrative.

The final two sections of *She Tries Her Tongue, Her Silence Softly Breaks* extend and consolidate the displacements made so far. In "Testimony Stoops to Mother Tongue," Philip looks again at how African women are judged by the aesthetic standards of beauty defined by Western patriarchy, asserting that "the confusion of centuries that passes / as the word / kinks hair / flattens noses / thickens lips / designs prognathous jaws / shrinks the brain / to unleash the promise / in ugly / the absent in image" (1989, 78). Rather than being a passive describer of what is, the word forms what is by assigning value. The "absent in image," the beauty of African women, erupts in the poem and provokes the poet to ask whether "in my mother's mouth / shall I / use / the father's tongue / cohabit in strange / mother / incestuous words / to revenge the self / broken / upon / the word" (1989, 82). In the final section, which shares its title with that of the book, Philip begins, as in the first section, with a quotation from Ovid, but the poems in this last section go beyond reenactment of a Greek myth: "loosed from the catapult pronged double with history / and time on a trajectory of hurl and fling / to a state active with without and unknown / i came upon a future biblical with anticipation" (1989, 84). The "i-mage" of loss returns here as a state of absence, the "without and unknown," that is essential if history's holes are to be made visible. But this is also a state of the absence of the word as defined by the Western tradition—a state of silence the poet searches in hope that "one song would bridge the finite in silence / syllable vocable vowel consonant / one word erect the infinite in memory" (1989, 90).

By displacing the word with silence, Philip creates the psychological, historical, and textual "space" in which the body speaks through the word rather than the word speaking through the body. The future Philip imagines, "biblical with anticipation," will displace the word as God and logos—as that which defines what is—with the body as the material site of history:

> That body should speak
> When silence is,
> Limbs dance
> The grief sealed in memory;

That body might become tongue
Tempered to speech
And where the latter falters
Paper with its words
The crack of silence
(1989, 98)

In *She Tries Her Tongue, Her Silence Softly Breaks,* Philip confronts us with silence, but this silence has two different origins—one imposed and one earned. To be silenced by command and to remain silent in order to listen to the body are very different experiences. Philip says, "*She Tries Her Tongue* was the call, and *Looking for Livingstone* was the response" to the confrontation with silence in both its senses (1996, 26). If the first book emphasizes the disruption of silence imposed, the second emphasizes the silence earned as a result of the struggle to displace the legacy of patriarchal colonialism in the Caribbean.

As its subtitle, "An Odyssey of Silence," and its dedication, "For the ancestors who have been silent for too long and whose Silence is. Always," indicate, *Looking for Livingstone* is very much concerned with silence and with the transition from imposed to earned silence. In many ways, this work is her most adventurous in terms of its form—mixing narrative prose, verse, travelogue entries, and letters together. Although the book is advertised as being a novel, Philip calls it "a long poem. It was written as a long poem in prose and poetry, and it was the decision of the publisher to market it as a novel. I think there's good reason for that because we live in an age of fictions. The attention poetry needs—to do it, to read it and absorb it—is so rare in today's world. . . . I also think that because it's a quest—there's a beginning, a middle, an end—all these qualities lead one to think of it as a novel . . . but certainly I have always thought of it as a long poem or as prose poetry, and I will insist that that's what it is" (1996, 29). I have used the term *poetic investigation* as a way of including work that is not readily identifiable as verse in this study, and Philip's *Looking for Livingstone* represents a good case in point. It may be important for marketing purposes to assign a work to a particular genre, but to understand the scope and variety of contemporary investigative poetry, it is equally important to allow works to transgress the boundaries between genres.

Looking for Livingstone tells the tale of a black woman, known only as the Traveller, searching the continent of Africa for the Scottish explorer,

Dr. David Livingstone. Her search takes place in an "alternative" time frame, beginning on "THE FIRST AND LAST DAY OF THE MONTH OF NEW MOONS (OTHERWISE KNOWN AS THE LAST AND FIRST MONTH) IN THE FIRST YEAR OF OUR WORD" (1991, 7) and concluding "IN THE EIGHTEEN BILLIONTH YEAR OF OUR WORD, WHICH IS THE SAME AS THE END OF TIME, WHICH IS THE SAME AS THE FIFTEENTH DAY OF JUNE, NINETEEN HUNDRED AND EIGHTY SEVEN IN THE YEAR OF OUR LORD" (1991, 60). Since the historical Livingstone was exploring Africa in the 1850s and 1870s, the narrative could be seen as taking place between 1850 and 1987 in the time of "OUR LORD." In terms of the calendar of "OUR WORD," the Traveller's quest transpires over eighteen billion years. This alternative time line has at least two significant effects. First, it displaces the Christian drama as the benchmark of time and history; rather than calculating time from the advent of "OUR LORD," in *Looking for Livingstone* time is calculated from the advent of "OUR WORD," which I take to be the symbolic moment when the silence imposed on Africans by the Western world is lifted. Second, this alternative time line gives the work the feel of an allegorical journey that takes place "outside" of time as we normally conceive it. The Traveller's quest, then, becomes the search not of a single individual but of an entire race and culture, and Livingstone becomes a symbol for the arrogant claims of the West to have "discovered" Africa.

The narrative begins with the Traveller's first journal entry:

My own map was a primitive one, scratched on animal skin. Along the way, some people had given me some of theirs—no less primitive—little pieces of bark with crude pictures of where they thought I would find what I was searching for. I also had some bones and various pieces of wood with directions incised on them. And a mirror. Where was I going? I had forgotten where I had come from—knew I had to go on. "I will open a way to the interior or perish." Livingstone's own words—I took them now as my own—my motto. David Livingstone, *Dr.* David Livingstone, 1813–73—Scottish, not English, and one of the first Europeans to cross the Kalahari—*with* the help of Bushmen; was shown the Zambezi by the indigenous African and "discovered" it; was shown the falls of Mosioatunya—the smoke that thunders—by the indigenous African, "discovered" it and renamed it. Victoria Falls. Then he set out to "discover" the source of the Nile and was himself "discovered" by Stanley—"Dr. Livingstone, I presume?" And History. Stanley and Livingstone—white fathers of the continent. Of silence. (1991, 7)

A number of the work's important themes appear in this first paragraph: that the Traveller is not quite sure what she is searching for, but that her search entails opening a path to the "interior," which for her is her own interior, not the interior of a continent, as was the case with Livingstone; that the "discoveries" of the West were at best appropriations and were aided by indigenous Africans; and that Stanley and, more significantly, Livingstone are the "white" fathers of Africa and of the silence thereafter imposed on that continent and its indigenous people. The Traveller's discovery of the interior is, therefore, a displacement of the Western appropriation and representation of Africa and its cultures.

Following this first journal entry are two pages of verse that depict the birth of earned silence from the seed of imposed silence:

> I have retched
> —oh my mothers—
> upon its bile
>   whole
> swallowed
> touch prod kick
>   shove
> push
>   I have—
> stroked the kin
>   the stranger
> within it
> taken it to places secret
> with within
> from the between of thighs
>   expelled
> I have
> with the force of full
>   driven it
> —a giant birthing—
> from the hiding of its
> place
>   raw with inside
>   smell

of body
smell of birth

(1991, 8–9)

I take the antecedent of "it" here to be silence imposed by the other, the "stranger," in what may very well be a scene of rape. For Philip, rape in this case is not simply a sexual violation, nor is it necessarily unproductive. As she writes in *She Tries Her Tongue, Her Silence Softly Breaks*, "The linguistic rape and subsequent forced marriage between African and English tongues has resulted in a language capable of great rhythms and musicality; one that is and is not English, and one which is among the most vital in the English-speaking world today" (1989, 23). This poem, then, not only speaks of but stands as an instance of a way in which a violent act of imposition, a physical and linguistic rape of Africans, can be turned against the agent of that violence to give birth to a poetic language true to its historical circumstances.

And the link between sexuality and language is reinforced when the Traveller encounters the first of six bands of people, all of whose names are anagrams of silence. Bellune, the oldest woman of the ECNELIS, gives the Traveller her version of the creation and the fall from grace, from silence in this case:

> "God first created silence: whole, indivisible, complete. All creatures — man, woman, beast, insect, bird and fish — lived happily together within this silence, until one day man and woman lay down together and between them created the first word. This displeased God deeply and in anger she shook out her bag of words over the world, sprinkling and showering her creation with them. Her word store rained down upon all creatures, shattering forever the whole that once was silence. God cursed the world with words and forever after it would be a struggle for man and woman to return to the original silence. They were condemned to words while knowing the superior quality of silence." (1991, 11)

The differences between this cosmogony and the Biblical account are numerous. First, for the ECNELIS, the creator is female, not male. Second, silence was in the beginning, not the word. Third, the first word is not, as it is in the Gospel of John, equated with or created by God; according to Bellune, humans gave birth to the first word. And fourth, in the Biblical account, the unreachable origin is the state before good and evil were introduced as a result of Adam and Eve's transgression, but this state is not one of silence since language was given to humans by God prior to the fall; for the ECNELIS, the acquisition of language is the fall, and the longed-for origin is silence. In the poem following this prose section, Philip writes of the effects this fall has on women in particular: "it bound the foot / sealed the vagina / excised the clitoris / set fire to the bride . . . the ache in chasm / stretched the word / too tight / too close / too loose / nestled in the flesh / grounded / in the or of either" (1991, 13). Thus, the word is anything but an abstract, spiritual entity; rather, it is a physical and psychological tool that exercises power over "dis place" in particular and over women's bodies in general.

Yet as *Looking for Livingstone* progresses, Philip also figures sexuality and reproduction as "i-mages" of reconciliation. Shortly after her first sighting of Livingstone, the Traveller recounts two recurring dreams. In the first, "HE—LIVINGSTONE—AND I COPULATE LIKE TWO BEASTS—HE RIDES ME—HIS WORD SLIPPING IN AND OUT OF THE WET MOIST SPACES OF MY SILENCE—I TAKE HIS WORD—STRONG AND THRUSTING—THAT WILL NOT REST, WILL NOT BE DENIED IN ITS SEARCH TO FILL EVERY CREV-ICE OF MY SILENCE—I TAKE IT INTO THE SILENCE OF MY MOUTH." Although the sex here seems consensual, Livingstone is clearly in the dominant position. But shortly after the sex act is complete, we find Livingstone weeping and telling Stanley "MY WORD, MY WORD IS IMPOTENT . . . WITHOUT MY WORD, THE CONTINENT IS BEYOND ME" (1991, 25). If we recall that the historical Livingstone's major justification for "penetrating" Africa was to bring the "word" of Christianity to the savages, then the fact that his word, at least in the Trav-eller's dream, is impotent suggests that Christianity will bear no fruit on the continent. In the second dream, however, the Traveller dreams she is "HUGE AND HEAVY, BLOWN UP LIKE A SOW ABOUT TO FAR-ROW—THE FRUIT OF HIS WORD. . . . KEENING AND WAILING I TRY TO BIRTH THE MONSTROUS PRODUCT OF HIS WORD AND MY SILENCE" (1991, 26). Although the product of this birth is never explicitly revealed, I suggest that she gives birth to a continuum of expression similar to the one discussed earlier. Here, though, the opposite poles of that continuum are speech and silence rather than standard En-glish and the Caribbean demotic.

But any possibility of reconciliation will require a more balanced rela-tionship between the poles of those two continuums. Before such a balance can be reached, the Traveller must be cleansed of the word in order to truly discover what she seeks—the silence earned rather than imposed. In her stay with the CLEENIS, the Traveller is required, as are all visitors to that society, to spend time in a sweat lodge where words are purged out of the body. Before she enters, she is told that she can choose three words that will survive the purge. "I spent a year . . . in the sweat-lodge, sweating words. How they fled—rushing from all orifices and openings, words evacuating, escaping—fleeing me" until she is left with only her three chosen words: birth, death, and silence. "I would need all three in the sweat-lodge, I had finally reasoned that night, as I lay in my hut and tasted my fear of the unknown and the sweat-lodge. That was all I had— birth, death, and in between silence—all I could call my own—*my* birth, *my* death, and most of all, *my* silence. My words were not really mine— bought, sold, owned and stolen as they were by others. But silence!—such devalued coinage to some—no one cared about it and it was all mine" (1991, 43). In her time in the sweat lodge, the Traveller discovers what she has been seeking all along—something that is hers and hers alone: silence. From this point on in the narrative, she is in possession of herself, her "i-mage," and it is this possession that enables her to encounter the putative object of her search, Livingstone.

Her search, spanning "eighteen billion years—the age of the universe; advancing deeper and deeper into Silence, my silence" (1991, 61), finally ends when she catches up to him in a clearing in the forest. Her meeting with Livingstone, "This old white man—tall, gaunt—my nemesis— half-blind, bronzed by the African sun, the indiscriminate African sun— malarial, sick or crazy" (1991, 61), and the discussion between the two that follows, is on her terms. She begins by thanking him for discovering her silence and starting her out on her journey to the interior, "the source of my silence" (1991, 63). She then cajoles him about his "discoveries" and the help he had from indigenous Africans, help he never acknowledged. And after extracting from him a promise to answer her questions honestly—"I am a man of my word," he replies (1991, 68)—she confronts him with her ultimate question: "Didn't you advocate the destruction of African society and religious customs so you could bring European commerce more easily to the Africans, and then Christianity?" And after a prolonged silence on his part, he admits, " 'Yes, I did, but I had to, don't you see, I had to—my work—' I raised my hand and he fell silent" (1991, 68–69). Her final gesture is significant since she imposes silence on him and thereby displaces him as the source of authority.

Yet the book does not end on this note. After their discussion, which leaves Livingstone on the edge of death, the Traveller reaches

out   my hand   felt the evidence   of SILENCE all around   around me
original primal   alpha *and* omega   and forever   through its blackness
I touched something warm familiar   like my own   hand   human
something I could not   see in the SILENCE   reaching out   through
the SILENCE of space   the SILENCE of time   through the silence of
SILENCE   I touch it   his hand   held it   his hand   *and* the SILENCE
(1991, 75)

Philip has been criticized for ending the book this way, with a silent gesture of reconciliation, and she initially thought that criticism might be all too accurate. But then she "read the entire work through and thought, no, this is what the Traveller has to do. She has come to this point, and she's now her own agent. She can reach out and take Livingstone's hand or not take it. She chooses to take his hand, and it all ends in this Silence. Upper case silence speaking to something larger than both of them. But I think we have to be prepared to enter those moments where we don't know what will come next—that's what the silence means at the end" (1996, 26). The fact that the Traveller chooses to take Livingstone's hand—her "nemesis"—and that Philip endorses this gesture indicates that Philip's poetic investigation amounts to much more than a simple reversal of the established hierarchies between men and women, blacks and whites, silence and the word: reaching out to Livingstone entails a *displacement* of hierarchy, not a *replacement* of one with another. If we recall that this final scene in *Looking for Livingstone* occurs "IN THE EIGHTEEN BILLIONTH YEAR OF OUR WORD, WHICH IS THE SAME AS THE END OF TIME, WHICH IS THE SAME AS THE FIFTEENTH DAY OF JUNE, NINETEEN HUNDRED AND EIGHTY SEVEN IN THE YEAR OF OUR LORD," then I suggest that Philip's Traveller brings us to our present state in contemporary culture—a state "where we don't know what will come next" in the relations between races and genders, where the holes in history have been exposed and a gesture of reconciliation may be at hand.

Such gestures are essential, as are those that come from the other "side," if we are to overcome the crisis in contemporary culture in which underrepresented groups strive to be heard while others strive to impose silence on them once again. But, as Ernesto Laclau and Chantal Mouffe argue, "the form in which this crisis will be overcome is far from being predetermined, as the manner in which rights will be defined and the forms which struggle against subordination will adopt are not unequivocally established. We are faced here with a true polysemia" (168). Like Philip, we do not know what will come next, but I contend that her poetic investigations—along with the work of Susan Howe, Nathaniel Mackey, Lyn Hejinian, and Kamau Brathwaite—articulate possibilities for overcoming this crisis by writing history poetically in ways that do not reduce the "true polysemia" of our situation to a single category of analysis—be it race, class, or gender—or to a single language-game—be it verse, fiction, or critical prose.

In my introduction, I claimed that contemporary investigative poetry is an active participant in the struggles against imperialism and the attempts to roll back the gains made by underrepresented groups in the last thirty years. The five writers discussed in this book refuse to present history as a seamless narrative of Western progress or as a seamless simulation generated by consumer capitalism. Instead, they deploy an array of innovative poetic tactics to subvert both of those views of history and to awaken those who are "sleepwalking through history," to recall Haynes Johnson's phrase. But it would be a great mistake to see the work of Howe, Mackey, Hejinian, Brathwaite, and Philip as mere negations of the dominant ways of representing history. As I have demonstrated throughout this book, each of these writers, in distinct yet related ways, offers a positive alternative vision of the complex process by which underrepresented groups make room for themselves to speak and write in contemporary culture. Without such compelling alternatives, we may indeed end up with Ron Headrest as poet laureate as well as president.

Notes

Introduction

1. For these and other details concerning Max Headroom, see Lili Berko, "Simulation and High Concept Imagery: The Case of Max Headroom," *Wide Angle* 10, no. 4 (1988).

2. Small Press Distribution (1341 Seventh Street, Berkeley, CA 94710, phone [510] 524–1668) is an excellent source for these and other small press books.

3. "Contemporary investigative poetry" seems to me to be a more accurate term than either "language poetry" or "postmodern poetry" for a number of reasons. First, language poetry may be an accurate description of Hejinian's work, but Howe and Mackey, although they publish in the same circles as Hejinian, are not directly part of that movement, and it would be far too appropriative to subsume the work of Caribbean writers like Brathwaite and Philip under that term. And calling the work of these five writers "postmodern" raises more questions than it answers. Does postmodernism refer to a particular historical period that begins either in the late 1950s (Leslie Fielder and Ihab Hassan) or the early 1970s (Fredric Jameson and David Harvey)? Or does it refer to a philosophical debate about Enlightenment rationality (Jürgen Habermas and Jean François Lyotard) that begins with Friedrich Nietzsche in the nineteenth century and culminates in the present with Michel Foucault and Jacques Derrida? Does postmodernism signal a discontinuous rupture with its modernist past or a continuation of it? If the latter is true, does that continuity signify a genuine extension and revision of modernism or a watered-down, made-for-TV repetition of it? Does postmodern art—poetry, in this case—have the capacity to offer a critique of the culture in which it exists, or is it so complicitous with its culture, whether intentionally or not, that it is incapable of offering anything but an affirmative response? Finally, does postmodernism question the possibility of answering any of the questions just raised, or does it offer new, although local and specific, answers? At this point in the debate, I am not sure anyone could or should address all those issues— which may be a sign that the term has become too amorphous to be useful. Furthermore, a number of the writers examined in this book make it very clear that they do not consider their work to be postmodern.

4. My reading of Benjamin is particularly indebted to Susan Buck-Morss's *The Dialectics of Seeing,* Richard Wolin's *Walter Benjamin,* and Julian Roberts's *Walter Benjamin.*

5. For a thorough account of Benjamin's relation to surrealism, see Margaret Cohen, *Profane Illumination* (Berkeley: University of California Press, 1993).

6. See Richard Sieburth, "Benjamin the Scrivener," in *Benjamin: Philosophy,*

Aesthetics, History, ed. Gary Smith (Chicago: University of Chicago Press, 1989) for an excellent analysis of Benjamin's practice of quotation.

7. I do want to acknowledge that my comments about the situation of the working class in the United States may not all apply to the situation in the Caribbean, which is the primary culture for Kamau Brathwaite and M. Nourbese Philip; in short, the relationship between the artist and the working class may be significantly different for these two writers.

8. This rejection leads Steven Best and Douglas Kellner to conclude that Ernesto Laclau and Chantal Mouffe "collapse non-discursive into discursive conditions and privilege discourse over practices and institutions." But Laclau and Mouffe do not necessarily "collapse" one term into another in order to "privilege" one over the other; rather, they reject "the distinction between" the two terms. Best and Kellner, *Postmodern Theory* (New York: Guilford Press, 1991), 203.

9. See the chapter "Force and the Understanding: Appearance and the Supersensible World," in G. W. F. Hegel, *Phenomenology of Spirit,* trans. A. V. Miller (Oxford: Oxford University Press, 1977), 79–103.

10. The obvious exception here is the recent *Norton Anthology of Postmodern American Poetry,* edited by Paul Hoover, which was compiled specifically to counteract the prevailing canon of contemporary American poetry and includes all three of the American poets I discuss. This anthology is not only a welcome exception to the rule but a clear sign that this kind of poetry is indeed infiltrating the institutions that regulate poetry. I should also mention Douglas Messerli's monumental anthology, *From the Other Side of the Century: A New American Poetry 1960–1990,* as another instance of this revisionist moment, but that is published by Sun & Moon Press, which is not primarily in the business of producing textbooks and anthologies for the collegiate market.

Chapter 1

1. Susan Howe's work has received a great deal of critical attention recently. See George F. Butterick, "The Mysterious Vision of Susan Howe," *North Dakota Quarterly* 55 (Fall 1987); Rachel Blau DuPlessis, " 'Whowe': On Susan Howe," *The Pink Guitar* (New York and London: Routledge, 1990); Marjorie Perloff, " 'Collision or Collusion with History': Susan Howe's "Articulation of Sound Forms in Time," *Poetic License: Essays on Modernist and Postmodernist Lyric* (Evanston, IL: Northwestern University Press, 1990); Linda Reinfeld, *Language Poetry: Writing as Rescue* (Baton Rouge: Louisiana University Press, 1992); Peter Quartermain, "And the Without: An Interpretive Essay on Susan Howe," *Disjunctive Poetics* (Cambridge: Cambridge University Press, 1992); Lew Daly, *Swallowing the Scroll: Late in a Prophetic Tradition with the Poetry of Susan Howe and John Taggert* (Buffalo, NY: M, 1994); John Taggert, *Songs of Degrees* (Tuscaloosa: University of

Alabama Press, 1994); Ming-Qian Ma, "Poetry as History Revised: Susan Howe's 'Scattering as Behavior toward Risk,'" *American Literary History* 6 (1994), and "Articulating the Inarticulate: Singularities and the Counter-method in Susan Howe," *Contemporary Literature* 36, no. 3 (Fall 1995); John Palatella, "An End of Abstraction: An Essay on Susan Howe's Historicism," *Denver Quarterly* 29, no. 3 (1995); Peter Nicholls, "Unsettling the Wilderness: Susan Howe and American History," *Contemporary Literature* 37, no. 4 (Winter 1996); Hank Lazer, *Opposing Poetries*, vol. 2 (Evanston, IL: Northwestern University Press, 1996); Megan Williams, "Howe Not to Erase(her): A Poetics of Posterity in Susan Howe's Melville's Marginalia," *Contemporary Literature* 38, no. 1 (Spring 1997); Lynn Keller, *Forms of Expansion: Recent Long Poems by Women* (Chicago: University of Chicago Press, 1997); and Michael Davidson, *Ghostlier Demarcations: Modern Poetry and the Material Word* (Berkeley: University of California Press, 1997).

2. As Peter Nicholls contends, Howe knows that "such [historical] contexts can never be made fully present—the recurring figures of these texts are those of the dark night, of the 'confusion' of the past, of forests and wilderness—but it is that impossibility which redefines the hermeneutic drive as a search for what Howe calls 'trace-stories' rather than for origins" (588).

3. Howe is not only familiar with Benjamin's work, but she is very taken by it. As she tells Keller, "I love his interest in very short essays, his interest in the fragment, the material object, and the entrance of the messianic into the material object" (1995, 29).

4. Although I am reading Howe's embrace of transcendence as a sign of an antiessentialist approach to gender, that desire for transcendence can also be read as part of the religious impulse that animates much of her work. For a reading along these lines, see Lew Daly, *Swallowing the Scroll.*

Chapter 2

1. The phrase is Ezra Pound's, although he claims to derive it from Rudyard Kipling. For a history of this phrase and of three American poems that attempt to tell such a tale, see Michael Bernstein, *The Tale of the Tribe* (Princeton, NJ: Princeton University Press, 1980).

2. These are not the only traditions woven together in Mackey's poetry; elements of European, Arabian, Latin and South American traditions also make their presence felt in the poems.

3. I should point out that these issues are fully addressed in Mackey's third book of poetry, *Whatsaid Serif* (San Francisco: City Lights, 1998), which appeared after I had completed *Poetic Investigations*. I pursue this line of inquiry in "'Some Ecstatic Elsewhere': Nathaniel Mackey's *Whatsaid Serif*," in *Boxkite* 3 (1999).

Chapter 3

1. For reprints of the first three volumes of this magazine, see *The L=A=N=G=U=A=G=E Book,* ed. Bruce Andrews and Charles Bernstein (Carbondale: Southern Illinois University Press, 1984).

2. For other useful accounts of language writing, see Marjorie Perloff's essays on language writing in *The Dance of the Intellect* (Cambridge: Cambridge University Press, 1985), *Poetic License* (Evanston, IL: Northwestern University Press, 1990), and *Radical Artifice* (Chicago: University of Chicago Press, 1991); Lee Bartlett, "What Is 'Language Poetry'?" *Critical Inquiry* 12, no. 3 (1986); Andrew Ross, "The New Sentence and the Commodity Form: Recent American Writing," in *Marxism and the Interpretation of Culture,* ed. Cary Nelson and Lawrence Grossbert (Urbana and Chicago: University of Illinois Press, 1988); George Hartley, *Textual Politics and the Language Poets* (Bloomington and Indianapolis: Indiana University Press, 1989); Linda Reinfeld, *Language Poetry: Writing as Rescue* (Baton Rouge and London: Louisiana State University Press, 1992); Alan Golding, *From Outlaw to Classic* (Madison: University of Wisconsin Press, 1995); Bob Perelman, *The Marginalization of Poetry* (Princeton, NJ: Princeton University Press, 1996); and Hank Lazer, *Opposing Poetries* (Evanston, IL: Northwestern University Press, 1996).

3. I do not believe Kristeva's emphasis on the "trans-linguistic" puts her at odds with Laclau and Mouffe's emphasis on "discourse" since their definition includes both language as a system of signs and the "actions" that accompany that system. In short, "discourse," for Laclau and Mouffe, is similar to what Kristeva calls the "signifying process," which includes, as we will see, the "semiotic" and the "symbolic."

4. Jane Flax's *Thinking Fragments* (Berkeley: University of California Press, 1990), Susan Rubin Suleiman's *Subversive Intent* (Cambridge: Harvard University Press, 1990), and a collection of essays on the topic, *Feminism/Postmodernism,* ed. Linda J. Nicholson (New York: Routledge, 1990), are the most informative books I have encountered on feminism and postmodernism.

5. For critical work on *My Life,* see Marjorie Perloff, *The Dance of the Intellect* and *Radical Artifice;* Michael Davidson, *The San Francisco Renaissance* (Cambridge: Cambridge University Press, 1989); Rae Armantrout, "Feminist Poetics and the Meaning of Clarity," *Sagetrieb* 11 (Winter 1992); David R. Jarraway, "My Life through the Eighties: The Exemplary L=A=N=G=U=A=G=E of Lyn Hejinian," *Contemporary Literature* 33 (Summer 1992); Craig Douglas Dworkin, "Penelope Reworking the Twill: Patchwork, Writing, and Lyn Hejinian's *My Life,*" *Contemporary Literature* 36, no. 1 (Spring 1995); Juliana Spahr, "Resignifying Autobiography: Lyn Hejinian's *My Life,*" *American Literature* 68, no. 1 (March 1996); and Lisa Samuels, "Eight Justifications for Canonizing Lyn Hejinian's *My Life,*" *Modern Language Studies* 27, no. 2 (Spring 1997).

6. The numbers in brackets are mine.

7. For a detailed review of *Oxota,* see Marjorie Perloff, "How Russian Is It?" *Parnassus* 17, no. 2 and 18, no. 1 (1992).

Chapter 4

1. Brathwaite makes great use of different fonts and point sizes in *Barabajan Poems* and in most of his work in the 1990s; I have tried to approximate the look of his "Sycorax Video Style."

2. I should note that I disagree with Brathwaite's evaluation of modern American poetry; I think he would see a more successful break with the iambic line if he considered Williams, Stein, and Zukofsky rather than Whitman, Cummings, and Moore.

3. Given the visual dimension of "Sycorax Video Style" of Brathwaite's third trilogy, I have reserved an account of that trilogy for a collaborative article written with my colleague, Bruce Maylath, an expert in document design and computer-based composition.

Bibliography

Adorno, Theodor. 1977. "Letters to Walter Benjamin." Translated by Harry
  Zohn. *Aesthetics and Politics*. New York: Verso.
Aronowitz, Stanley. 1990. *The Crisis of Historical Materialism*. Minneapolis:
  University of Minnesota Press.
Bagdikian, Ben. 1992. *The Media Monopoly*. Boston: Beacon Press.
Bakhtin, Mikhail. 1981. *The Dialogic Imagination*. Translated by Caryl Emerson
  and Michael Holquist. Austin: University of Texas Press.
Baudelaire, Charles. 1964. *The Painter of Modern Life and Other Essays*.
  Translated by Jonathan Mayne. New York: Da Capo Press.
Baudrillard, Jean. 1983. *Simulations*. Translated by Paul Foss, Paul Patton, and
  Philip Beitchman. New York: Semiotext(e).
———. 1989. *America*. Translated by Chris Turner. New York: Verso.
Beckett, Tom. 1989. "The Difficulties Interview." *The Difficulties* 3, no. 2.
Benjamin, Walter. 1968. "Theses on the Philosophy of History." *Illuminations*.
  Translated by Harry Zohn. New York: Schocken Books.
———. 1978. "Surrealism." *Reflections*. Translated by Edmund Jephcott. New
  York: Schocken Books.
———. 1989. "N." Translated by Richard Sieburth. *Benjamin: Philosophy,
  Aesthetics, History*. Chicago: University of Chicago Press.
Bennett, Tony. 1990. *Outside Literature*. New York: Routledge.
Bernstein, Charles. 1992. *A Poetics*. Cambridge, MA: Harvard University Press.
Bérubé, Michael. 1994. *Public Access*. New York: Verso.
Brathwaite, Kamau. 1971. *The Development of Creole Society in Jamaica*. Oxford:
  Oxford University Press.
———. 1973. *The Arrivants*. New York: Oxford University Press.
———. 1977. *Mother Poem*. Oxford: Oxford University Press.
———. 1982. *Sun Poem*. Oxford: Oxford University Press.
———. 1987. *X/Self*. Oxford and New York: Oxford University Press.
———. 1990. *Shar*. Mona, Jamaica: Savacou Publications.
———. 1991. "An Interview with Kamau Brathwaite." *Hambone* 9.
———. 1993a. *The Zea Mexican Diary*. Madison: University of Wisconsin Press.
———. 1993b. *Roots*. Ann Arbor: University of Michigan Press.
———. 1994a. *Trench Town Rock*. Providence, RI: Lost Roads Publishers.
———. 1994b. *Barabajan Poems*. New York: Savacou North.
———. 1995. Unpublished interview at the University of Memphis.
———. 1996. "Note(s) on Caribbean Cosmology." *River City* 16, no. 2.
Buck-Morss, Susan. 1991. *The Dialectics of Seeing*. Cambridge and London: MIT
  Press.
Butler, Judith. 1990. *Gender Trouble*. New York: Routledge.

Butterick, George F. 1987. "The Mysterious Vision of Susan Howe." *North Dakota Quarterly* 55.

Chamberlin, J. Edward. 1993. *Come Back to Me My Language*. Urbana: University of Illinois Press.

Cohen, Margaret. 1993. *Profane Illumination*. Berkeley: University of California Press.

Cole, Johnetta. 1997. "Gender, Culture, and Caribbean Development." In *Gender: A Caribbean Multi-Disciplinary Perspective*. Edited by Elsa Leo-Rhynie, Barbara Bailey, and Christine Barrow. Kingston: Ian Randle Publishers.

Coleridge, Samuel Taylor. 1951. *Selected Poetry and Prose of Coleridge*. Modern Library College Editions.

Davidson, Michael. 1989. *The San Francisco Renaissance*. Cambridge: Cambridge University Press.

de Certeau, Michel. 1984. *The Practice of Everyday Life*. Translated by Steven Rendall. Berkeley: University of California Press.

DuPlessis, Rachel Blau. 1990. *The Pink Guitar*. New York and London: Routledge.

Eagleton, Terry. 1981. *Walter Benjamin*. London and New York: Verso.

Engels, Friedrich. 1978. *The Marx-Engels Reader*. New York: W. W. Norton.

Falon, Janet Ruth. 1989. "Speaking with Susan Howe." *The Difficulties* 3, no. 2.

Foster, Ed. 1992. "An Interview with Nathaniel Mackey." *Talisman* 9.

Fraser, Nancy, and Linda J. Nicholson. 1990. "Social Criticism without Philosophy: An Encounter between Feminism and Postmodernism," in *Feminism/Postmodernism*. New York: Routledge.

Funkhouser, Chris. 1996. "An Interview with Nathaniel Mackey." *Callaloo* 18, no. 4.

Glissant, Edouard. 1981. *Caribbean Discourse*. Translated by J. Michael Dash. Charlottesville: University Press of Virginia.

Golding, Alan. 1995. *From Outlaw to Classic*. Madison: University of Wisconsin Press.

Gould, Stephen Jay. 1981. *The Mismeasure of Man*. New York: W. W. Norton.

Griaule, Marcel. 1965. *Conversations with Ogotemmêli*. Translated by Ralph Butler. London: Oxford University Press.

Hartley, George. 1989. *Textual Politics and the Language Poets*. Bloomington: Indiana University Press.

Hatlen, Burton. 1986. "Crawling in Bed with Sorrow: Jack Spicer's *After Lorca*." *Ironwood* 28.

Hejinian, Lyn. 1984. "The Rejection of Closure." *Poetics Journal* 4.

————. 1985. "The Rejection of Closure." *Writing / Talks*. Carbondale and Edwardsville: Southern Illinois University Press.

————. 1987. *My Life*. Los Angeles: Sun & Moon Press.

———. 1991. *Oxota*. Great Barrington: The Figures.

———. 1994. *The Cold of Poetry*. Los Angeles: Sun & Moon Press.

hooks, bell. 1990. *Yearning: Race, Gender, and Cultural Politics*. Boston: South
  End Press.

Howe, Susan. 1985. *My Emily Dickinson*. Berkeley, CA: North Atlantic Books.

———. 1990a. *Singularities*. Hanover and London: Wesleyan University Press.

———. 1990b. *The Europe of Trusts*. Los Angeles: Sun & Moon Press.

———. 1993. *The Birth-mark*. Hanover and London: Wesleyan University Press.

———. 1995. "An Interview with Susan Howe," conducted by Lynn Keller.
  Contemporary Literature 36, no. 1.

Huyssen, Andreas. 1986. *After the Great Divide*. Bloomington: Indiana
  University Press.

Jackson, John G. 1994. *African Civilizations*. New York: Citadel Press.

James, William. 1987. *Writings 1902–1910*. New York: Library of America.

Jameson, Fredric. 1991. *Postmodernism, or The Cultural Logic of Late Capitalism*.
  Durham, NC: Duke University Press.

Johnson, Haynes. 1991. *Sleepwalking through History*. New York: Anchor Books.

Jones, Ann Rosalind. 1985. "Writing the Body: Toward an Understanding of
  l'Écriture féminine." In *The New Feminist Criticism*. Edited by Elaine
  Showalter. New York: Pantheon Books.

Jones, W. T. 1975. *A History of Western Philosophy: The Twentieth Century to
  Wittgenstein and Sartre*. New York: Harcourt, Brace, Jovanovich.

Kalaidjian, Walter. 1989. *Languages of Liberation*. New York: Columbia
  University Press.

Keller, Lynn. 1997. *Forms of Expansion: Recent Long Poems by Women*. Chicago:
  University of Chicago Press.

Kristeva, Julia. 1984. *Revolution in Poetic Language*. Translated by Margaret
  Waller. New York: Columbia University Press.

———. 1986. *The Kristeva Reader*. Edited by Toril Moi. New York: Columbia
  University Press.

Laclau, Ernesto, and Chantal Mouffe. 1985. *Hegemony and Socialist Strategy*. New
  York: Verso.

Lechte, John. 1990. *Julia Kristeva*. New York: Routledge.

Mackey, Nathaniel. 1985. *Eroding Witness*. Urbana and Chicago: University of
  Illinois Press.

———. 1990. "Gassire's Lute: Robert Duncan's Vietnam War Poems, I."
  Talisman 5.

———. 1991a. "Gassire's Lute: Robert Duncan's Vietnam War Poems, II."
  Talisman 6.

———. 1991b. "Gassire's Lute: Robert Duncan's Vietnam War Poems, III."
  Talisman 7.

———. 1992. "Gassire's Lute: Robert Duncan's Vietnam War Poems, IV and V." *Talisman* 8.

———. 1993a. *School of Udhra.* San Francisco: City Lights Books.

———. 1993b. *Djbot Baghostus's Run.* Los Angeles: Sun & Moon Press.

———. 1993c. *Discrepant Engagement: Dissonance, Cross-Culturality, and Experimental Writing.* Cambridge: Cambridge University Press.

———. 1993d. "Song of the Andoumboulou: 18." *Poetry Project Newsletter* 149.

———. 1993e. Personal letter to the author.

———. 1994a. "Song of the Andoumboulou 16." *River City* 14, no. 2.

———. 1994b. Personal telephone conversation with the author.

———. 1994c. "Wringing the Word." *World Literature Today* 68, no. 4.

———. 1995. *Strick: Song of the Andoumboulou 16–25.* Memphis: Spoken Engine.

———. 1997. *Bedouin Hornbook.* Los Angeles: Sun & Moon Press.

McGann, Jerome J. 1988. *Social Values and Poetic Acts.* Cambridge, MA: Harvard University Press.

McKee, Margaret, and Fred Chisenhall. 1981. *Beale Black & Blue.* Baton Rouge: Louisiana State University Press.

Moi, Toril. 1985. *Sexual/Textual Politics: Feminist Literary Theory.* New York: Routledge.

Mullen, Harryette. 1992. "Phantom Pain: Nathaniel Mackey's *Bedouin Hornbook.*" *Talisman* 9.

Nelson, Cary. 1989. *Repression and Recovery.* Madison: University of Wisconsin Press.

Nicholls, Peter. 1996. "Unsettling the Wilderness: Susan Howe and American History." *Contemporary Literature* 37, no. 4.

Olds, Sharon. 1990. *The Living and the Dead.* New York: Alfred A. Knopf.

Owens, Craig. 1983. "The Discourse of Others: Feminists and Postmodernism." In *The Anti-Aesthetic.* Edited by Hal Foster. Port Townsend, WA: Bay Press.

Pearce, Roy Harvey. 1969. *Historicism Once More.* Princeton, NJ: Princeton University Press.

Perelman, Bob. 1994. *The Trouble with Genius.* Berkeley and Los Angeles: University of California Press.

Perloff, Marjorie. 1990. *Poetic License: Essays on Modernist and Postmodernist Lyric.* Evanston, IL: Northwestern University Press.

———. 1992. "How Russian Is It?" *Parnassus* 17, no. 2 and 18, no. 1.

Philip, M. Nourbese. 1989. *She Tries Her Tongue, Her Silence Softly Breaks.* Charlottetown: Ragweed Press.

———. 1991. *Looking for Livingstone: An Odyssey of Silence.* Stratford, Ontario: Mercury Press.

———. 1992. *Frontiers: Selected Essays and Writings on Racism and Culture 1984–1992.* Stratford, Ontario: Mercury Press.

———. 1994. "Dis Place   The Space Between." *Feminist Measures*. Edited by
    Lynn Keller and Cristanne Miller. Ann Arbor: University of Michigan Press.
———. 1996. "A River City Interview with M. Nourbese Philip." *River City* 16,
    no. 2.
Pound, Ezra. 1968a. *Literary Essays of Ezra Pound*. New York: New Directions.
———. 1968b. *The Spirit of Romance*. New York: New Directions.
———. 1973. *Selected Prose: 1909–1965*. New York: New Directions.
Rahim, Jennifer. 1997. "Trinidad and Tobago Women's Writing, 1929–69." In
    Gender: A Caribbean Multi-Disciplinary Perspective. Edited by Elsa Leo-
    Rhynie, Barbara Bailey, and Christine Barrow. Kingston: Ian Randle
    Publishers.
Reinfeld, Linda. 1989. "On Henry David (Susan Howe) 'Thorow.'" *The
    Difficulties* 3, no. 2.
Roberts, Julian. 1983. *Walter Benjamin*. Atlantic Highlands, NJ: Humanities
    Press.
Said, Edward, W. 1993. *Culture and Imperialism*. New York: Vintage Books.
Scholem, Gershom. 1991. "Walter Benjamin and His Angel." Translated by
    Werner Dannhauser. *On Walter Benjamin*. Cambridge and London: MIT
    Press.
Showalter, Elaine. 1985. "Feminist Criticism in the Wilderness." *The New
    Feminist Criticism*. Edited by Elaine Showalter. New York: Pantheon Books.
Sieburth, Richard. 1989. "Benjamin the Scrivener." *Benjamin: Philosophy,
    Aesthetics, History*. Chicago: University of Chicago Press.
Spahr, Juliana. 1996. "Resignifying Autobiography: Lyn Hejinian's *My Life*."
    American Literature 68, no. 1.
Spicer, Jack. 1980. *The Collected Books of Jack Spicer*. Santa Barbara, CA: Black
    Sparrow Press.
Stevens, Wallace. 1957. *Opus Posthumous*. New York: Vintage Books.
———. 1974. *The Collected Poems*. New York: Alfred A. Knopf.
———. 1981. *Letters of Wallace Stevens*. New York: Alfred A. Knopf.
Strand, Mark. 1990. *Selected Poems*. New York: Alfred A. Knopf.
Suleiman, Susan Rubin. 1990. *Subversive Intent*. Cambridge, MA: Harvard
    University Press.
Taggart, John. 1994. *Songs of Degrees*. Tuscaloosa: University of Alabama Press.
Trudeau, G. B. 1990. *Recycled Doonesbury*. New York: Andrews and McMeel.
Tuma, Keith. 1997. " 'Chisselin Darkness Writin In Light.' " *River City* 17, no. 1.
von Hallberg, Robert. 1985. *American Poetry and Culture, 1945–1980*. Cambridge,
    MA: Harvard University Press.
Weinberger, Eliot. 1992. "News in Briefs." *Sulfur* 31.
White, Hayden. 1973. *Metahistory*. Baltimore: Johns Hopkins University Press.
Whitman, Walt. 1970. *An American Primer*. San Francisco: City Lights Books.

Wills, Garry. 1988. *Reagan's America.* New York: Penguin Books.

Wittgenstein, Ludwig. 1968. *Philosophical Investigations.* Translated by G. E. M. Anscombe. New York: Macmillan Publishing.

Wolin, Richard. 1994. *Walter Benjamin.* Berkeley: University of California Press.

Index

Adorno, Theodor, culture industry described by, 29–30
African-Caribbean writers, 15–17
Afro-Asian Music Ensemble, 91
American imperialism
  for Brathwaite, 142–44, 148, 165–68
  contemporary investigative poetry as fighting, 41
  Howe's poetry investigating, 43, 54–56
Andoumboulou
  as draft of human beings, 77
  song of, 76–78
Aronowitz, Stanley, 31
Ashanti nation, treatment in Brathwaite's work of, 151–52

Bagdikian, Ben, 6
Bakhtin, Mikhail, theories of language and authorship of, 46, 49
Baudelaire, modernist dictum of, 22
Baudrillard, Jean
  diagnosis of Reagan by, 4–5, 41–42
  difference between real and simulated for, 10, 42
Benjamin, Walter
  alternative to Pound of, 20, 22–23
  angel of history of, 25–26
  author as witness for, 54
  authorship as collaboration with reader of, 56–57
  class for, 29
  dialectical images for, 21–27, 56–57
  history for, 20–21, 24–25, 169
  Howe's appreciation of works of, 203n.3
  portrayal of culture by, 69–70
  theory of collective unconscious of, 29

Works:
  "Surrealism," 20
  "Theses on the Philosophy of History," 20–22, 25–26, 57
Bennett, Tony, 37
Bernstein, Charles, cultural difference for, 39
Bérubé, Michael, fears of reactionaries described by, 41
Brathwaite, Kamau, 10–11, 138–73
  "Adam" as representing his childhood for, 164–68
  betrayal of the gods in West African civilization for, 149–50
  Caribbean heritage from Barbados in call to poetry of, 139–41, 164
  gender issues explored by, 158–60
  international and Creole perspectives included in way of seeing for, 138
  Legba described by, 95
  links between African and Christian ceremonies for, 153–63
  magical realism of history for, 168–70
  manscape for, 158
  movement from divine to human agency in, 150–52
  nation language of, 15–16, 29, 144, 157–58, 161, 164, 168–69
  sense of music of, 140–42, 144, 146–47, 173
  significance of name changes for, 142–43, 146
  "Sycorax Video Style" of, 205n.1, 205n.3
  talking drum for, 153, 157
  tidalectic pattern of movement for, 144–45, 157, 162, 173

213

Hejinian, Lyn, 106–37
androgyny of desire stirred by language for, 107
breakup of Soviet Union for, 127–28
construction of the self explored by, 117
"I" investigated by, 106–13, 119, 121–26, 134, 137
inaccuracy of memory for, 122–23
lack of punctuation in, 129
language writing of, 107–8, 119, 134
metaphor and metonymy for, 131–33
number for, 117, 121
open text of, 14, 108–9, 116, 123–24, 128–29, 133, 136–37
poetic policy of glasnost toward form for, 127–29
reality as mutable for, 133
repetition as intrasectional and semantic for, 120–22
struggle between impulse toward closure and open-ended response to world for, 121
as subject of her work, 107
understanding of truth by, 130–31
Works:
"Guard, The," 15
My Life, 10, 107, 117–26, 137, 204n.5
My Life in the Early Nineties, 117
Oxota, 10, 107, 117, 126–33, 137, 205n.7
"Rejection of Closure, The," 107, 108
Historigraphy, poetic, 27
History
Benjamin's image-based philosophy of, 20–27, 169
essence of Western philosophical, 11
Howe as unsettling, 12
Philip's exposure of holes in, 192

poetic expression of, 11, 17, 42, 43, 53, 138, 169, 176, 185, 200
world-poems of tribes including holes in, 72
Horkheimer, Max, culture industry described by, 29–30
Howe, Susan, 43–70
anonymous voices explored by, 52–53, 69–70, 96
approach to writing history poetically of, 53–55, 58
authorship as collaboration with reader of, 56–57
Benjamin's works for, 203n.3
challenge to structure of authority in, 14
contrast between linguistic landscape of Stevens and, 59–60
critical attention to works of, 202n.1
exclusion from formalism of, 52–53
gender investigated by, 65–69
as not embraced by mainstream feminist criticism, 63–65
objection to tools of grammar and spelling of, 55–56, 58
"order" attained through poetic use of language for, 69
poetry of, as investigator's search, 9, 203n.2
power relations in construction of meaning for, 12, 61
silence of the ruled for, 13, 62, 69
Spicer's poetic landscape like that of, 60–61
stammering quality of poetic logic of, 60–62
transcendence of the individual by, 68, 203n.4
transgression of limits of pure poetry by, 54
Works:
Birth-mark, The, 10, 58

"Incloser," 57–58
My Emily Dickinson, 10, 62–67
Singularities, 52
Thorow, 52–56, 58–59
Huyssen, Andreas, avoidance of post-
  modernism debate by feminist
  criticism noted by, 115

"I"
  as author disrupted by open text,
    108–9
  biological determinants not articu-
    late about, 116
  distinguishing Kristeva's concept of,
    112
  explored in Brathwaite's work, 157
  explored in Hejinian's work, 106–13,
    119, 121–26, 134, 137
  female, 115
  history of, 107
  revolutionary text representing, 109
Images, dialectic of, 21–23
Impure poetry, 45
Inward migration of poetry, 7–8

Jameson, Fredric
  aesthetic of schizophrenic fragmen-
    tation of language writers noted
    by, 134–35
  assessment of postmodern cultural
    productions of, 41–42
  pastiche for, 138
Johnson, Haynes, 2
Jones, W. T., mysticism defined by, 79
Joyce, James, aesthetics of "stasis" of,
  22

Kalaidjian, Walter, 6–7
Kamau, Edward. *See* Brathwaite,
  Kanau
Kant, Immanuel, phenomenal and
  noumenal realms for, 37
Keller, Lynn, Howe's illumination of

language's oppression of women
  described by, 68
Kristeva, Julia, 109–14
  chora for, 111, 113, 114
  feminine for, 114
  genotext and phenotext for, 113–14
  Hejinian's work illuminated in
    Revolution in Poetic Language by,
    109
  materialistic dialectic of, 112
  modern poetic language for, 113,
    204n.3
  as poststructuralist, 110, 112
  semiotic modality in notion of self
    of, 110–12, 135
  symbolic modality of, 113–14, 135
  textual experience for, 112–13
  thetic phase for, 111–12

Laclau, Ernesto
  abandoning the thought/reality
    opposition for, 33–34, 36
  enlargement of poetic and political
    fields by, 35, 62
  history written poetically in model
    of, 29–31, 33
  ideality of phenomenal realm for, 37
  poetic elements of discourse for, 67
Language writing
  critical analysis of, 204n.2
  Jameson as noting schizophrenic
    fragmentation in, 124–35
  McGann's description of, 108, 135
  as philosophy of composition, 107–8
  restlessness of language for Hejinian
    depicted in her, 136
Language-games, 10–12
  explored by contemporary inves-
    tigative poets, 33, 169, 177, 185–
    87, 200
  intervention in culture by connect-
    ing divergent, 67

Lechte, John, Kristeva's nature of language analyzed by, 110
Legba, 94–95
Lewis, Furry, minstrel shows for, 102–3
Literary texts of modern poetry, 113
Lorca, Federico García, 49
Lyric poetry, transcendent moment in, 80

McGann, Jerome
    language writing described by, 108, 135
    oppositional politics of language writers noted by, 134
Mackey, Nathaniel, 71–105
    aesthetics of accessibility for, 13, 38
    analysis of Brathwaite's treatment of African civilizations by, 149–50
    Angel of Dust of, 92–95
    categorization of work of, 90–91
    challenge to structure of authority in, 14
    collaboration of Hartigan, Modirzadeh, and, 90–92
    complexity of race issue for, 13
    concern for silenced voices in history of, 13
    counterpoint in poetry of, 89–90
    discrepant engagement between cultures for, 73–75, 78, 105, 203n.2
    fascination with absence or nothingness in, 100
    gender and sexuality for, 83–84, 88, 98
    issues of race for, 101–4
    minstrel show imagery of, 101–3
    mired sublime of oppositions for, 94, 97, 104
    postmodern dilemma of, 100–101
    song in works of, 72–73, 77
    stuttering in works of, 85–86

    transcendence for, 77–78, 80–88, 93, 98
    world-poem vision of, 72, 74
    Works:
        Bedouin Hornbook, 71, 92, 94, 95, 98–99, 101
        Discrepant Engagement, 71
        Djbot Baghostus's Run, 71, 92, 94, 95, 98, 100, 101, 103–4
        Eroding Witness, 71, 92, 93
        From a Broken Bottle Traces of Perfume Still Emanate, 10, 92, 94, 99
        Gassire's Lute: Robert Duncan's Vietnam War Poems, 72, 74, 75, 84
        Moment's Notice, 71–72
        School of Udhra, 71, 84–85, 87
        "Slave's Day Off, The," 96
        "Song of the Andoumboulou 1–15," 13–14, 72–73, 76, 81–90, 92, 98
        "Sound and Sentiment, Sound and Symbol," 86
        Strick: Song of the Andoumboulou 16–25, 71, 90–92
        "Third Leg of the Sun," 94–95
        Whatsaid Serif, 203n.3
Marxism
    accounts of how artists intervene in culture in, 34
    of contemporary investigative poets, 28–29
    reality shift for, 37–38
    upset of Hegelian philosophy by, 36–37
    working-class shift from tenets of, 30
Media ownership, consolidation of, 6
Modernism
    differences between contemporary writing and, 20

"heroic" or "elitist," 19
Modernists
  differences between surrealists and
    other, 23–24
  modern poetic language of, 113
  politics of, 28
  textual practices of, 18
Monopoly, decline of competition
  through, 6
Montage, 25, 169–70, 172
Mouffe, Chantal
  abandoning the thought/reality
    opposition for, 33–34, 36
  enlargement of poetic and political
    fields by, 35, 62
  history written poetically in model
    of, 29–31, 33
  ideality of phenomenal realm for, 37
  poetic elements of discourse for, 67

Nation language of Brathwaite, 15–16
  cultural voice of, 161
  of infiltration of English by linguis-
    tic "noise" of remnants of African
    cultures, 144
  montage style of, 168–69
  not accessible to working class, 29
  poetic tactic of, 157–58
  in prose poetry, 164
  refusal to submit to rule of iambic
    pentameter of, 144
Nelson, Cary
  assessment of Quinn's poetry of, 38
  study of modernism of, 27–28
Nicholson, Linda J., biological de-
    scriptions of gender and sexism
    dismissed by, 115–16

Odomankoma, 151, 156
Oglotemmêli
  connection between language and
    sexuality for, 84

Griaule's discussions with, 82–83
Olds, Sharon, "Miscarriage" by, 8–9
Olson, Charles, *Maximus Poems* as
  world-poem of, 75
Open text
  of Hejinian, 14, 108–9, 116, 123–24,
    128–29, 133, 136–37
  issues of gender at work in, 109
Owens, Craig, postmodernism and
  exclusion of women described by,
  115

Pearce, Roy Harvey, Stevens's dialectical compromise described by,
  47
Perelman, Bob, 19, 135
Perloff, Marjorie, Hejinian's way of
  writing about self described by, 128
Philip, M. Nourbese, 174–200
  assertions of identity in "i-mages"
    for, 176–78, 180–81, 184, 185, 188,
    190–92, 197
  body speaking through word for,
    192–93
  confrontations between Western
    and Caribbean values and forms
    for, 180, 182–84, 189–91, 196–99
  connection of grammar and power
    for, 185
  contrast between Pound and, 18–21
  demotic tradition used by, 178–81,
    197
  "dis place" for female genitalia for,
    174, 181, 190
  grammar used in its context for, 188
  lifting of silence imposed on Afri-
    cans pinpointed by, 194, 196,
    199
  neglect of works of, 179–80
  relation between poetry and politics
    for, 20
  role of black women noted by, 174